MAKING A SMALL FORTUNE

Surviving publishing, parenting, and porphyria

M A T T H E W   S P A U R

Notes and Acknowledgements

Some names in this book have been changed to protect privacy and for clarification.

A portion of this book was previously published in slightly different form in
Microsoft in the Mirror, 2003, Pennington Books. Karin Carter, editor.

Print ISBN: 978-1-66785-346-8
eBook ISBN: 978-1-66785-347-5

Printed in the United States of America

TABLE OF CONTENTS

COTTONWOOD BAY

Two days before marrying my third wife for the second time, I found her and her oldest son Brad crying in our kitchen. I was carrying bags of groceries through the back door from the car. Connye stood by the sink and Brad by the refrigerator. Both were bleary-eyed and sniffling. This was a Saturday in July 2000, back when I was a millionaire. I set the bags on the wooden cart in the middle of the kitchen. "What's going on?" I asked with my man-in-control voice.

Connye uncrossed one of her arms and rubbed the tip of her cheerleader's nose with the wad of tissue in her hand. "Brad says that he's gay and wants to move back here, with us."

I turned to Brad. During the three years I had loved his mother, Brad lived with his dad and stepmom in Las Vegas. Connye sent him to the desert when her second marriage, to the father of Brad's half-brothers Walt and Christian, grew rocky.

Brad scrunched his face. His eyes grew wetter. His lips quivered and he thrust his chin forward. This was a historic event for a slender 14-year-old boy who already stood inches above his mother and me. Connye re-crossed her arms and looked to me.

"Are you sure?" I asked Brad. I meant about living with us in Spokane, not about being gay. I'm not sure that's how he took it.

Brad dipped his chin down and back up.

"Well," I said, "I don't want to sound flip, but is that all?"

They both widened their wet eyes.

"You're acting like it's the end of the world." I turned to Brad. "You're always welcome here."

"So, you don't have a problem with Brad moving in?" Connye asked.

I shrugged. In times of stress, I tend to focus on practical matters. Emotions can come later. "You'll probably have to give up your office," I told Connye. The front bedroom of our 1928 bungalow was her room for writing. "Unless you want to give Brad the TV room in the basement. Or make Walt and Christian share a room."

Connye shook her head. "No, the boys need the space, especially in the winter. Brad can have my office."

"We can share mine," I said. My office occupied the upstairs bedroom too small to hold a queen-sized bed. I turned to Brad. "Have you told your dad yet?" Again, I meant about moving to Spokane, not about being gay.

He shook his head.

"You two will have to tell him soon. I'm sure there'll be a battle about that."

"I'll tell him," Connye said.

After a pause, I asked, "So, is everyone OK?"

They both forced small smiles to their lips. We three hugged, and then I continued with unloading groceries and other chores in preparation for our wedding.

That night Connye and I fell into bed for nearly the last time as two people living in sin. On our bedroom ceiling shone constellations of glow-in-the-dark stars: Cancer, Pisces, Cepheus the Whale. After I thumbed constellations onto Christian's bedroom ceiling as part of a decorating project, Connye said that they reminded her of camping. We made love under Christian's stars one evening when the three boys were gone. Soon after that, I surprised Connye with her own bedroom sky.

She looked at me in the twilight and asked, "Are you sure about all this?"

"All what?"

"We moved into this house together barely a year ago. We started publishing a newspaper three months ago. In two days, you're getting married, and now you're parenting a gay teenager full-time. It won't be too much?"

I put my arm around her. I hadn't strung it all together. Still, no bride wants to hear her groom hesitate. "Nobody's forcing me. I knew you came with kids. The house is big enough, plus it won't be for long. Brad turns 15 next month. It'll be fine."

We spooned together and slept while our stars slowly went dark.

"Can we kiss yet?" Connye interrupted.

Everyone laughed. When it's your third marriage, you can relax and do things differently. First weddings are anxious. Second weddings are like a patient in a hospital gown, exposed and embarrassed and wanting it all over soon. By the third wedding, most of the nerves and shame are gone. Connye wore a dusty blue dress with pearl-white beads. She squinted her cornflower eyes against the glare from the lake. July 11, 2000 would be hot.

On any other morning like this she'd wear sunglasses and baggy shorts. The bright sun highlighted her dyed blonde hair, which she wore in a pixie cut because it had grown too brittle to keep long. She was only 34, but seemed to embrace a third marriage. On our refrigerator at home hung a magnet with a retro 1950s cartoon woman winking beside a caption that read, "The first two husbands are just for practice."

Although Connye and I and the three boys and three cats already lived together, I felt nervous about standing before my family and doing the marriage thing—again. At 37, this was my third marriage as well. My parents, sister, and brother had all remained in their marriages for decades. So, what was my problem? I certainly didn't want to fail again. I tried to alleviate my embarrassment by referring to our entire wedding week as "the weenie roast." Luckily, the logistics of a wedding provided lots of practical challenges to distract me from my feelings.

Connye and I decided that we weren't getting married as much as creating a new family, so we designed our wedding week around our families. We rented a huge house on Cottonwood Bay, a small, developed stretch along the southeast shore of Lake Coeur d'Alene in northern Idaho. For the week, at least 25 parents, grandparents, aunts, uncles, cousins, nieces, and nephews spread out in eight bedrooms on three floors. The house had so many rooms I doubt I saw them all. The brochure claimed the place could sleep up to 40. The living room's two-story windows overlooked the wrap-around deck and sloping yard leading down to the water. Just the center part of the deck stood wide enough for rows of white plastic chairs to seat all our guests for the ceremony. Extra couches, grills, and refrigerators we pushed to the sides.

"No kissing yet," Connye's brother Randy grinned. He was an ordained Southern Baptist minister, which can be handy to have in the family. Connye stood to one side of Randy, with her sister Dayna next to her. Christian, her youngest boy and soon be nine years old, leaned against her. He clutched a white stuffed seal he'd received the previous winter after breaking his arm (he fell from a ski lift after his dad failed to guide him off the chair). I stood to the other side of Randy with Brad and Connye's middle son Walt, who was newly 10. Connye dressed all her men in khaki pants and polo shirts ordered from Lands End. I didn't want to complain, but I looked horrible in that shirt. Even now I see the pictures and wince. Partly the shirt was to blame: wrong color, wrong cut, wrong weight of fabric. But the shirt merely accentuated my flab. Too much work, stress, and cooking-for-kids meals without any exercise raised my weight to more than 200 pounds. I've always been stocky, but that was too much for a guy of thoroughly average height.

In keeping with our theme of family, we asked our parents to each read a passage from a collection of love and marriage writings. Their selections included passages from Robert Browning, George Eliot, and a Buddhist marriage homily. Connye's father was a lawyer and the most churchified of our parents. He picked his own reading from the book, a lengthy piece from the Coptic Orthodox marriage service full of *beseech this* and *betrothal that* and all sorts of King James verbs. Soon enough, Connye and I answered, "for richer or for poorer, in sickness and in health" with "I do." Because we did. We kissed. After three years of dating and living together, we were now officially married. My brother-in-law rang the ship's bell hanging above the deck.

Within an hour, our families changed out of formal attire and into shorts and t-shirts. White and red and orange and yellow floaties grew on the green lawn as people huffed and pumped to inflate them. Dire Straits replaced organ music on the portable stereo. My brother slid his Jet Ski into the lake and then dove in.

The caterer delivered food from Coeur d'Alene, a resort town at the lake's northern end. While many couples spend $25,000 on just a wedding day, we managed to house and host both our families for a week for less than $5,000. In such a family affair, catered food on our wedding day was a luxury. Nothing fancy: hors d'ouevres and pasta salad and salmon, plus three small cakes— one chosen by each of the boys. Connye and I provided breakfast and lunch for the week, and each night a different set of relatives cooked dinner. Cooking we counted as our wedding gifts. With our home already bulging with the kids and pets and furniture and books and dishes from a combined four previous marriages, we didn't want any more. Plus, putting new relatives together in the kitchen helped build family.

In the afternoon, more guests arrived for our reception / lake party. Most we knew either from graduate school at Eastern Washington University, where we had met, or from the weekly newspaper we published. Some came with suit and towel to play in the lake. Others sat on the deck, drank, and enjoyed our wedding as an excuse to extend their summer weekend into Monday. Down on the dock, kids argued over who could float in which inner tube or drive the Jet Ski next. The band arrived as we were warming up the grill. "Band" sounds big. Two guys, a duo with guitars and Birkenstocks, covered John Prine and John Hiatt and The Grateful Dead as the trashcans filled and the drink coolers emptied.

In a final, gentle poke at tradition, Connye and I had asked everyone to wrap and bring something funny or useless or ugly for a tacky gift exchange. Once the sun eased into a late twilight, we piled the gifts around the rock fireplace in the living room. All the guests drew numbers. When someone's number came up, they could either unwrap a gift or take a gift that someone else had already unwrapped. If someone took your gift, you could open another. Fierce swapping developed around a four-foot tall, wooden tiki god that my oldest nephew finally won.

One morning while driving from the lake to work, I saw the low, wide, furry form of a badger crouched on a grassy side road near the lake house. Badgers are rare around Spokane, rare enough to make me consult a field guide after our week at the lake was over. I'm no expert, but I'm convinced I saw a North Columbian badger, a species officially endangered in British Columbia and probably threatened in Washington and Idaho. Maybe Badger was a sign, like Raven or Coyote in the stories from the Coeur d'Alene and other area tribes. But a sign of what—ferocity? determination? a guiding spirit for stocky, hairy guys like me?

And yes, I was working the week of my wedding. We owned a new small business, after all. Connye and I entered the newspaper business because we believed it was the best way for us to build a life for our family in Spokane. We believed stories could overthrow the stultifying provincialism of Spokane. We believed that the right people wanted something intelligent and funny to read, and that advertisers would pay to reach those people. We believed that a new newspaper could counterbalance the power that Cowles Publishing—local monarchs of newspaper, television, commerce, real estate, and philanthropy—held over the region's culture and dialog. Our newspaper would be our ten-year project, a force for change, our legacy to the community, and our springboard to greater things. We committed to investing all our talent, sweat, and money in building a business for our family and our community.

My day's struggle at the office pitted me against our local phone company, US West (sarcastically known as US Worst). In the three months since we had started service with them, our main phone number—the one published in our paper, on our business cards, on stickers and banners and ads—had been silent for more than a month. Every time we asked them to correct a problem with our voice mail, our main line went dead and stayed dead for days after.

"Your screw-ups and delays are hurting my business," I argued, pacing the floor and talking into a headset.

"Oh, I doubt that," the customer service agent in Seattle replied.

"Are you kidding? My customers can't call me for weeks, and you don't think that's hurting my business?"

"Well, I'd have to research that."

I wrote down that agent's name, plus the date and time of our call.

Our newspaper shared office space temporarily with the Internet service company who hosted our website and built our computer network. They specialized in providing Internet connections that filtered obscene and pornographic content. It made sense. Spokane likes to consider itself the last notch west on the Bible Belt. The Internet service guys just shook their heads at me as I paced. In the afternoons, they would convert their in-house network into one large tournament of *Unreal*, a bloody shoot-'em-up video game. Over the sounds of simulated machine gun fire, I heard them laughing and swearing and shooting at each other. We eventually received $3,700 rebated for our phone service before switching to another phone company. The US Worst regional vice president told me that my customer service agent was "sent for retraining." I envisioned a Maoist political center hidden among the drippy fir trees of western Washington and smiled.

Late one night at the lake, Brad came screaming through the front door of the house carrying his youngest brother. "Mom! Mom! It's Christian!"

"In here," Connye called. We were just getting ready for bed.

Brad stomped down the hall from the foyer, into our room, and laid his brother on our bed. Christian appeared to be deeply asleep despite all the commotion and lights. A couple of spittle bubbles clumped at one corner of his mouth.

"We can't get him to wake up," Brad said.

"Why were you trying?" I asked. "It's midnight."

"He didn't look right. Look at him."

I checked Christian's breathing, which was normal. He didn't seem in pain. In fact, he seemed very comfortable. Connye jiggled him by his shoulders and talked to him. "Mr. Chris. Chrisser. Wake up."

No change.

"Maybe he's just really tired," I said, resisting Brad's sense of the dramatic. All the sons at the wedding who were old enough for a sleepover stayed just across the gravel driveway in the trailer home that came with the rental. Its dark paneling, old appliances, and sculpted shag carpet reminded me of a trailer where my dad, brother, and I stayed one fishing weekend in Louisiana when I was the boys' age. Late nights of video games and scary movies ruled the boys' annex. Christian was the youngest of the group. He was ridiculously competitive and determined to party just as hard as boys nearly twice his age. After long days swimming in the sun and sleepless nights staring at the old console TV, maybe he'd just given out.

"Come on, Chrisser," Connye said as she shook him gently. "Wake up." Christian's eyes remained shut.

It did seem odd. Anyone who was simply asleep would have woken up by now. I wished my mom the nurse was on hand. My parents brought their travel trailer with them on this trip and camped about 20 miles away. They'd already left for the night.

"Maybe he's having a seizure or something," Brad worried. No one in the family had a history of seizures.

I focused on the practical. "He's not tensed up at all. Really, he could just need the sleep. You guys have been up late every night."

"But we were like screaming his name in his ear and nothing."

"Well, let's not try that in here."

Connye kept stroking Christian's head and talking to him. "Maybe Brad's right," she said.

"Maybe," I said. "But he's breathing, he's comfortable, he's not convulsing. If he's having a seizure, there's not much more that anyone would do for him."

"Should we take him to the hospital? What about his tongue?" Connye asked. "Can't he swallow it?"

"Look in his mouth and check."

Connye opened Christian's mouth. Nothing wrong. She kept stroking his hair and talking to him.

"What are we going to do?" Brad said.

"Like I said, there's nothing much to do at the moment."

Christian opened one sleepy eye, blue like his mom's, and murmured momentarily. Connye looked him square in the face. "Christian, are you okay?"

Another murmur. Christian rolled onto his side.

"He's just tired," I repeated. "Let's put him to bed." Brad and I carried him back across the driveway and tucked him into bed. When the other boys asked about Christian, I restated my theory of exhaustion and chased them all to bed. They'd been up too late for too many nights.

I felt tired, too. Connye and I had been trading off hosting the wedding and working at the newspaper. She was the editor, and we had an issue coming out the following week.

When I returned from the boys' annex, Connye asked, "You think he'll be okay out there? Maybe we should take him to the hospital."

"And ask them to do what—a CAT scan? An MRI? Admit him? I doubt an emergency room would get worked up over him right now."

"You think he's just exhausted?"

"It's the best explanation that I can see."

"Maybe he should sleep in here with us."

Children were not sleeping anywhere near my honeymoon bed. "Chrisser will be fine." I kissed Connye. We spooned together. "And if he isn't, I'm sure we'll hear about it."

If anything was wrong with Christian that night, it remained a medical mystery. The next morning, he woke as he normally did, tussled and grumpy. He didn't recall anything between falling asleep and waking. Connye tried to monitor him throughout the day, but all the family commotion distracted her.

I still wonder what that badger signified, if anything. With everything that happened after that week, I'd like to know—in case I ever see one again.

EMOTIONAL EDUCATION

I moved to Spokane seeking literary training and an emotional education.

I don't know how actors do it, replicating emotions, when I've found it hard enough to experience them the first time around. With the rootless nature of a military childhood guided by Depression-baby parents who praised stoicism, perseverance and chores, I felt that I was emotionally muted. I'm not sure I had a vision of what this emotional education would be like, only that I needed it. It's in my personality to always want a plan, but sometimes my plans are rather vague. "Get an emotional education," is hardly specific. On the other hand, it's far-fetched to compose a checklist of emotions that you want to experience: anger, fear, triumph, love. And sometimes plans are merely a starting point, a structure intended to flex. Being the child of my Depression Baby parents meant that I faced my problems with stoic determination, giving little attention to emotional reaction or reflection. While outwardly I appeared to have it all—marriage, career, home, wealth—I also had a big problem. I was married to Susan and Susan was depressed.

We met at Microsoft in 1988, shortly after I transferred to the division of the company where she worked. I was 23 and already divorced from a short-lived mismatch. I liked Susan's bright blue eyes, her sharp mind and her mischievous sense of humor. After several months of dating, we moved in together to housesit for friends who were going to study for a year in Belgrade. Once our friends returned, we bought and remodeled a house in the same neighborhood.

In the fall of 1992 Susan and I wed in a small ceremony at our house. A judge officiated and just family attended. Even at the time I had a faint, vague feeling that getting married was a mistake. During the previous year, Susan had grown increasingly melancholy. Our sex life dwindled. Had I been a more emotionally reactive person, I think that I would have pushed harder and louder for some sort of answer about her withdrawal. As it was, I gave her space and time and support, even my promise of fidelity. How's that for self-denial—promising sexual fidelity to someone who would barely consent to sex.

When I left Microsoft in March 1994, Susan and I took an extended vacation for the rest of the year. I finished a series of night-school courses in creative writing. We spent three weeks in Britain, including hiking from Stratford-upon-Avon southward to Bath. My brother and his wife invited us to spend a summer week at Priest Lake in northern Idaho. It was just the sort of recharge that I needed. I was out on a think, as one of our bed-and-breakfast hostesses in England put it. Mostly I was mulling the notion of graduate school. By the end of the year, though, I was back at Microsoft working as a freelance writer, doing basically my old job with my old group of colleagues. I'd stay there for another year.

Susan and I continued to sink deeper into a sad complacency. She wouldn't own up to the severity of her depression, or confess its origins, or claim her need and responsibility to address this medical condition. Depression ruined her sleep patterns, her ability to feel joy, our sex life, and a lot of our communication. Her muted emotions exacerbated my already repressed nature. I felt like I was often wrong, even as I was trying to be right. Nothing satisfied her, because she was medically incapable of feeling satisfaction. I still recall the sting when people asked us when we were having children. It probably seemed like a perfectly normal question. After all, we were apparently successful, wealthy, married, and settled. Honestly, I've never had the urge to have a child of my own. I was always tempted to reply, "We'd have to have sex first," but I knew the hell I would pay if Susan learned I'd mentioned her depression to anyone. Depression is a hard blight to survive; I've watched my father struggle with its darkness. Looking back later, I could see that I was dangerously close to depression myself.

At first it was just a battle to get her to admit to being depressed. I remember nights turning over in bed, turning away from a barely communicative wife, to look out the window into the evening. Sometimes in those late northern summers a great blue heron would perch atop a nearby utility pole, its black silhouette distinct against the deepening blue. I'd stare at the shape and enjoy the moment's Zen respite from sadness before drifting to sleep.

At one point Susan confronted me by saying that we lived more like roommates than husband and wife. I froze for a moment. It was one of those emotional charged moments that as a child I'd learned to ignore. She was right. I sat on our stairs and said that I thought she'd withdrawn. She admitted that maybe she was depressed. When I suggested counseling or medication, she refused. I offered to find a self-help book, and she agreed to try. But I was the one that read the book, alone. After another confrontation about no progress being made on regaining a life together, I again offered to find a counselor. She agreed to try.

My first editor at Microsoft had spoken positively about her therapist, so I asked for a recommendation. The therapist worked out of her house, a blue, well-landscaped bungalow with office space in the daylight basement. For most of the appointments, Susan went by herself. On one occasion, though, she asked me to attend. From that session I don't remember much, except for one statement. At some point the therapist said, "Susan says that she'd be happy to never have sex again. How do you feel about that?"

I was caught off-guard. How can you respond to a near-stranger relaying a message like that from your wife? That was probably my opportunity to finally discuss what was happening with Susan, but I blew it. I froze, wordless. Ignore the moment and it will pass. I didn't know how to locate any feeling. Maybe that was shock, although I shouldn't have been shocked. Maybe I was overwhelmed by the acknowledgement of the problem. How was I supposed to feel? I could have been elated to finally address the problem, or sad she felt that way, or annoyed that she'd discussed this issue more with a therapist than with me. I could have wondered what was wrong with me or explored why I had stayed so long thus far in a relationship that had little joy with a woman who admitted to not wanting sex ever again. (Why did I stay? Partly I think it was that perseverance handed down from my Depression Baby parents, and partly determination to not fail at marriage for a second time.)

And I'm still confused about that moment. Did Susan want the therapist to tell me what she couldn't? That's a very enabling therapist, if that was the situation.

I think that I eventually stammered some sort of reply. The subject didn't come again after that. Soon Susan said that the therapist wasn't actually helping anything and stopped going.

I was surprised at the end of 1995 when Susan consented to me applying for graduate creative writing programs around the Pacific Northwest, which meant the possibility of moving out of Seattle. Moving to me represented a major commitment to working together and to our relationship. Moving for her would mean the first time living in a different city than her family. It might also mean having less scrutiny while she worked through her depression.

When Eastern Washington University in Spokane accepted me for their Masters in Fine Arts program, I told Susan that we'd be gone two years, that it wasn't that far away from our families, and that after I graduated we could go wherever she wanted.

To our friends we said that we were moving to Spokane so I could attend school. I didn't tell anyone that I was also looking for an emotional education. I didn't confess my desire for some adventure, to escape the uncomfortable rut I'd been living in, enduring a depressed wife while living in a too-familiar town and having no real purpose or identity. By 1996 I'd lived 11 years in the same city, five of them in the same house. To a military kid, that means it's time to move.

I was also seeking a way to force myself into facing some new emotions, although I wasn't successfully facing my current feelings of frustration, isolation, and despair. The challenge of graduate school, the risk of failing at something as personal as creative writing, could definitely spur some new feeling. Partially I thought that learning to write characters and scenes could put me in touch with emotions and form a good portion of my emotional education. Moving to a new town could definitely generate some new vibes by forcing myself into new communities and new terrain. And maybe moving together with Susan was a way to possibly force us to handle something together, to get us out of the rut of her depression. Sure, moving and attending school could probably do all that, but honestly it was also a way for me to avoid addressing my emotional struggles.

That summer Susan and I crisscrossed Washington for our move. Even though we could afford professional movers, we were both frugal enough to insist on doing it ourselves. We rented out our house in Seattle and bought a fixer house on the south side of Spokane. Our new house sat on a corner lot with cedar and chestnut trees along the sidewalk.

Spokane carries with it a sense of isolation. It's the only metropolitan area for 300 miles or more in any direction. While it's not unique among cities of the American West for geographic isolation, Spokane feels like that isolation has possibly warped its culture more so than other western communities. Spokane in the mid-90s was a particularly loony place. Neo-Nazi groups featured prominently in the news, thanks to Richard Butler's local headquarters for the Aryan Nations. People with strange motives were robbing banks and bombing places like Planned Parenthood clinics and the city's only synagogue. Right after Susan and I moved into our house, a police deputy gunned down his wife in the park closest to our house, and then claimed that two black men were the assailants. We started referring to Spokane as "The Gateway to the Fringe."

In our first autumn in our new city, I found depression still waiting for me at our new house. I'd return home from class full of new learning and new acquaintances, or come downstairs after an afternoon's immersion in Eliot or Faulkner, to find Susan still stuck in monotone, sitting on our couch watching mysteries on A&E or PBS. We couldn't see our neighbors from our house and didn't meet many of them. Susan didn't seem interested in finding friends. She didn't click with any of my fellow students. Shortly after moving she had applied for a job as a tour leader with a large educational travel company in town. Susan had a Masters degree in Slavic culture, spoke Russian and Polish, and had led several economic tours of the old Soviet Near East. After a couple interviews and weeks of waiting, they finally offered her a part-time, temporary desktop publishing job at $10. That day I came home to find her in tears. This appalling slap seemed to confirm her low self-esteem.

Our first Thanksgiving in Spokane brought a few feet of snow and a major ice storm. More than 100,000 people lost power, some for up to three weeks. Many of the city's power lines run down alleys behind the houses, alleys lined with ponderosa pines and magnolias and lilacs. The weight of the ice and snow pulled trees down onto the power lines, which collapsed. Utility crews had to restore power one house at a time. Somehow, we kept our electricity throughout the storm, save for a few hours on Thanksgiving Day. People living one block west of us went without electricity for three weeks during severe cold weather.

The storm accentuated the differences between us. Susan cocooned deeper into her depression. She stayed inside most of that winter quilting, drawing, reading gardening books. For a couple of months freelance work from Microsoft kept her busy. I, on the other hand, found the ice and snow a wonder. Sunlight was prismatic. Through waist-deep snow in our backyard I tromped out to our ramshackle, detached garage. "Fall down damn it," I muttered as I pushed against its walls. With all the snow on the roof I hoped the thing would collapse. Then my homeowner's policy could rebuild it. And getting to class was an adventure. The city was muffled. People were secretly enjoying being intrepid or having a vacation in a motel paid for by their insurance company.

Homework and snow, and a small secret crush on a classmate, got me through that first cold winter.

Spring thawed the massive snowpack in the mountains and swelled the Spokane River to flood levels. The pedestrian bridges crossing the river downtown were closed because of spray soaking the bridge decks, making them slippery. My garage didn't collapse, so I made plans to right it once classes were out for the summer. Susan decided that she'd had enough of office work for a while. She wrote a resume reflecting her horticultural interests—she had been a master gardener in Seattle—and landed a job at a plant nursery near our house. As part of a bigger plan, the nursery experience could help her if she eventually decided to pursue her own landscaping-related business.

I was happy that she'd found something to do, even if the pay was low and the work sometimes purely manual. Maybe Nature could fix what her nature had wrought. And it seemed to work. Each week the weather warmed a little more. Forsythia bushes started blooming yellow, then the lilacs that give Spokane its nickname budded. In the afternoon, Susan would come through the back porch door into the kitchen talking about rude customers and new friends at the nursery. She was animated for the first time in years. One colleague in particular, Deanna, came up often in conversation. I told Susan that I was happy she'd found a new friend.

But as spring welled up towards summer, Susan started slipping back. She withdrew again and stopped eating. Instead of melancholy, now she seemed tense, worried. One night we ate dinner in front of the TV, sitting on the floor around our coffee table. Susan was tight lipped. She hadn't touched her food. As she walked towards the kitchen after not eating, I asked her, "Is everything alright?"

She turned back towards me and broke into tears.

I patted the couch cushion next to me. She crossed the room and sat down. "It's Deanna, isn't it?" I asked.

She nodded and sobbed.

"You're in love with her, aren't you?"

She nodded again and cried harder. To my surprise, she let me put my arms around her.

"How did you know?" she asked.

"It's hard for anyone to hide something like that, especially after being sad for so long." I hugged her a little tighter. "It's okay. You haven't wanted me as a husband for a long time."

Outwardly I was supportive, caring, but her revelation left me frustrated. I was irked that I'd cooked dinner for her and Deanna just a few weeks earlier. I spent years forsaking all others while being forsaken at home. When I wasn't working on my studies, I was demonstrating my continued devotion through performing ugly chores like re-roofing the garage or driving to Seattle to chase rodents out of our rental house there. In my male mind, these things demonstrated my continued support of her and our relationship.

Although for years the idea of giving up our marriage had seemed like one way to end the emotional ache I kept trying to ignore, divorce wasn't what I had wanted. I was tired of the secrecy, the lack of joy, the isolation, but at the same time I didn't want the stigma of being twice divorced before I was 35 years old. I could accept that my first marriage ended in part because I wasn't emotionally educated enough to be married. But what was my fault this time? At worst, I hadn't stood up for myself. I'd married Susan when she was depressed, and I didn't look out for my own needs or health. About this time Susan admitted that she remembered choosing me in part because she knew that I'd put up with her depressive behavior. If my first wife had married me because she thought I was the stability she needed, Susan married me in part because she thought I was the patsy who wouldn't fight her problems.

Susan said that she'd let me file for the divorce, since I was the injured party. I wanted her to file the papers, since she was the one who said that she wanted out. I ended up doing it. Of course, it was a do-it-yourself project, being as frugal as we were. I proposed a division of assets, trying to be equitable. Susan would get the house and the newer car, a Ford Ranger pickup truck. She'd need the truck for her landscaping pursuits. I'd get the older car, a Volkswagen Jetta, and a large proportion of our investments.

I hadn't envisioned mourning a relationship, again, as part of my emotional education. But if a desire for women lay at the root of Susan's misery, maybe she'd be happier now. A woman's body, a woman's touch, was the one thing in the world that I couldn't offer. But I could learn that I can't always make someone else happy. If another woman was what Susan needed to be happy, so be it. And if I need an emotional education, my schooling had just started.

SANTA MARIA
DEI MIRACOLI

Connye saw me months before I noticed her.

In February of my first year in graduate school, when I was still married to Susan, I was asked to participate in a campus reading series. The graduate writing students of Eastern Washington University gave monthly noon performances of their work on the main campus in Cheney, 20 minutes outside of Spokane. Faculty, undergraduates, and other graduate students came and ate lunch during story time. One of the "traditional" students (younger and with a teaching assistantship) couldn't make it and I, one of the "non-traditional" students (older and no assistantship), substituted. I was working up new material after my first quarter of classes stripped away most of my previous thinking about writing. What the hell, I wondered; I might as well go and read the new stuff. My stomach churned as I stood at the front of the small lecture hall—it was my first public reading.

For inspiration, I reached back to something Ray Bradbury wrote in a book called *Zen and the Art of Writing*. He said that anger wasn't a bad place to start a story. Anger resembled, but not exactly, my feeling when entering the shampoo aisle in the grocery store. It's only hair, for God's sake. Sometimes during the solitary years of my second marriage, I fantasized about the women in shampoo commercials, but that's beside the point. How can so many companies put so much research, labor, materials, and marketing into hair? All that shampoo seemed like wasted resources to me. So, I wrote a story called "The Shampoo Aisle," about a guy who gets promoted to grocery store manager and starts clearing the excess and duplicate products from his shelves. At first, he does it for efficiency. Then he starts experiencing little vacations of magic realism inside his store. My voice quavered. I felt a little foolish, reading a story about a store manager disappearing because of Apple-Mango Cream Rinse. The audience seemed to like it, though.

Connye attended my reading. She was also a non-traditional student, a senior at the time majoring in liberal studies. Eastern was her ninth school in 13 years. Connye later said that she wore a bright red wool coat and matching beret that day, but I didn't notice individual members of the audience while I stood at the lectern. She told me that my story showed I was aware, that I cared. She said she knew, even on first sight, that I was someone she wanted to know and someone who would be important in her life. And now my memory has a flash of red among the students shuffling out of that stuffy February classroom.

Connye and I officially met three months later, in May. EWU housed their Masters of Fine Arts in Creative Writing program, along with several other departments, in a converted bank building in downtown Spokane. One warm afternoon I went downtown to register for fall quarter. As I left the registration desk in the cavernous former bank lobby, a petite, blue-eyed woman with straw blonde walked up to me. She seemed a little younger than I, and a hand's length shorter. "Are you Matt?"

"Yes. Hi." I offered her my hand.

She rubbed her palm on her corduroy overalls. "I just got out of the darkroom. I'm Connye. Are you registering for the MFA program?"

"Second year." At the time I couldn't see how I would finish all my classes and my thesis in another 12 months.

"I'm just starting. I get my B.A. this spring."

I congratulated her. I noticed three things about her voice. One, she'd grown up in Texas; no matter how long she'd been away or how she covered it, the land of cicadas, tornadoes, and pump jacks still tinged her words. Two, she had a very slight lisp, like someone who had needed a few sessions of speech therapy in kindergarten. (I had.) And three, I liked it. I liked her voice.

"Are you the one running the writer's group?" she asked

I confessed I was. Did she have all the information? She tugged at a copy of my flier among her books and papers. "Great," I smiled. We shook hands again and went our ways.

In June, once classes ended and the lilac blossoms began to fade, Connye arrived at Susan and my house for the first group meeting. All the members of my writing group for that first meeting were women: a TV reporter from Long Island, a feminist from Peru, a technical writer from Spokane, an ESL teacher from Vermont, a Mennonite poet who'd grown up mostly in Ivory Coast, and Connye.

A writing group works with members taking turns distributing their works-in-progress for others to read and critique. We began the evening with introductions: your name, where you were from, what you were writing. We made a list of our addresses and phone numbers, and a schedule of who would hand out their work at which meetings. Normally, you distribute your manuscript at one meeting, and receive feedback at the next. Since this was our first meeting, I asked if anyone had some poetry that we could work on that night. Poetry was short, something that we could tackle in an evening.

Connye volunteered and passed around some photocopies. Her poems that night were raw, confessional. In one she compared herself to a smashed china cup. The longest poem dealt with stomping on penises and spitting on her grandfather's grave. The group decided to focus on this one. My man radar warned me that this was a test. How would the only guy in the room handle such material?

My main comment focused on the word *penis*. "Too clinical," I said, "especially for such an angry tone. Plus, I've never liked the word."

"What do you suggest?" Connye asked.

"Cock, maybe, or dick. They're stronger, one-syllable words, with that hard -k sound." I assumed I passed the test.

After we quit for the night, all us writers stood around the front yard and enjoyed the long glow of the June evening. The former reporter announced, "I'm going to have a smoky treat." She dug a cigarette and lighter from her purse.

"Can I have one of those?" Connye asked. She puffed and said, "I quit over a year ago, but it just sounded good." Another puff. She laughed with her Texas accent. "'Smoky treat' was what we called pot in high school."

I watched all the women at least feign a knowing laugh about marijuana memories. Having never been a toker, I kept quiet and played a male mental game. Maybe I'm a pig, but I know that other men play this game, too: Which One Would I Sleep With? You can pick more than one, if you're into that sort of thing. That night in my head game, there was really only one choice: Connye.

In July we held our writing group at the apartment of Carolina, the feminist from Peru. She was older than the rest of the group, a generation older than some. She and her stories had poise and elegance from growing up surrounded by long-held traditions, unlike us Americans with our abbreviated history and hodge-podge culture. Carolina's manuscript that night dealt with rebellion against those traditions. After a women's rights protest, a Peruvian feminist drives to the coast with her lover and nearly drowns in an undertow.

When the meeting broke up, Connye and I stood and talked in the parking lot of the apartment complex. The heat and light from July lingered late into the night. I was separated from Susan by then, living alone with no reason to be home. She asked me if the tone and subject of some of her work bothered me. I shrugged no. My place wasn't to tell her or anyone what to write, but to help them write it better if I could.

That night, by way of explaining the memoir she'd planned to write in graduate school, she confessed a lot to me. She grew up in Graham, Texas, the daughter of a lawyer in a small town on the edge of the oil fields. In high school she was an honor student, a cheerleader, and champion debater. As a junior, she played the school mascot Ol' Blue, which meant she wore a large paper maché steer head atop her cheerleading uniform. I thought, only Texans would hide one of the most attractive girls in school under a cow head. Like many of her peers in the early 1980s, she also smoked pot, drank beer, and snuck out late at night, motivated mostly by the boredom of being a bright kid in a dull small town. Weekends she spent at the reservoir waterskiing barefoot, dodging copperheads and jumping off cliffs. As a senior, she dated Jim, the dark-haired, broad-grinned quarterback of the football team.

In the fall of 1984, Connye and Jim both started classes at the University of Texas at Austin, Connye with a state academic scholarship. Her grades were just passable her first quarter, Bs and Cs. At the start of her second quarter, she got pregnant by Jim and dropped out of school. All her dad said during that phone call to Graham was, "Why don't you come home?" Her parents took her in again, barely looking up from reading their used paperback books, but said that they wouldn't pay for any more college. Connye swore to her father that she would earn her degree someday, no matter what. She and Jim married, against her parent's wishes, and moved to Altus, Oklahoma to live with Jim's grandmother. Connye gave birth to James Bradley II there and attended community college as well. She also attended college when they moved to Mobile, Alabama. At both schools she earned straight A's.

She divorced Jim in Mobile after he punched a hole in a wall while aiming for her.

At a 1987 Super Bowl party in a Mobile bar, Connye met Sam, another dark-haired athlete with a broad grin. Sam had joined the Army Corp of Engineers after being tossed out of Navy ROTC at Vanderbilt University. His tour of duty was nearly up. He and Connye married later that year and moved around while Sam established himself in chemical sales. Wherever they moved, Connye attended classes and earned straight A's. In October of 1990, when Sam's career took them from Carson City, Nevada, to Spokane, Washington, Connye had enough credits on her eight transcripts to be one year away from finishing her degree. But she also had to care for Brad, age five, and little Walt, age six months. In another year, Brad and Walt would be joined by Christian. Being a wife and mother replaced college student until the

1996-1997 academic year, when Connye enrolled to finally fulfill her promise to her parents and herself.

That evening in Carolina's parking lot, Connye also confessed that while traveling for work in 1994, she was assaulted in her hotel room by a co-worker. A group from her new job was attending sales training in Los Angeles. One night after class, they went drinking in the hotel bar. Connye stumbled drunk to her room and collapsed on her bed. Kevin must have followed her. He forced a pillow over her face until she blacked out. When she came too, he was just finishing raping her. After winning an out-of-court settlement against both her co-worker and former employer, she suffered a year-long bout of what doctors at the time surmised was post-traumatic stress disorder: nausea, vomiting, weight loss, depression, hallucinations, suicidal ideation. During this time, she also finally acknowledged that her grandfather had molested her when she was five years old during a visit to an abandoned ranch house. Her illness debilitated her to the point where her sister, Dayna, moved from Austin to Spokane and became her live-in caregiver.

In Connye's mind she could still see the vivid hallucination of her three boys' bloody bodies stacked in her bathroom like cordwood. She showed me the jagged scar across her left wrist. Six times in two years, she retreated to the adult psych ward of Spokane's Sacred Heart hospital. Eventually, she lobbied for and underwent electro-convulsive shock therapy. Her psychiatrist helped her find medication that tamed her depression and brought her back to normal life. She was still undergoing a therapy called Eye Movement Desensitization and Reprocessing (EMDR). In the EMDR sessions she focused on her feelings of fear and helplessness, and what helped banish them. Her husband Sam was little comfort throughout her rape and illness. Once, over dinner in a fancy downtown restaurant, he told her that life would have been easier for him and the boys if she had managed to kill herself. She didn't think that her marriage would last much longer.

I don't know why I wasn't scared off by Connye's story. Maybe it was, in part, because she wasn't scared. I felt sad for her troubles, but also astounded at her confidence. She told her events with the surety of a survivor, a conqueror even. She carried an air of wellness, of activity and joy and appetite. She seemed confident that her future held health and happiness and success.

We were still talking in the parking lot at one in the morning. Both of us were tired. After such a confessional conversation, I felt the urge to hug Connye. "Come here," I said, and wrapped my arms around her shoulders. She pressed her cheek against my chest and touched the tips of her fingers to the t-shirt clinging to the small of my back, where the muscles run parallel to my spine.

That touch. It remains a great, unexplainable event in my life. Although I was sweaty and tired from a sweltering day in my first Spokane summer, I felt energy spread the length of my body. There was arousal, yes, because I hadn't been touched with tenderness for years. But there was connection, transference of something that I couldn't, and can't, name. It threatened to overwhelm me. I've always feared abandoning myself to emotion, so I slowly released our hug and said goodnight.

She told me that her husband traveled a lot for work, and we could talk whenever we wanted. I had her number from the writing group roster. "Call me anytime."

When I moved out from Susan, I found an apartment in a historical home built as a duplex in 1908, a rare thing for the time.

My apartment occupied the second story, two bedrooms and a bath with hardwood floors, leaded glass windows, antique push-button light switches, box-beam ceilings, and a built-in butler's pantry. Above me was a garret apartment made from the original servant's quarters. The building owners lived below me, on the first floor. Laundry, storage, and another small apartment comprised the basement. An interior spiral staircase connected all levels of the house, its curves matching the spiral metal stairs of the building's fire escape. The place was sparsely furnished. I didn't take much from the house when I moved out. The windows in the living room, dining room and larger bedroom had no curtains or shades, making my new apartment airy and light. Squares of northern summer sunlight glowed on the polished floors. When I looked out at the leafy branches, I felt I lived in an Art Deco tree house.

My new apartment, coincidentally, stood about 10 blocks northwest of Connye's house. Moving closer to Connye made it easier to continue our friendship. On a hot August afternoon, I joined her and her two smaller boys, Walt and Christian, at a public pool in a neighborhood park. We both read books and talked while she also kept an eye on the boys. She explained that her son from her first marriage, Brad, had gone to spend middle school with his dad in Las Vegas.

Soon I started inviting Connye to my apartment for lunch. My kitchen was small. Together we'd assemble some pasta and a salad. If the day had warmed by noon, we'd carry our plates down the secret spiral staircase and out onto the back patio. We'd talk about writing, Spokane, and divorce.

After one lunch I walked Connye down the stairs to my front door. As I reached to open the door for her, she leaned against the wall, with her hands behind her back. There was desperation in her eyes, and pain, and want. People who discount chemistry and telepathy and other intangibles in human relations need only remember a first kiss. It's still possible for two people to beg, confide, confess, dare, and desire without saying a word. I'd spent several years married to a depressed woman, years without a passionate kiss, but I still remembered that look. If I would ever find my way back to passion, it would be in accepting what Connye's look yearned to offer. I let go of the doorknob, pressed Connye against the wall with my body, and kissed her. Her lips were warm, almost pillowy, but determined to seek mine out and enjoy them. She showed no fear as a married woman kissing another man. We put our hands on each other's ribs, felt chests expand and fall. Her skin radiated from our lunch in the sun. Although I'd been married twice, certainly no virgin, my heart pounded like prom night. And then it was over. She definitely had to leave, to pick up her boys at their friend's house and be home. I'm sure we looked both emotionally spent and eager.

I invited Connye for a picnic lunch at Lake Roosevelt, the body of water behind Grand Coulee Dam. In a brown paper grocery bag, I packed bagel crisps and hummus, individual cheese wheels, a thermos of tea, baby carrots. Clouds quilted the sky by the time we reached the pine-lined shore. We cruised northward, eyeing the lake through the trees, until we passed a place where we could pull off the road. Our relaxed chatter stopped, and we sat up a little straighter. I needed another minute to find a stretch of two-lane road straight and long enough for oncoming drivers to see my clearly stupid U-turn. I parked. Connye and I crossed the road holding hands and picked our way down to the lake.

A small but steady breeze pushed little waves across the brown water. We brought a single blanket to sit on; we didn't think it would be this cool. Sitting with our backs to the wind, we dug into the picnic. I don't remember exactly what we discussed.

Likely we started talking about upcoming classes and graduate school in general. She probably told me more about Christian and Walt and Brad, who would also start school soon, and her eroded faith in Sam. We made love for the first time. Connye lay on top of me to stay off the cool ground. She remained mostly clothed. A poem I wrote to her afterward refers to me crying. Now, I don't remember why.

After that, we made love whenever we had the chance. Both of us had spent years in sexless marriages and wanted to make up for lost time. She would cover her mouth with her hand to muffle her moans. The arm that she used to cover her mouth also pressed against her breast, accentuating its curve. My apartment stood one block away from railroad tracks and in bed we could hear the train whistles. Connye came to associate train whistles and sex. For our first Christmas, she gave me a framed Art Deco poster announcing Britain's Night Scotsman train with service from King's Cross station each evening at 10:30. But it wasn't just sex we craved. Romance had been absent from our lives as well. One night Connye put an Aretha Franklin CD into the stereo. She placed several lit candles around the bathroom and filled the tub with steamy water and vanilla bubbles. I hopped in and slowly reclined. At first the porcelain felt cold on my back. Connye climbed in and lay against my chest. I could smell her hair and knead her shoulders. I felt another knot in my soul loosen. This was how life should be. I'd waited 35 years to share a moment like this.

When Connye was at my apartment, occasionally we'd look down through the leaded-glass windows and see her husband Sam drive slowly past the building. My heart would race. I didn't know Sam. All I knew was that he was bigger than I was, he had been in the Army, and I was sleeping with the woman who was still legally his wife. Connye was braver than I. One evening after I'd made us dinner, she saw her husband drive by. She picked up my white cordless phone and called Sam's cell phone. "Please don't come around keeping tabs on me…Sam, it's over…It's been over for quite a while…I've found some happiness again and it's just over." Her voice didn't quaver the way mine would have. I don't think I've ever been the one to announce, "It's over." Usually I'll know that a relationship is over, but not admit it fully. In the past I'd hung on, hoping that things will somehow miraculously improve without any awkward discussions or tearful scenes.

I didn't fully feel how barren living with my second wife had been until Connye took a shower at my apartment one morning. She'd spent Friday night with me and had a wedding to attend on Saturday. I was in my tiny kitchen cooking us scrambled eggs and hash browns, toast and tea. I wore my green bathrobe and brown leather slippers as I cooked. Meals with Connye were still a luxury. I walked through the butler's pantry and into the dining room to set our tea on the table. At the same time, Connye was finishing her preparations and opened the bathroom door. Her perfume mixed with the mist of her shower, and a warm, moist fog of sweet scent rolled down the small hallway and into the dining room. I stopped and inhaled deeply. Roses, the room smelled like roses, or the way that roses should smell. It was the sweetest smelling salts I'd known, because I woke up again. It had been years, I suddenly realized, since I'd noticed the smell of perfume on a woman, years since I'd been around a woman who wanted to wear perfume, put on lace occasionally, and actually enjoy the company of a man—to enjoy my company. In that moment an entire, submerged part of me resurfaced. This was why women were so appealing, I remembered now. I soaked in that perfumed moment. I was too enthralled to analyze the moment, or else I would have been terrified at how dead I'd been for so long.

This domestic moment, cooking breakfast and smelling perfume, marks in my mind the start of my life with Connye. It would be another few weeks before she'd move into the main floor apartment below me. The owners were moving across the street, into a house that they had recently added to their kingdom of rental properties. Connye and I christened our duplex "The Shack," after a B-52s song. Walt and Christian thought it was the coolest house, with the spiral staircases inside and out. It reminded them of Batman's lair. Once they introduced me to their friends by saying, "This is Matt—he lives on top of our mom."

In the duplex, Connye and I each had our own spaces and lives away from the draining marriages of the past. We had quiet times and places to write, to read, and to reclaim who we were from who we had become to survive. We attended classes together. And we shared a secret spiral staircase. We ate together often. On Friday afternoons we'd have lunch in her apartment while listening to *This American Life* on National Public Radio. We'd wash dishes together and read together and sleep together the nights when Walt and Christian were with Sam.

The summer of '98 was hot. I'd finished my thesis, the first half of a comic novel about a guy applying his MBA skills to modernize a family-run cemetery. Connye blossomed as a writer during her first year in graduate school and would soon spend two weeks writing at the Hedgebrook women writer's community in Puget Sound.

Summer meant that school was out and Connye could garden. Outside her kitchen door on the south side of The Shack waited a couple of square feet of neglected dirt. I helped her clear the weeds, mix in new soil, and plant some okra starts she had found at the local garden and pet store. (With its parrots and alligator, that pet store was the closest thing Spokane had to a zoo.) Connye loved fried okra. Growing up in north-central Texas meant that fried okra was comfort food, served after church on Sundays. In one essay, she wrote, "I grew up in a part of Texas where fresh, chopped okra dipped in corn meal, deep fried in Crisco— preferably in a cast iron skillet over a gas stove and covered with a whole shaker of salt—is as daily as bread." It's still that way when the Miller clan gathers. Lots of people don't like okra. When boiled it becomes thick and gummy. It's the vegetable that thickens gumbo. But fried okra is a whole 'nother story. Fried, okra becomes popcorn with an aubergine center. Heaped next to fresh corn on the cob and barbeque chicken—that's summer perfection, especially with cold watermelon for dessert. I may be a Yankee, but on the food front I'm Southern friendly. Bring on the barbeque and sweet tea.

Most every night we'd come out of The Shack after dinner to check our okra while the house exhaled the heat of the day. Summer nights in Spokane cool off graciously, dipping 30 or more degrees from the daily highs. The cool nights make it easier to sleep. Despite her Texas childhood, Connye had never seen an okra plant. Neither had I—okra didn't grow in the dank Tacoma of my childhood. Okra flowers resemble pale yellow hibiscus flowers. The foliage is dark and sturdy. And with a new love in my life, I did notice that okra pods look somewhat phallic.

One evening Connye and I were out admiring our plants while Walt and Christian played in the yard. She bent down to smell the flowers, although they aren't fragrant, and to check on the progress of the pods. "Come here," I said to Connye, grabbed her hand, and led her off the patio and around to the grassy side yard.

Moisture from the Pacific, 300 miles to the west, had somehow crossed the Cascade Mountains and central basin desert. Clouds mixed in the declining heat of sunset to build charcoal-black thunderclouds tinged with vermilion. We lay down in the lawn with our fingers interlaced behind our heads and watched. Between the clouds, patches of deepening sky still shone through. Tiepolo could have used it as a background.

"I hope it storms," she said. She missed the thunderstorms rolling into Alabama from the Gulf of Mexico.

Cicadas chirred in the trees. We shared our childhood memories of cicadas, their husks left on trees after their molting. Their buzzing formed the white noise of our respective childhood summers, every Texas summer for Connye and for me just the two summers I spent in Louisiana. On evenings like this Spokane approached an inner ideal for me, a city of bungalows along streets lined with sycamores and elms, a city where I could transform into a writer daydreaming on a porch, strolling sidewalks under elms, weekending at a lake cabin, and expanding into the artist I hoped to become. I imagined myself as professorial, scholarly, visionary, doing for the Northwest what Faulkner did for the Deep South.

A blessing of dragonflies gathered in the air above the yard. In the stormy light they might have been jewels dangled from the rooftop of The Shack, with crystal wings and tapered ebony bodies and eyes cut from rubies. They seemed like little flying tubes of joy. It was one of those spontaneous romantic moments that guys rejoice in capturing for once. We counted more than 50 dragonflies. Soon we got up and pointed out the congregation to Walt and Christian. The four of us started playing a little baseball. Occasionally we'd look up and see the dragonflies still dancing above our heads. We laughed and chased and rolled on the lawn. As dusk fell the clouds slowly darkened and the house inhaled the night. Walt and Christian eventually lost interest in our game, and the dragonflies drifted away.

I decided that Connye and I should talk about money. Connye knew that I had worked for years at Microsoft. She didn't know the financial implications of job. I had been able to move to Spokane with a sizeable amount of cash. My recent divorce wasn't a financial hit to either one of us, other than I had to accustom myself to dealing with relatively smaller account balances. They were exclusively my balances, no longer communal, but still they were smaller. The financial boom of the '90s rolled on.

I brought Connye into my apartment office, the bigger of my two bedrooms. Above my desk—really just a door lying across two sawhorses—I taped pictures related to the funeral industry, which had been the subject of my thesis. Economic secrets and disparity can wreck a relationship, I told her, and I didn't want that for us. She didn't seem that concerned about the issue.

With a few mouse clicks I started my personal finance computer program and generated a net worth statement. The liabilities section held no student loans, car loans, mortgages or credit card debt. The assets section contained mutual funds, retirement accounts, individual stocks, and cash accounts. I pointed to the bottom-line figure on the computer screen. The sum looked something like $1,083,647.83.

Connye hesitated a moment, then looked at me. "Yes?"

I didn't think that she'd fully counted all the numbers and commas. She'd always known me as a frugal person who shopped sale items, did my own repairs, and cleaned my own house. "That's a little over a million dollars."

I told her that, as a Microsoft employee, my best way to save money for future time to write was stock options—the chance to buy shares of the company's common stock tomorrow at today's price. With time and work and luck, the value of the stock would rise but the option price would remain fixed. Any increase in value translated into profit. As part of my November 1986 employee review, the company awarded me the option to buy 1000 shares of Microsoft stock at $30 a share. The option took full effect, or vested, gradually over the next four and a half years and remained good for ten years. (At a few subsequent employee reviews I received additional options, though never as many as the first time.)

The company posted the stock price on the computer network every weekday afternoon, usually around 3 p.m. Its appearance was something of a watershed. If the afternoon was going well—no deadlines hanging over my head, no meetings, little or no email to answer—the posting of the closing stock price meant soon I'd be commuting homeward, into the sunset, across one of Seattle's floating bridges spanning Lake Washington. It's hard to imagine a more scenic traffic jam.

But, if work was awful—another twelve-hour day spent rewriting chapters to accommodate last minute redesigning of the software—I would close my office door and repeatedly check for the arrival of the day's quote. Once the stock market delivered a figure, I entered it into a spreadsheet and let the magic of computers do the math in a nanosecond: subtract option price from current price, multiply the remainder by number of shares, deduct percentages for income taxes and retirement savings, and display the final result at the bottom of the page. For a few minutes I'd fantasize about how I might live off that much money if I quit right then. But at that point the thought of quitting was just a crutch. I'd sigh, close my spreadsheet, and return to work.

On rare and wonderful afternoons, seemingly every other year in the spring, electronic mail would arrive announcing a stock split. At the news people would whoop out of their offices, jump down the halls high-fiving each other, and telling those still at their desks to check their mail. A split meant that the board of directors had decided to give everyone who held stock in the company, say, one additional share for every one share they already owned. Splits happen mainly because the price per share has risen too high for most investors. This doubled the number of shares, but made each one worth half as much. Mathematically, it's no change in value and no big deal.

But a split also affects stock options. Those 1000 shares I was granted at $30 would become 2000 shares at $15. As Microsoft kept growing and the stock kept splitting, my grant would become 3000 shares at $10, then 6000 shares at $5, and so on. If the stock reaches $100 a share, splits down to $50, and then rises again to $100, the value of stock options has gained another $100 per share. Multiply that by thousands of shares, and you get some serious money.

Little did I know that my hazy plan about writing would work out the way it did with Microsoft. My office mate there, Christopher, referred to the early history of Microsoft as "the financial freak show." Plenty of other people who were just as smart and industrious as those at Microsoft never received the ridiculous amounts of money given to us software workers. I can't pretend that all that wealth resulted from my individual merit. I just lucked out. But when the freak show called for me, I didn't turn it down. What cascaded my way I managed reasonably well and didn't spend all at once. After 11 years of writing software manuals,

I was in a position to execute that hazy plan of taking time off for literary endeavors.

Connye looked again at my computer screen. "I figured you had some money, but nothing like this."

"I just thought you should know." I explained some of the things I was doing at the time, like selling down my portion of Microsoft stock to balance my holdings.

"It doesn't really change anything," she said.

For Christmas 1998, our second Christmas together, Connye gave me a small, wrapped box. We were sitting on the wool rug next to her couch. When I opened the box, colored stones spilled out along with a few chocolates and something gold.

Connye picked up the gold. "I didn't know if I should give you this, or how." She handed me a gold ring with stars embossed around the outside. "Can you read what it says?"

I took the band. An inscription ran along the inside. I must have held it upside down, because I couldn't make out the script.

Connye took back the ring and held it so I could read the writing. *"Many are the stars I see,"* she said, *"But in my eye no star like thee*. It's Shakespeare."

She took my right hand and slid the ring onto my third finger. "I want you to marry me. Not right now, but some day. I know that you're the one I want."

I said yes, we'd get married—someday. At the moment, a third marriage was hard to imagine with her in school, no jobs, three kids, and her divorce barely final. Marrying her meant becoming a stepparent. It meant dealing with her ex-husbands. It meant the possibility of hurt and grief and losing my self again. But it also meant her love for me.

"That's all I'm asking," Connye said. "Someday."

In the spring we bought real rings. Connye chose a custom-designed yellow gold band with a raised white gold setting. The setting held two half-carat diamonds flanking a three-quarter-carat cubic zirconium. The cubic zirconium in the center appealed to my frugality. We could replace it with a real gem on a future anniversary. I felt some hesitation about spending thousands of dollars on a ring. The previous summer I'd watched Connye throw her wedding ring from Sam into Iceberg Lake in Glacier National Park. Ten thousand years from now, maybe someone would find her ring and wonder how it came to the bottom of a mountain lake. Maybe they'd find a bunch of rings. I prayed that this ring wouldn't end up tossed into a lake.

I choose an heirloom ring. It was a simple gold band with small, embedded stones, a blue sapphire flanked by two diamond chips. The ring was made in England around 1910 and still bore the jeweler's hallmark. It was inexpensive, but I liked its age and the fact that it came with a small story. We wore our rings on our right ring fingers to show our engagement.

By Connye's 33rd birthday in February 1999, we'd decided to buy a house. Between us we paid nearly $1,200 a month in rent at The Shack. That rankled me. Mostly we had kept two places so that Walt and Christian would have their own space, with their mom and without me, during the first year that their parents were apart. The divorce was hard enough. The boys didn't need the confusion of another man living with them right away. But they seemed to like and accept me. If I was making a commitment to Connye, I was also making a commitment to Brad and Walt and Christian and Spokane, which meant staying put another 10 years while the boys finished school. Buying real estate made economic and logistical sense, in addition to the emotional sense of having our own home.

We liked our general neighborhood, the south hill of Spokane, and looked for a house fairly close to Sam's. Connye and Sam shared equal custody of Walt and Christian, so we wanted easy movement between the houses. We drove past a peach-colored bungalow for sale about ten blocks southeast of Sam's place. In walking through the house, we both loved the hardwood floors, the walls painted the color of hubbard squash, and the gumwood trim still intact from 1928. Connye wasn't sure that the house had enough room, though. Upstairs held three small bedrooms, a simple kitchen, living room, dining room, and an outdated bathroom. The basement was finished but not laid out well. The front third consisted of a single, long, carpeted playroom. The central third held the furnace, water heater, and a small shop area. In the back third there was a bathroom and laundry area, plus stairs down from the kitchen and up into the back yard.

I saw the potential. With my previous wives I'd completed major and minor remodeling projects in three other houses. By waving my arms around a little, I described how the basement floor plan could mirror the upstairs layout and make another two bedrooms while keeping a family room. Connye believed me and we made an offer. I paid cash for the house and we put both our names on the title. I still wasn't employed after grad school, so I managed our basement remodeling with help from a couple contractors. Connye and I laid a tile floor in the center third of the basement and painted the rooms.

We moved from The Shack to our new house at the end of March 1999, the same week that *Wisconsin Review* offer to publish my story about shampoo. Connye felt immediately at home living with me in our bungalow. She puttered around in her ratty favorite shirts, one from the Mangy Moose saloon in Wyoming and another from the *Mystere* show in Las Vegas. Every day, she'd do her stretching and exercise routine in the living room. Daily activity was part of her continued recovery and stress management. At night she disappeared into her office to work on her thesis, since she would graduate in another two months. I was at home, too, finally enjoying living with a woman who loved me for who I was, just as I was. As the days started to warm up, Connye strolled around her yard, planning what to plant and where. "I hope we can grow okra again," she said.

Connye received her MFA diploma on a warm, clear Saturday in June. She opted for the full ceremony with black gown and mortarboard. Because the Master of Fine Arts is considered a terminal degree—you can't get a higher degree in the arts—she also wore an academic cowl. The cowl for writing was crimson with a white strip in the center. The layers of black nylon gathered the heat of the morning as she sat amongst all the graduates arranged in rows on Eastern Washington University's football field. The black mortarboard on her head acted like a solar collector.

The boys and I stood in the stadium with Connye's parents. At first, we had difficulty spotting her and the few other MFA graduates who bothered with commencement (I skipped mine). Walt and Christian fidgeted in their seats, obviously bored with the slow, adult ceremony. Connye's mom smiled and chattered away in her high-pitched Texas twang. She's the type of grandmother to dig to the bottom of her purse looking for month-old Lifesavers, just to have something to share with the kids. Connye's father,

Dayne, told the boys to quit their fussing. Their mom attended
all their school events; they could attend one of hers. Connye
wanted her boys to see their mother acknowledged, wanted them
to glimpse the college education that she hoped they would have,
wanted to put an exclamation mark on her pledge to finish her
education. Saying "Boy, howdy" is as expressive as Dayne got;
graduation was a "Boy, howdy" day. After the ceremony, we
posed for pictures, and then dropped Walt and Christian back at
Sam's house.

The next morning, Connye started perusing the Sunday
newspaper ads for a job. We were in no danger of starving, but
after two divorces she wanted and needed to build her own résumé
and her own assets. Plus, she had student loans to repay. Even
as a straight-A student with a graduate degree and experience
serving on the boards of local non-profits, she struggled to find a
decent job. Over the summer 40 resumes went out, but no calls
came back. She suggested we consider buying a business. Before
attending EWU, she owned her own business making and selling
handcrafted dolls. That business had grown too quickly, though,
and she eventually burned out on the handwork. She scanned
franchise opportunities on the Internet, and for a while thought
that we should buy a legal self-help franchise.

I found myself perusing the business-for-sale ads in the
Sunday paper. Without realizing it, I had grown restless. Writing
was still enjoyable, but my novel wasn't panning out. The first half
was good enough to seal my degree, but the finished tale wasn't
good enough to publish. I found myself looking for something in
addition to writing and parenting the boys. Owning a business had
never been a burning desire of mine, but the idea started to appeal.
Even if our business covered just salaries and expenses, that would
be enough. For a while I explored becoming a certified financial

planner. My own experience with Microsoft's rewards taught me quite a bit about investments, portfolios, and financial planning. My ex-wife still called me for financial advice. I researched different types of planning businesses and what certifications I needed to be credible and legal. The legal requirements eventually dampened my enthusiasm. Managing my own finances was one matter, but ultimately I wasn't enthused enough to accept fiduciary responsibility for other people's finances as well.

One Sunday, I saw an ad that the local second-run movie theater was for sale. The Garland Theater stands as the last grand single-screen movie hall in Spokane. It showed movies for a dollar, nothing rated "R," usually two to four different movies every week. With Spokane's family culture and low wages, it served a good niche. Connye and I could get excited about providing affordable entertainment to families. Plus, I thought it feasible to divide the hall in two parts to make a second theater. That would alter the original character of the Garland, but with two screens you could make decent money. In the movie business, the economic engine is really the concession stand. The more people you can drive to eat and drink, the better. Maybe one screen could show family movies and the other R-rated movies or foreign films or a repertoire schedule. Midnight movies could pull in students from the area's three universities and four community colleges. We started planning how we could offer profit sharing to help student employees get through college.

Negotiations uncovered that the seller didn't control the building, main projector, screen, or seats. Those he leased from the cinema-turned-real estate company in Seattle that owned the entire city block under the building. The seller did own the popcorn popper, sound system, backup projector, office equipment, and giant trash compactor behind the building. I analyzed the financials in Microsoft Excel and saw that the payout to the seller had decreased in each of the previous three years. None of this looked promising for an asking price of more than $300,000. We offered and counter offered. I wrote reports, complete with charts, to justify how much we were willing to spend. The seller wouldn't go below $235,000. The value just didn't seem to be there. We abandoned the theater dream. We moped around the bungalow for days. Connye half-hearted lick envelopes for resumes. Eventually another woman used her inheritance from her grandmother to pay the seller's asking price for the Garland.

Connye did find two part-time jobs to earn a little money and add some recent experience on her résumé. One job placed her on a watchdog committee overseeing the county's public mental health system. The Quality Review Team, or QRT, consisted of three part-time workers operating out of a closet-sized office and earning barely more than minimum wage. She loved the investigative part of the job. It was muckraking for the cause of mental health, something she could be passionate about given her history. She supplemented her QRT work by teaching early morning classes in vocational English at Spokane Community College. Her students consisted of aspiring hairdressers and auto mechanics. She imagined that on her first day teaching, the class would erupt into the musical "Grease."

With two jobs, her pay was low and schedule scattered. She kept looking.

One thing I did with my restlessness was teach myself some Italian. Being frugal, I researched my options before investing any money in the project. Gonzaga University in Spokane, a Jesuit school, offered Italian classes for $2,100 a quarter, and an extensive study abroad program in Florence, Italy for $25,000 a year. Clearly, Gonzaga was not in my budget. Instead, I found a computer program that could teach the basics of 25 different languages: Arabic to Chinese, Tagalog to Greek, English to Italian. Every day, I worked a little further into the lessons.

Connye suggested that we actually go to Italy. Here I was, wealthy and unemployed, studying Italian from a CD-ROM, and the thought had never crossed my mind to actually go to Italy. I can be cheap with myself, a symptom of growing up with hand-me-down clothes and brown bag lunches. But I could justify the trip if it were for both of us, a honeymoon for the as-yet-unmarried. When she asked where I would go in Italy, my first response was Verona: it's a smaller town with a huge concentration of Roman ruins and a prominent place in Shakespeare's stories. Connye said she had dreamed of seeing Venice since she was a little girl. Her grandmother in Texas had a plastic model of a Venetian gondola. Connye loved to plug in the model and watch the lights glow.

Venice it was.

I financed our trip by trading options on Microsoft stock that I planned to sell anyway. Through the Internet, I found a studio apartment we could rent just one canal off St. Mark's Square. We went to a travel agent for plane tickets, since we'd have to travel through four airports to reach Venice from Spokane. I switched from my language computer program to taking night classes at the community college. A little Italian grandmother taught there, and one of our neighbors attended her classes. I finished five lessons before Connye and I boarded the plane in mid-October. I hoped I knew enough.

As our water taxi pulled away from the airport at Mestre, Italy, we could see the skyline of Venice in the middle of the

Venetian lagoon. Stone spires and cupolas rose above the choppy, steel gray waters. It was tangible magic. As an American, I had to fight the feeling that I was heading towards an attraction built by Disney. Connye looked out the boat's spray-soaked windows, and then back to me. She grinned.

Venice in many ways is diametrically opposite from America: ancient, historic, uniform, ornate, worldly, compact, devoid of cars. At times the city is hard to comprehend, and comprehension must be abandoned for awe. Like sitting in a café at lunch watching burly Italian stonemasons mixing red wine and *acqua minerale gassata*, then ending their lunch with the tiniest demitasse cups of espresso delicately pinched between their meaty thumbs and forefingers. Other times, Venice can be utterly pedestrian. October is the month of floods in Venice, we discovered. One morning a foot of water covered the courtyard outside our building's front door. I had to wade away from our building barefoot, with my pant legs rolled up and carrying my shoes, to find us rubber boots. No one lives at street level in Venetian buildings. Main floors are reserved for shops, or occasionally museum lobbies. Natives smiled and chatted under umbrellas as stores ran sump pumps to remove the foot or so of water. My feet were freezing, but I grinned for being on an adventurous chore. I managed to find two pairs of rubber boots and a couple of bumbershoots as well.

We spent our days in Venice roaming the city on foot. In the mornings, we'd pick a direction or district or destination that we hadn't seen yet and set off. If we wanted to cross a major canal into another district, we'd thread our way towards a bridge or pay the small fee for a *trajetti*, a type of public-transportation gondola, to ferry us across. After hours of sightseeing and shopping and exploring, we'd collapse into a café for lunch lasting at least an hour, maybe two or three. At one of our first and favorite *tavernas*

Connye discovered *profiterole*, round puff pastry filled with cream and served with chocolate mousse. For the rest of the trip, she insisted at every restaurant we patronized that I ask in rudimentary Italian, "*Per favore, ha lai profiterole?*" We managed to walk and eat and shop our way through the entire city. We bought masks and glass jewelry and lace, all Venetian specialties. We bought watches, necklaces, leather coats, and art. Mostly, Connye bought. I was the one worried about money and how we'd manage to haul everything back to the other side of the world. She argued that we'd probably never be in Venice again and should take advantage of whatever presented itself. She was right. And at the end of our daily excursions the *vaporetto*, Venice's water-borne bus, brought us down the Grand Canal and back to St. Mark's. We spent the evenings in our studio playing cards over a light supper or, if lunch had been late, long and large enough, no supper at all.

Like many Venetian visitors, we rode in a gondola. I thought this was definitely something Disney would love. At nearly $100, it seemed expensive, but Connye argued that we'd regret not doing it. She was right, again. Our gondolier showed us Venice at dusk, no motors masking the sound of water lapping against stone. He took us past the house of Marco Polo, explorer and businessman and a memoirist like Connye wanted to be. When we told our gondolier that we were engaged (it was the easiest way to explain our relationship), he told us about Santa Maria dei Miracoli, the church where Venetians married. In a town with 70 major historical churches for a population of just 50,000, we decided that we needed to see the church that the locals favored for weddings.

Our guidebook likened Santa Maria dei Miracoli to a jewel box. Although the church wasn't far from our apartment, it was difficult to actually find. As we got closer, we could spot it from the peaks of *ponti* (bridges) spanning the canals. In relation to other churches in the city, it's hardly more than a chapel, barely four stories tall including the dome above the altar. White fluted columns separated the exterior marble panels of pink and gray and okra-flower yellow.

Connye and I paid the few lire admission charge and entered wearing our parkas and rubber boots. I doubt 150 people could fit in the pews. The church was built in the 1480s to house Nicolo di Pietro's painting "The Virgin and Child," which was believed to have miraculous powers. The painting formed the center of the altar atop a grand staircase. The interior marble panels were more colorful and complex than the exterior. A barrel-vaulted ceiling arched over the pews. Embedded in the ceiling rested 50 portraits of saints and prophets, each one a star in a gold and green firmament.

We browsed for a few minutes, whispering to each other and pointing, before sitting in a pew. The beauty and serenity of the spot silenced us. I glanced around. A couple other tourists walked slowly around the perimeter of the church. Looking up the aisle and the staircase to the altar, I could see why Venetian brides wanted their weddings here. Any bride would want to stand atop those marble stairs with the white train of her wedding dress fanned below her, surrounded by family and friends and pink marble and gold.

Connye and I had each been married twice before. We hadn't yet discussed when or how we might get officially married, although we knew our commitment to each other. My gut told me now was the time. I slipped my heirloom band off my right ring finger. I nudged Connye to get her attention, and then put my ring in her hand. I looked at her ring on her right hand. She didn't understand my plan, so I took her right hand and slid her ring off her finger. I shifted in the pew to fully face her. Without a word, I lifted her left hand with mine, palm to palm, and placed her ring on her third finger. She must have figured out what I was doing, because when I looked up from her hand, tears welled in her eyes. She took my left hand with hers, palm to palm, and slid my ring onto the third finger of my left hand. Gazing up again, she smiled and sniffed and wiped away a tear. We kissed gently and sat in our pew for another minute holding hands, silent.

Outside Santa Maria dei Miracoli, we met an American couple standing in the campo admiring the church. Connye asked them to take our picture, rubber boots and all. After pushing the shutter button and returning our camera, the husband resumed complaining to his wife about paying the church's admission fee.

I smiled at them and said, "You've flown halfway around the world to be here. You'll probably never be back here again. What's a couple of lire to see the church where Venetians get married?" Connye must have been proud to hear me.

The wife looked at her husband, and they entered the church.

EARLY HISTORY OF THE PLANET

After we returned from Venice, Connye answered the following ad in *The Spokesman-Review*, the city's daily paper:

> JOURNALIST WRITERS wanted to cultivate & define new editorial coverage in the NW. Qualified candidates should have strong interviewing skills & a lively alternative writing voice. Please send clips or writing samples along with pay requirements c/o Journalist, 505 E. Third Ave., Ste. B, Spokane WA 99202.

The ad did not mention the company's name. The address belonged to a half-vacant strip mall on the edge of downtown. Connye's cover letter started with, "I usually don't answer blind ads, especially ones addressed to half-empty strip malls." But she loved newspapers, loved reading even Spokane's mediocre daily newspaper. She'd finish every investigative piece that lost me at the page jump. Molly Ivans and Jim Hightower were her Texan heroes. Journalism could feed her passion and her family.

The ad was for *The Local Planet*, an alternative weekly newspaper being started by a computer wholesaling company.

They wanted a place for their computer-reseller customers to advertise. One company employee, Mitch, had worked at a monthly computer magazine in town before it folded. Mitch was tall enough to fill a doorway, with a goatee and as much of a Georgian accent as Connye's tinge of Texan. He drank Mountain Dew from sunrise to midnight and supplemented his caffeine with cigarettes. He had little education, nothing beyond a GED, but some native talent for graphic design. Mitch convinced his employers that another computer-oriented publication wouldn't survive in Spokane. The market simply wasn't large enough. But an alternative weekly newspaper could work and would appeal to young, tech-friendly readers who were not necessarily geeks but still bought a lot of computer gear.

Spokane already had one established weekly newspaper, *The Pacific Northwest Inlander*, in its crowded media landscape. Aside from weeklies, the local metropolitan area of barely half a million people also supported two daily papers, two business journals, two classified shoppers, three billboard companies, two cable TV systems, five television network affiliates, and 25 radio stations. That's nearly as much major media as Seattle, a metropolitan area at least five times as large.

Connye landed the job, and rejoiced to have full-time work that she believed in. Her starting pay was low, $24,000 a year. She recruited her graduate school and community college colleagues to staff her "penthouse" of writers. She didn't like the industry cliché of "a stable of writers." I wasn't working at the time, so I tagged along as well, contributing my experience for free to help this venture get off the ground.

The first issue of *The Local Planet* came out on Connye's 34th birthday, February 17, 2000. The publication plan called for distributing the paper every other Thursday to start. We worked straight through Tuesday night and into Wednesday morning to ready our pages for the printer. Mitch was a disorganized artist, and he didn't want to relinquish any of the page designing. We missed our first printing deadline by more than 12 hours, after spending nearly 40 hours trying to combine words and drawings and photos and ads into 32 pages of readable material.

That first issue held enough passion to counterbalance the typos and lack of ads. Page four contained the following Letter from the Editors, signed by Connye and Mitch:

> We promise that we won't habitually quote dead white guys, but Plato wrote that the purpose of art is to inform and delight. And that's our intent: to leave you informed and delighted.
>
> Personally, we're delighted to bring a fresh alternative magazine to the Inland Northwest. There is a wealth of creative energy in our region. That's what we'll show-case: local innovation. Many gifted individuals, writers, visual artists and musicians make this region their home. We hope to bring you their words, their images, their sounds as a way to reflect on the large and small issues that affect our lives.
>
> This one-paper town needs a new sheriff to shake up the establishment. Think of us as riding in on a news-print palomino, wearing a fuchsia hat and packing one humongous word processor.
>
> We need you. Our noble experiment won't fly without vigorous, intelligent discussion. It's a two-way deal. Gone are the days of ivory-tower journalists dummying down their take on the world and calling it gospel. You get a say in writing our history here.
>
> We want to hear from you.

To start, we reported mostly on the pocketbook issues all readers feel: wages, prices, making ends meet, getting ahead. Paulette, a community-college teacher who joined our staff, wrote the first cover story. She detailed the life of union members on the picket line outside Kaiser Aluminum. Members of the United Steelworkers local 338 picketed to protest plans to replace union jobs with non-union outsourcing. In turn, Kaiser illegally locked out the workers and refused to negotiate. The lockout had already lasted more than two years. The loss of thousands of union-scale jobs gutted the Spokane economy. Among the other stories in that first issue, Connye contributed a personal essay built around her memory of accidentally flushing a $5 bill down the courthouse toilet during a recess in her divorce hearings with Sam. I wrote an editorial about creating an economically diverse city that replaced imported products with local goods, and then exported those goods to other cities. I also reviewed Windows 2000, Microsoft's new operating system, and started a weekly personal-finance column under the pen name Proper Lincoln.

Connye's new job honeymoon didn't last long. After two issues, she realized that the parent company leadership consisted of one dumb guy (finance), one spineless guy (operations), and one drug addict (president). Being a freelancer at the time, I wasn't in the office much and didn't see all the insanity these three generated. I did hear the stories, though, from Connye and the other employees. Occasionally, random pairings of the top three went to the back parking lot and slugged it out, either for fun or as an alternative method for making decisions. On paydays, the dumb one gave the addict the checks. The addict signed them and put them his desk drawer. Employees had to come to him and request their pay. When asked why he did this, the addict answered that maybe someone would forget, and the company could keep the money. The addict wanted the newspaper to trade ads with a

florist so he could give flowers every week to the receptionist he
was screwing--this while he had a wife and newborn baby at home.
He repeatedly made one of the newspaper sales staff shuttle his
receptionist/mistress to and from liaisons. Another newspaper
salesperson complained that during a one-on-one meeting,
the addict said, "I've got a gun on you right now." When the
salesperson looked through the leg hole of the president's desk, he
saw a handgun resting in the addict's lap. The staff told me that the
gun went off once in the office during business hours. The bullet
lodged in a filing cabinet.

After three issues, the newspaper staff decided they'd had
enough. Mitch knew I had some money and asked if I wanted
to buy the paper. I'd never owned a business before, not even a
lemonade stand. Negotiating for the movie theater was the closest I
had come. But here was publishing, a business where Connye and
I knew something. We knew that we'd be in Spokane for another
10 years, until Christian was out of high school. We believed
that Spokane would be a better place in those 10 years if voters,
shoppers, parents, and business owners were engaged by real,
relevant stories instead of the ad-separators that passed for editorial
content in most of the region's media. We believed that democracy
didn't work in Spokane because Cowles Publishing controlled too
much of the local media. Connye carried a strong sense of social
justice, and she believed in journalism as an instrument of that
justice. Me, I'd never ached to be a journalist, never attended a
journalism class, never written more than the occasional review
for a newspaper. (My most infamous piece of journalism to date,
written for my college newspaper, defended the campus screening
of the soft-core movie *Emmanuelle*. I wrote preemptively, figuring
someone else would write in to complain about the eroticism of the
movie. No one did. My lone defense made me look like a pervert.
A fellow English major wrote in after me, though, and thoroughly

skewered me. Touché.) But I was looking for an endeavor and looking to do something with my wife. Her dream became my dream. Owning a newspaper could be the way Connye and I built our life and family and community together.

We also believed a business opportunity existed because the established newsweekly, *The Inlander*, didn't reach an audience much different than that of the daily paper. One day in graduate school, I realized that I represented *The Inlander*'s prime audience— mid 30s, college educated, progressive, a reader and writer—but I hadn't picked up one of their issues in years. After reading them as my potential competition, I decided that they didn't know why they were publishing a newspaper in Spokane. One-third of their cover stories could be published by any weekly paper in the country. Another third of their covers were "special" issues, projects like menu guides, shopping guides, "Best Of" guides, skiing guides, all aimed purely at selling advertising. Only a third of *The Inlander*'s cover stories concerned the community in which they wrote, and those stories were timid and unenlightening. Editorials are where the vision and purpose of a newspaper finds expression. Every week, *The Inlander* farmed out their editorial, sometimes to a syndicated writer but most often to a retired professor of governmental studies from Eastern Washington University. His editorials were so ill conceived, boring, and riddled with cliché that I seriously considered turning in my degree from EWU. No one locally was publishing the stories that would appeal to a 31-year-old Spokanite with dyed hair and a pierced nose who was also a college graduate and parent.

Musing about the power of stories and the mediocre content of *The Inlander* comprised the sum total of our market research. With far more gut instinct than knowledge, we agreed to buy *The Local Planet*. Our plan, such as it was: we could spend several hundred thousand dollars getting the paper started. People said that we would need about three years to break even. At the end of ten years, we should have been collecting salaries and a profit for at least seven years and be positioned to sell the paper to the employees. We'd get our money back out, or at least enough of it. That way, *The Local Planet* would remain a voice in Spokane. With the paper sold and Christian graduated from high school, Connye and I could depart Spokane for new, grand adventures in writing and travel.

Mitch told the addict on the first Friday in April that the entire newspaper staff was quitting. Mitch towered over the addict. He explained that someone was interested in buying the paper for what the company could show it had invested. If the addict didn't want to sell, he could re-staff the paper or fold it. The addict claimed we were staging a coup but agreed to sell. Mitch said that his contract with the company gave him 20% of the newspaper upon its sale. Connye and I never actually saw that contract, but we trusted Mitch. The dumb one and the spineless one, the company employees who actually negotiated the sale, didn't contradict Mitch's contractual claim.

In the next five days we closed the purchase of the newspaper, found temporary office space, secured phone lines through U.S. Worst, and loaded all the desks, chairs, filing cabinets, computers, monitors, keyboards, mice, printers, scanners, cameras, phones, copiers, fax machines, and lamps into borrowed vans for the drive one mile west to our new home. Our new offices occupied the top corner of the Holley-Mason building in downtown Spokane. The Holley-Mason was six stories of solid brick built in 1905 as a hardware store and warehouse, something like the Home Depot of its time. The building towered just on the wrong side of the elevated freight rail tracks that divide the offices-and-restaurants part of downtown from the dicey-shambles-for-homeless-people part. It was also Spokane's first fireproof building thanks, in part, to its concrete columns. That design meant that, 90 years after its construction, the Holley-Mason had survived four major fires and stood burned out and boarded up.

Rob, the building owner, told me that he was able to purchase the building plus the parking lot and Camp Fire Girls headquarters behind it, for significantly less than $500,000. He restored the first five floors as the temporary home for Lewis & Clark High School while the historic school five blocks to the south underwent renovation. Rob was younger than we were, with brown curly hair and a boyish face. He made some money in Washington, DC real estate, and came home to Spokane to make more. Rob was also gay, and Connye hoped that he might be a positive role model for Brad. The sixth floor of the building was partially finished, and we moved there into 400 square feet of space shared with an Internet service company.

In that frantic week of closing and moving, we also published our fourth issue featuring my cover story about wages in Spokane. Like my fictional shampoo story, I wrote this cover story partly out of anger. Many Spokane employers paid wages below the national average, claiming that the city's cost of living is cheaper than elsewhere. I compared costs in Boise, Idaho; Salem, Oregon; Spokane and Seattle by combining U.S. Census data and Chamber of Commerce survey statistics. My findings? In examining 1997, the most recent and complete year of data available at the time, Spokane's per-capita income lurked 12% below the national average, while prices ran about 2.5% to 5% above average. Buying a house in Spokane was cheaper than in Seattle. That's the only thing that was cheaper, and that wasn't a fair or direct comparison. Matched against comparable markets like Boise or Salem, Spokane housing wasn't any cheaper. Gas, food, cars, car insurance, medical care, clothing, electricity, natural gas, water, garbage, cell phones, phones, cable, dry cleaning, and all the other costs of life in Spokane mirrored national averages. These pocketbook stories did surprisingly well. Copies leapt from our distribution racks and we heard good anecdotal information about buzz around town.

In June 2000, we ran an exposé of the Cowles family. For our cover we ripped off the daily paper's page A-1 design. (Our newspaper was tabloid format—it more resembled a magazine—while most daily papers have a longer, folded page style known as broadsheet.) A headline on our mock front page joked "Stacey—He's a guy!" William Stacey Cowles was the fourth-generation publisher of *The Spokesman-Review*. He was also the family's fourth William in a row and thus used his middle name. As scion, he should have been a very public figure for the town's leading family. But because he was so ineffectual at representing his paper and his family, and because his middle name looked like a woman's name, many people in town didn't even know his gender.

At the time, the Cowles family was also remodeling their downtown shopping center. The public-private partnership carrying out the work relied in part on loans backed by the community's grants from the federal Department of Housing and Urban Development (HUD). One of our exposé segments questioned the social justice of using public grants to finance a wealthy family's mall housing stores like Godiva Chocolates. Some single pieces of Godiva sold for more than a gallon of milk, and plenty of people in Spokane relied directly on grants just to buy milk. Later we learned that, during the week of our exposé, the entire Cowles clan had coincidentally gathered in Spokane to reorganize their family corporate structure. Stacey kept control of the paper; his sister Betsy controlled most everything else. A

Philadelphia bond attorney with Spokane connections told us that a segment about the Cowles's domination of Spokane, based partly on our reporting, made the short list of potential news stories for the CBS news magazine "60 Minutes."

We tried placing environmental stories on the cover of *The Local Planet.* Early stories included the fate of wild salmon in dammed Northwest rivers and pollution in the Spokane River that runs over waterfalls smack in the middle of downtown. (In fact, the city's original name was Spokan Falls). Environmental covers didn't entice readers to take a paper from the rack, even in a community so obviously connected to its landscape. We published a nature essay, "Nakedness and the River," about the Spokane River. To illustrate the story, our art director digitally clipped Adam and Eve figures from a 1507 Albrecht Dürer painting and digitally placed them in photographs of the river. Both wore fig leaves but Eve was bare-breasted—and she was on the cover.

You'd think we published pornography. One distribution point refused to carry that issue. Another tossed out our rack and paper altogether. The computer expo advertiser called to complain about the pictures. His ad ran on the left-hand page facing Eve and the opening of the nature essay.

"But you do realize that's Eve?" I said. "She's supposed to be naked."

"I know who it is and I still don't want my ad next to bare breasts."

So much for Christian iconography in a Catholic town.

By Labor Day we'd outgrown our temporary, shared office space. We were staffing up to switch to weekly publication, and needed a larger, permanent office space to accommodate our growth. We employed 15 people but still occupied just 400 square feet: one 15x15' room for editorial and design, one former storage area for sales, and part of the Internet company's lobby for distribution and administration. We wanted to stay in the Holley-Mason building. We even paid an architect to design a new space in the empty portions of the sixth floor, but Rob kept dragging his feet about starting the project. Eventually, we decided to move.

For our second corporate move in six months, we went north three blocks. Once again, everyone on staff labeled and boxed their desks, chairs, computers, monitors, keyboards, boxes, and anything else to move. We packed and unpacked in one weekend so we wouldn't disturb high school classes in the building during the week. Despite my own back problems the weekend of the move, everything went surprisingly smoothly. No one dropped a computer or monitor.

We leased an entire floor of a Wells Fargo bank building. Our new address was once the site of Spokane's first "skyscraper." Before that, in the 1880s, it was the block of opium dens, just south of Dutch Jake's saloon and brothel. Nearly everyone had a private office with a window and door. In the center of our floor, we built a break area and a production area to hold the scanner, printer, network server, copier, and fax machine. Instead of cheap cordless phones and US Worst, we leased our own digital phone system and PBX with voicemail, conference calls, and more. Now we could put people on hold, just like a real company. Near the elevators we had two bathrooms: Women's and Handicapped. We felt like an honest-to-God newspaper now and could get down to publishing every week. In her new corner office, Connye leaned back in her chair, feet up on her new desk, arranging a photo shoot of two drag queens for our first weekly cover.

That September Saturday when the company moved to permanent offices, I stayed home flat on our couch with muscle spasms in my back. My back never failed because of dramatic effort, like trying to single-handedly muscle a desk into an elevator. Usually, it happened when I bent over to put on or remove my underwear. I told myself that my back problems stemmed from a track-and-field injury in junior high school, or maybe the stress of new marriage and new family and new business. Any excuse was easier than admitting that I was overweight and out of shape.

Connye took Brad shopping that Saturday after the move. Shortly after lunch, as I lay grimacing on the couch and listening to National Public Radio, they walked through the back door from the car. Connye carried something black and unmistakable. Christ Almighty *no*, I thought. A puppy.

Connye had talked for several months about getting a dog. She raised the subject soon after we bought the house, before we owned the paper. Now that we had a house and a fenced yard, why not have a dog? A family needed a dog. The boys needed a pet to play with. They needed something at our house that wasn't at Sam's. She and the boys still missed Greta, their keeshond. Greta herded and guarded the boys when they were little. When the kids played in Sam's front yard, she lay between them and the curb and kept watch. She let the boys watch her raise a litter of puppies. Then, one day in 1995 during Connye's bout of hellish illness and depression, Greta started shaking in the hallway and collapsed against the wall. In a few days she died, the vet said, of a stroke. Every Christmas, Connye hung an enamel ornament of a keeshond with a halo on our tree.

Connye and I would sit on our bed and debate: dog, no dog, dog. Originally, I objected because she and the boys would be at work and school, and I'd be stuck caring for a creature I didn't want or have the energy for. Two boys and three cats seemed enough to me. Then we grew to three boys with Brad's return, plus a business. Finally, not long after our lake wedding, I told Connye,

"Look, I can't command you to not get a dog. I don't want that kind of marriage. But I'm begging, please, not now and especially not a puppy."

"Isn't he cute? Here." She put the black, curly, wriggling puppy on my chest. I immediately got a tongue bath. "I just fell in love with him. He's a miniature poodle. Isn't he sweet? Right when he looked at me, I knew. You should have seen his brother. He was apricot, and he was jumping straight up and down on all fours all the time we were there. This little one looked like he was begging us to take him away."

I flailed my arms. "I don't want him on me. I thought we talked about this. Who's going to take care of him? What's he going to do while we're all gone? What about the cats?"

Connye took back the dog. "I can come home at lunch—it's not very far. Or he can come to work with me. See, he's calm and quiet, not like the other poodles. Aren't you?" She let him lick her face. "What should we call him?"

I wondered to myself if you could name a dog "Refund." Another husband might have thundered to take the damn thing back. I struggled to get off the couch. The black support belt helped my back, some, that and the ice packs. "Henry," I grunted.

"Why Henry?"

"I don't know." I shuffled off to our bedroom to lie down in peace.

"My sister had a beagle once named Henry."

That afternoon Walt and Christian seemed excited by the novelty of the event. Walt got down on all fours so he could be right in Henry's face. "Here Henry Here Henry Here Henry arf Arf ARF!" The dog hid among the chair legs under the dining room table.

"Walt," I said while stirring macaroni and cheese, "get out of the dog's face. You're scaring him."

"Here Henry Here Henry Here Henry."

"Walt, did you hear what I said? Stop. He's not going to like you if you keep that up."

The cats hissed and swatted at Henry before leaving to hide in the basement. He snuck down there after them and soiled the carpet on the landing. He slept with us that night.

On Monday morning the boys all left for school. I minced down the back steps, a little chilly in just a t-shirt and pajama pants, and tossed treats out in the lawn for Henry. I want to get him accustomed to sniffing in the grass. Henry liked the treats but didn't get the connection. He didn't look like he'd get it anytime soon, either. I could hear Connye blow-drying her hair for work and wished I were standing in her perfumed steam. When time came for us to leave, I put the dog in his crate in the upstairs hallway near the bathroom. In went a couple of towels, in went his stuffed pink poodle, and I closed the door. He started yipping before we walked out of the house.

Snow came early and stayed late that winter. In fact, Spokane set a record with 110 straight days of snow on the ground. Henry was slow to housebreak. His legs were short and the snow deep. Several times a day I'd stand in the white back yard with him, urging him to "go piddle." Occasionally throughout the winter he'd sneak into the basement and "go piddle" at the foot of the stairs. I carried a lot of resentment towards Connye about bringing home the dog. I even asked a neighbor if she wanted Henry, because I didn't and she'd had a small poodle before. She didn't take him.

Before our lake wedding, Connye asked me if I was taking on too much. If she had asked me now, I might have admitted that I had—and the dog certainly didn't help. The signs were there for me to notice. I was tired. Moving, parenting, and returning to working full time had been quite a switch from the life I led just a year earlier. More and more I was carping on Walt and Christian and chaffing against routines that were already set or coordinated with Sam. The stress affected our marriage. Connye wanting the happy companionship of a dog should have been a sign. Our sex life slowed down, as well. We held a running debate about the quality of people that we got with the purchase of the newspaper. Connye wanted to fire nearly all of them and start over, or just fold the business. It sapped a large amount of money every month.

I had volunteered for all of this. Maybe it was my enthusiasm for being in love again, of having found a love and a life and a purpose again. I still felt my inexperience was part of the paper's problem, and that things I could do as president of the company were part of the solution. Everyone at the paper was green, but they were working hard and deserved more of a chance. Even enthusiasm can get tiring, though. We planned to publish a double issue at the end of the year, so that the staff could take time off at the holidays. That issue would feature a cover drawing of a newsprint palomino, like the one mentioned in our first Letter from the Editors. I needed a vacation.

OUT IN COSTUME

Connye described her oldest son Brad by saying, "That boy came out of me in costume." Several childhood pictures featured him in some sort of get-up. One formal portrait captured him kneeling in a homemade costume of Batman's sidekick Robin. In another, he reclines next to a pond while wearing a white cowboy hat, white Western shirt, and new blue jeans. That one helped Brad land a few child modeling and acting assignments through a local talent agency. When I met Connye, she had just moved Brad from her home in Spokane to Las Vegas, to spend middle school living with his dad, Jim. Her second marriage was falling apart in loud, noisy chunks, especially after her rape and subsequent depression a couple years prior. Brad didn't need to endure the tension and fights. He should enjoy one of a few advantages of having a parent living in another city.

In some ways, Las Vegas was good for Brad. He could enjoy being his dad's only child. Jim installed a giant stereo system in his bedroom and drove him to weekend snowboarding trips in the Sierra Mountains. His stepmom, Molly, bought him enough Izod polo shirts and Nordstrom khakis to snap the rod in his closet. Middle school in Las Vegas spanned grades six through eight, so Brad graduated from elementary school a year earlier than if he had stayed in Spokane. He didn't always turn in his homework, usually because he was too busy socializing to remember. On weekends, he hung out with neighborhood friends. He talked with his mom often by phone and wrote her cards and letters.

Jim pushed Brad into playing football: like father, like son seemed the hope. Jim was always appalled at Brad's lack of interest and ability in sports. After his first week of team practices, Brad told his mom over the phone that football was just a bunch of fat old men yelling at boys about fitness. The sports photographs that Connye received along with Brad's correspondence seemed incongruous. Her son's smooth 12-year-old face smiled inside the dark cage of a plastic helmet. His shoulder pads towered around where his ears should have been, monstrous like a Halloween outfit. He suffered a concussion halfway through his first season and didn't join the team the next year.

Connye and I flew south a few extra times during the school year to visit Brad. Mostly, we wasted time at Circus Circus, waiting for the few hours when Jim would let us see Brad. We spoiled him with go-cart racing and burgers at Sonic Drive-In. We attended one of his football games and laughed at the fat men yelling. In the rental car to or from an outing, Brad chattered about his classes and school government and the latest bands that he and his friends listened to. At least once, we arrived in Las Vegas on a pre-arranged visit only to have Jim forbid us to see Brad. Jim declared a last-minute family trip to Disneyland in Los Angeles, several hours away by car, to keep us apart.

During that first year with his father, Brad fought the realization that he was attracted to boys, not girls. School and socializing became ways for him to disguise his inclination. He earned leadership awards, won the election for class treasurer, and escorted visiting dignitaries around the open-air campus. Brad

cultivated a succession of girlfriends and accompanied many of
them to dances. So many girls came and went that Jim sensed a
type of desperation. At one point, he grounded Brad from social
activities with girls, at least until his grades rebounded. Behind
the scenes, Brad tried other ways to soothe the panic of his
realization. He started smoking when he was not even a teenager.
He drank, too.

In the summer, Brad gladly escaped the July heat of Nevada
for his scheduled visit to Spokane. With us he could wear what he
wanted, within reason. Out of storage came the clothes he was
forbidden to wear at his dad's: concert t-shirts and Levi 501s with
the knees worn out and black Chuck Taylor tennis shoes. We didn't
know yet about Brad's identity struggles. Jim didn't tell Connye
much about Brad's life with him, or include her in decisions such
as religion, counseling, and sex education. On those summer
nights, Brad's half–brothers Walt and Christian pleaded to sleep
in our basement TV room. School was out. They wanted to stay
up late every night watching cartoons and playing video games,
but they needed their sleep and Connye, Brad, and I wanted to
watch movies on our one TV screen of any size. Being literary
types, Connye and I rented the artsy movies that we could never
take Walt and Christian to see in the theater. During Brad's visit
that summer we repeatedly rented videos with a gay theme: *Gods
and Monsters*, *Death in Venice*. At the time, we even joked about our
homoerotic film festival. The poor boy must have wondered what
Connye and I knew and whether we were sending some sort of
covert message.

After he returned to Las Vegas, Brad blew his cover by
leaving downloaded gay pornography on his dad's home office
computer. Jim snapped. He did not want his son playing for
the other team, so to speak. He enrolled Brad in counseling

through Exodus, an organization that promised "freedom from homosexuality" through Jesus Christ. For a while Brad submitted to the sessions, hiding his feelings of rage and shame and rejection, just to keep the peace with his father. That fanned his anxiety, and his tobacco habit. Brad finally refused when Jim wanted to take him to San Diego for a father-son gay conversion retreat. Jim later confessed to Brad his own previous struggles with alcohol and strip clubs. But with the help of The Lord, he had put that behind him and built a marriage with Molly. The Lord would help Brad as well, if only he would let Him. Jim pushed harder to keep Brad from, as he saw it, choosing homosexuality. More and more, Brad knew that there wasn't a choice. Their silences grew longer and their fights louder.

After Brad came out to us, Connye battled Jim in court about Brad returning to live in Spokane. Although Brad had clearly stated his wishes, and as a 15-year-old the courts would give his preference a lot of weight, Jim did not want his son returning to us. He knew we wouldn't challenge Brad's homosexuality. Connye hired an attorney in Nevada to handle the flurry of child support filings. Just before Thanksgiving, she flew to Las Vegas for a custody hearing. When I called her that night, she ranted into the phone for nearly an hour. The judge forced her to listen to Jim read a 15-page diatribe into the court record. In his deposition, he alleged that Connye made his son gay by tying his shoes with pink shoelaces when he was a kid, letting him avoid sports, giving him one of the dolls she crafted as part of her home business, and accompanying him to a concert by Melissa Etheridge—"a confessed lesbian." Jim wrote, "Brad is only 15 years old and being encouraged to pursue a lifestyle that he admits to never experiencing himself." Isn't that everyone's virginal state, gay or straight? After several weeks and several thousand dollars, the legal aspects were settled. Brad would live with us. Jim would pay

$300 a month in support. Medical costs would be split between the two parents.

Once Brad legally resided in Spokane again, Connye grieved. Having a gay kid didn't bother her, but as a mother she dreaded the difficulties her son would face in life. The possibility of AIDS worried her. The reality of discrimination angered her. She mourned that her son might not ever live the American Dream life that all parents want for their children: a happy home, a constant love, an engaging career, friends and acceptance and family. Me, I was still oblivious enough to the cruelty of life that these things didn't cross my mind at first. I didn't yet fully accept the reality of violent and bigoted idiots. I heard news stories about Matthew Sheppard being beaten and left for dead tied to a Wyoming snow fence but didn't imagine gay bashing could happen to my stepson, even though once I had been threatened on a Seattle city bus by someone who merely thought I was gay because I was wearing a tie and leather shoes.

I'm sure that for most of my high school years my mom suspected that I was gay. I didn't take wood shop or auto body class. I didn't date but had female friends that I could talk with for hours on the phone. Much of my free time I spent with other guys from the swim team. We wore those skimpy Speedo swimsuits. For big meets at the end of the season, we shaved off all our body hair not covered by suits or caps. In truth, I was shy in high school, somewhat earnest and bookish, and as clueless as Brad was gifted about popularity and clothing and gossip. I didn't have a girlfriend until halfway through my senior year, although I had plenty of crushes on girls. Homework and sports and church and family kept my life busy enough to enable my emotional repression, or cowardice, however one might term it.

If I had stopped to think, I already had a reference point for the experience of growing up gay. When I worked at Microsoft in Seattle, I mentored Mike, a guy who grew up in Tennessee as the gay only son of a Southern Baptist family. High school had been hard for him. He slept with his male French teacher. Ick. His only friend had been the one openly bi-sexual girl in school; she wanted to sleep with the French teacher. My future apprentice grew up to be a disguised alcoholic. During the workweek he appeared smart, dedicated and professional. On weekends he would call, drunk, and slur away until he fell asleep on the phone. His mental agility helped him continue to drink while hiding from doctors, counselors, and himself, and exhausting the rehab benefits of two different health insurance plans. Finally, addiction counselors put him on the maximum dose of Anabuse, a prescription drug that turns alcohol extremely toxic in the body. While on medication, Mike decided to drink a bottle of red wine and watch an episode of *Seinfeld*. He spent the next three days in the hospital recovering and convincing chaplains that he wasn't suicidal. At least that's what he repeatedly told me. I still wonder whether he didn't protest that point too much. Mike eventually sobered up and found another job in Seattle's high-tech economy.

I could accept Brad and care for him as Connye's oldest son, but because we were so different, sometimes it was hard for me to understand him. Brad had a genetic desire for a big-budget lifestyle, in contrast to my frugality. As a boy, he printed out sheets of fake checks on the family computer and then made them out to himself for bazillions of dollars from famous people like Walt Disney and Michael Jackson. I started a savings account when I was seven and only deposited money, never withdrew. While growing up, I watched football games and war movies on TV; Brad watched E!, the fashion channel. I built model airplanes; he drew dress designs. He blew $160 on one pair of designer jeans; every day of high school, I wore the same banana-colored sweatshirt under my orange-and-white letterman's jacket. Spending two consecutive nights at home made Brad claw the walls; usually two nights out in the same week exhausted me. Maybe Brad's attraction to glamour and fashion, in part, explained why Connye wasn't surprised when he came out to us two days before our formal wedding. She had occasionally, privately, suspected that Brad might be gay.

At first, I told myself that Brad's sexual orientation was inconsequential to parenting. Raising a gay kid shouldn't be much different from raising a straight one. Connye and I still had to teach Brad good values, manners, and habits. We had to worry about setting rules and curfews, when to let him start dating, whether he wore a coat when it was cold or applied himself at school. In the end, our job as parents was to raise Brad to be a principled and independent person, gay or straight. The only difference, I thought, would be who called for dates on Friday nights.

Occasionally Connye and I discussed Brad with Rob, the former landlord for the newspaper we owned. Connye hoped Rob, who was gay, could be a role model for Brad. Rob was smart and industrious, building a small empire in Spokane real estate. Over lunch one day at the downtown mall, the three of us talked about raising a gay son. I interjected my philosophy about raising all kids the same. Rob corrected me. Gay kids lived in a subculture with harassment, confusion, and self-loathing, he warned, even drug habits and suicide. Ignoring that fact would be perilous, and probably impossible.

After that lunch, Connye and I worked harder at understanding Brad's role as a gay teen. We let him hang out with other gay kids, but no dating. We debated whether running a weekly newspaper left us time and energy to dedicate to the local chapter of PFLAG (Parents and Friends of Lesbians And Gays). We strove to accept that our family story was different, like when other parents asked if Brad had a date for the prom or speculated about grandparenthood potentially just a decade away. And then there was "the talk." How does a heterosexual parent talk with a gay child about sex? Connye managed this brilliantly. She did her homework as any good journalist would. She also felt very comfortable with her own sexuality, especially after all the counseling she had done following her rape. When she found gay skin magazines and DVDs in Brad's room, she didn't freak out as Jim had. She told Brad that porn wasn't healthy, but to her it seemed safer than him going God knows where to engage in sexual exploration with strangers. But please, she asked, keep the pictures and gadgets away from Walt and Christian. And stop taking her make-up.

Before catching the bus to high school, Brad always checked his look in our hallway mirror. Taking the stage of a new school clearly called for the right costume. He was back to tight t-shirts and Converse sneakers. He would change his black tennis shoes for the red ones, and then check his look once more. He might have missed his friends in Las Vegas and wondered if he could get elected to student government again. He might have also missed getting all the clothes and CDs and trips as the only kid in his dad's house. But Brad didn't miss fighting about or disguising who he was, and this was who he was: a gay teen anxious to look good in the crowd.

Most of his energy as a freshman went towards social and political activities. With a grant from the school district, he attended a conference in Chicago about gay kids in schools. The conference helped him establish Spectrum, a gay-straight alliance, and lead the group through its first year. Such alliances were becoming more common in high schools across the country as part of the diversity movement. Brad also attended Odyssey, a social and educational group for LGBTQ teens that Connye featured in a story for our newspaper. Odyssey didn't sound much different from the Presbyterian youth group I attended in high school, except for the AIDS lectures and the fishbowl of free condoms by the door. Still, they had to be secretive: no signs, no printed announcements. Secrecy helped maintain Odyssey's funding through county public health dollars. In Spokane, public officials wanted the plausible deniability of not fully knowing who attended Odyssey and why, in case some conservative blue hair got her knickers in a twist about tax dollars supporting homosexuality. A couple nights a week, we ducked our station wagon behind a downtown strip mall. We watched from the alley as Brad bounded up concrete steps next to a dumpster and entered a rusty metal door with a grated window.

Just after Brad started high school, Connye featured the upcoming drag show, starring the queens Bijou Matinee and Coco Marzipan, on the cover of our newspaper. Putting them on the cover didn't seem like a big deal to us. To me, it looked like a poster for a church production of an Agatha Christie mystery. Word did get back to us that publicly displaying drag queens unsettled many Spokane minds. But this wasn't a typical drag show of campy lip-synchers parading in sequined body stockings through a loud, smoky bar. Bijou held a theater degree, and her shows were scripted and rehearsed. Real singers in real costumes sang real songs. She hosted this annual fundraiser for the Northwest Pride Foundation at the Unitarian church next to the community college. The sanctuary was packed on show night, with the crowd spilling from the pews onto ranks of metal folding chairs. Most of the numbers were musical comedy or torch songs. The humor was mainly corny. For this year's show, Bijou had coaxed a famous female impersonator out of retirement from his ranch near

Yakima. Connye and I saw that drag was just theater, trying on different roles and costumes.

Brad didn't attend the show, but was starting to explore drag. He came home from thrift stores with wigs and belts and pumps that mingled with the dirty laundry that carpeted his bedroom floor. At Halloween, he went all out. A local gay-friendly salon gave him a free facial and taught him some basics about make-up and plucking. Luckily Brad had no whiskers, although he did inherit thick, black eyebrows from his dad's Greek heritage. The stylist loaned him a platinum blonde wig with flip curls and a shiny cobalt evening gown. With more curve to his cleavage, lips, and hips, he could have been a credible Marilyn Monroe. We snapped a Polaroid close-up of him for his first gay Halloween. His pale skin and platinum hair filled the frame.

THE GIFT OF AN
UNCALLED AMBULANCE

By his 10th birthday, my stepson Walt liked to boast about the times that he almost died. He could point to any one of his several minor scars and launch into a story.

When Walt was three, before I knew him, his family vacationed at Lake Pend Oreille north of Spokane. It's one of the largest lakes in America and they camped on the west side, away from any towns. Toddler Walt picked up a soda can and drank from it. A bee buzzing around the sugary insides of the can stung him on the tongue. Immediately his mouth and throat started to swell shut from an allergic reaction. His parents threw all three of their boys in their old Chevy station wagon and raced miles down dusty, unpaved logging roads to Sandpoint, Idaho, the nearest town. They reached the hospital just in time to keep Walt from suffocating.

I participated in some of Walt's near-death experiences. One sunny weekend shortly after we moved into our house, a couple of neighborhood boys knocked at our door. I opened the door and saw their bikes tossed down in our front yard. "It's Walt, in the park," they panted. "He fell and he's bleeding."

I grabbed the keys as I told Connye the news. We all got in the same old Chevy station wagon, now hers after divorcing Walt's dad, and sped the few blocks downhill to the park.

The boys navigated. "He's over by the duck pond."

When we pulled up, Walt was sitting calmly with another friend at the base of a rocky ledge strewn with pieces of jagged basalt. He gripped his bloody left forearm.

Connye and I got out of the car and crowded around him. "Are you alright?" I asked.

He opened his grip and showed me a deep gash about two inches long running lengthwise up the inside of his forearm. It would leave a good scar. "I fell and hit a rock," he said.

"Can you move your arm?"

"Yeah, I'm just cut."

Through my mind flashed the fact that, contrary to Hollywood portrayals, cutting not across the forearm but up it, like Walt had managed to do, was the more effective way to commit suicide. "Well, keep pressure on it." I recalled the scar his mom bore across the width of her left wrist from the depression that helped end her marriage to Walt's dad.

We loaded Walt, his bike, and all his friends into the station wagon and drove the few additional blocks down the hill to the hospital. We were fortunate to live a mile from the two largest hospitals in Spokane County. In fact, like many other things in Spokane, they are probably the largest of their kind for 300 miles in any direction. Walt walked into the emergency room like it was his homeroom at school. He smiled and laughed with the nurses, recounting yet another near-death experience. True, if he were alone in the wilderness and knocked unconscious by the fall that cut his forearm, he might have bled to death. Instead, he was playing by a neighborhood duck pond. The emergency room staff stitched his wound and sent him home.

I shared Walt's ease with emergency rooms. My mom spent four decades nursing, many of them in emergency rooms, which made hospitals part of our family routine. Mom volunteered to work holidays like Thanksgiving. We just celebrated a day later. She said it let nurses with families younger than ours have the day with their kids. For us, it meant extra holiday pay. But many families have one kid, like Walt for Connye, who gets seriously sick and injured the most. I was that kid in my family. While growing up I broke both collarbones and my left wrist, dislocated a toe, tore ligaments and tendons, and collected various scaring gouges, burns and abrasions. Childhood asthma landed me in the hospital while I was still a toddler. In ninth grade, I contracted a rare form of influenza that normally afflicted kids less than five years of age and killed 95 percent of them. I missed the last third of that school year. I still recall the icy antibiotic flowing into my hand through the IV that the doctor literally sweated to insert.

Then there was Walt on Christmas Day, 2000.

It was our first Christmas owning a weekly newspaper. Publishing a double issue at the end of the year gave us a week off at the holidays. We distributed that last issue for the year the Thursday morning before Christmas. As soon as our distribution drivers were stocked and on their way, I went home to stuff our three boys, Henry the poodle, our luggage and presents in our new Ford station wagon for the day-long drive to my parents' house.

I walked into a quiet and tense house. The curved glass door of the antique china hutch hung open and smashed. Connye stood in the kitchen, scrubbing counters with all her muscles tensed. "What happened?"

"Oh, a chair fell and broke the hutch," she sighed, turning and leaning one hip against the counter. "The boys were roughhousing. I told them to stop, but they wouldn't listen."

I was ready to cancel Christmas. One of my pet peeves of stepparenting was the boys not listening to their mom. Often, stepparenting was merely inconvenient or annoying. But if the boys wouldn't follow parental directions now, what sort of trouble would they get into in the coming years?

My parents lived in western Oregon, in a small town about 35 miles east of the state capitol of Salem. It's a long drive from Spokane: southwest through arid farmland to the Tri-Cities (one of the birthplaces of America's atomic bomb), then south to the Columbia River and west along the water to Portland. Where the Columbia cuts a gorge through the Cascade Mountains, the vistas remind me of Chinese scroll paintings: cliffs and banks, trees and mist, boats pushing through small waves. At Portland, we turned south to Salem and then east a short way. My parent's house stretched along the banks of the Santiam River, with picture windows facing the water.

This was my first visit to my parents as a full-blown family man: wife, kids, dog, and station wagon. I was nervous. My parents had new, cream-colored Berber carpets and Henry the poodle wasn't completely housebroken. I dreaded him leaving a big, permanent stain to mark our holiday. The boys had already destroyed furniture that day; how would they behave with a new family? But when we reached my parents' house and everyone was simply happy to see us, I unwound a bit. Henry made one small mistake on a throw rug that easily went into the wash. Walt and Christian laughed and played with my nephews. Brad seemed out of place in a small town in the woods, 40 minutes away from any mall or multiplex. Connye thoroughly relaxed by simply staring at the river from the hot tub. She also joined in all the card games my family played.

We decided to head home on Christmas afternoon, after opening presents. This returned Walt and Christian to their dad for the second half of their vacation, and got Connye and I back to work to take advantage of our off-week at the newspaper. I wanted to work on improving company operations—such as creating an easier, more accurate distribution tracking system in Microsoft Excel—without the additional pressure of publishing that week. I drove, with Connye next to me up front. Brad and Christian sat in the middle seat, with Henry in his carrier between them. Walt sat in the rear facing third seat, nestled in suitcases and presents. Empty grey pavement stretch from median to shoulder. Few people drove around after lunch on Christmas day. We passed through the southeastern Portland suburbs, and then turned eastward onto I-84, the interstate leading back down the Columbia Gorge towards the long empty stretches of eastern Oregon and Washington.

From the front seat Connye asked Walt a question, but got no answer. After she raised her voice and asked a second time with no reply, Brad unbuckled his seatbelt to peer over the seat and see if Walt was asleep.

"Oh my God stop the car right now there's something wrong with Walt."

I looked at Brad in the rearview mirror, to make sure he wasn't just fooling around. Brad did like the dramatic.

"Stop the car he's not breathing."

I steered onto the highway shoulder at the base of an off-ramp. Flashers on. "Stay in the car," I told everyone. The last thing we needed was someone getting run over. I stepped out of the stuffy car and into Oregon's brisk December air. Connye and Brad got out of the car anyway and followed me to the back. Trucks sped by.

I opened the hatch. Connye and I leaned in. Walt lay among toys and candies and new games. His brown eyes were open but vacant. His skin was white and his lips were turning blue. I held my hand under his nose, leaned my ear close to his mouth. He wasn't breathing.

Connye talked to him, "Walt, Walt wake up." He didn't answer.

With a couple fingers on his wrist, I checked his pulse. His heart was still beating.

Connye turned and joined Brad trying to flag down help.

I stroked Walt's hair. His lips were growing bluer, like ice as it gets colder. I didn't have a plan. Should I start artificial respiration? "Come on, Walt, breathe. Breathe."

Maybe because it was Christmas day, the gift of an uncalled ambulance appeared within a minute of our stopping. Connye told the paramedics what she knew. They lifted Walt onto a gurney, gave him oxygen, and loaded him into the ambulance. We followed them up the off-ramp and through a maze of suburban streets to a hospital.

By the time we parked the car and all walked in, Walt already lay behind curtains and doors, surrounded by nurses. Connye completed paperwork and tried to explain to Christian what might be going on. "They think Walt had a seizure. It's when your nerves and muscles go haywire for a little while."

Hospitals on TV are always dramatic places. People rush about and bark orders. In reality, hospitals are filled with waiting. I called my parents from a pay phone. My mom the nurse hadn't heard of the hospital where we were. She didn't ask a lot of questions, but she was impressed that on Christmas the hospital found a technician to perform and read a CT scan within an hour of our arrival. She doubted that the ER where she had worked in Salem, which was one of the busiest trauma centers on the West Coast, could have done that.

Eventually we learned the test results—Walt definitely experienced a seizure, but there was nothing abnormal on the CT scan. The EEG didn't show abnormality, either. We learned that EEG tests don't always show seizure activity. He was still asleep, exhausted after the work of a seizure that large. We could take him home once he woke up.

The afternoon light was fading quickly. In Oregon at Christmas, the sun sets around 4 p.m. Connye and I drove Christian and Brad back down the hill to a trucker's café for an early dinner. We still faced more than 300 miles that night to get home and I didn't want to make it any longer with a meal stop later on. Christian ordered chicken strips, like he did at every meal in every restaurant on every road trip.

Walt looked groggy when the hospital released him. He'd lost consciousness for approximately 45 minutes, and then slept another couple of hours.

"Are you hungry?" Connye asked, stroking his brown hair.

"No."

"Has this ever happened before?"

He explained that many times he twitched and flexed before falling asleep. Sometimes he woke up and found his shirt or sheets wet from his drooling. It had always been part of his life, so he thought that it happened to everyone.

Walt and Christian switched seats for the ride home. We wouldn't have Walt sitting where we couldn't see him or facing backwards—that odd visual stimulus can start seizures in some people. Once we returned to eastbound I-84, Walt fell asleep slumped against the car door. Christian and Brad were quiet. Connye kept calling back to Christian in the rear-facing seat, making sure that he was all right. She and I talked for a while, rehashing what we thought we knew about seizures and epilepsy. Even with the newspaper, we'd have to make more time to care for Walt.

Just past the off ramp to Boardman we turned north, hummed through Umatilla, and bridged the Columbia River near McNary Dam. We entered Washington state and a huge bank of thick fog. It was hard to see the nose of the car. The road twisting from the river up to the Tri-Cities was a four-lane, divided interstate. I slowed to 40, 30, 20 miles an hour. The pace seemed interminably slow—we still had another 150 miles to cover—and yet always too fast for the fog. We could rear end a stalled car before we ever saw it. Walt woke up and the boys started griping at each other. Connye told them to knock it off. They were all tired and wanted to be home; she felt the same way. But the driving was very dangerous and they'd have to be quiet so I could concentrate. I don't think we saw another car in the hour that it took us to cover the 26 miles from the river to the Tri-Cities. Just outside the Tri-Cities, the fog lifted as quickly as it had appeared. Night in the central basin lay cold and starry. We arrived home at midnight after covering 350 miles in 11 hours.

Once we returned to Spokane, we needed to see a neurologist for a precise diagnosis. Connye researched Walt's case and conditions and thought that his symptoms most closely followed something called benign rolandic epilepsy. Doctors disagreed with her assessment, but never offered a definite diagnosis. They prescribed Dilantin to lessen the chance and severity of future seizures. It couldn't guarantee that Walt wouldn't have another seizure. But the neurologist explained that the brain could develop a habit of seizing. As the habit grew stronger, so would the seizures themselves. Keeping the brain out of the habit while Walt matured was our best hope.

For the next few years, Walt experienced episodes every four months—Christmas vacation, spring vacation, and summer vacation—until he outgrew the problem. He stopped boasting about the times he nearly died.

MONEY MAKES THE PLANET GO 'ROUND

A columnist for Spokane's daily newspaper, *The Spokesman-Review*, told me a story about his first job in journalism. His editor sat him in a conference room and asked, "Doug, what is the purpose of a newspaper?"

In reply, Doug expounded on the concepts of free speech, the fourth estate, community voice and identity, an informed electorate, primary source for history, conveyors of culture, and so on. The editor dutifully outlined Doug's response on the chalkboard.

Once Doug's monologue wound down, the editor asked, "Is that about it?"

"I think that covers it," Doug answered.

Then the editor picked up an eraser and wiped the board clean. He wrote a giant "S" in the middle of the chalkboard and drew two vertical lines through it: a dollar sign. "Doug, the purpose of the newspaper is to make money. If we don't make money, we can't do all those other things."

Like Doug, my first journalism job taught me the role of money in the media. From the content of the nightly local news to the corporate structure of America's largest companies, money shapes what Americans hear, see, and know.

The media doesn't make money by selling time on its channels or space on its pages. Time and space are generic. Media companies sell the types of audiences that come to those channels and pages. More specifically, it sells the audience that will see those channels and pages in the future, which is when the advertiser's next message will appear. Advertisers want to know that, when they sign an advertising contract, they'll have a consistent stream of predictable people seeing the content and therefore their ads. Next week's eyeballs, I told *The Local Planet* sales force. This is why media salespeople make sales calls equipped with reams of information about audience composition: size, average age, gender split, racial makeup, income levels, types of occupation, highest level of educational attainment, car ownership, home ownership, percent married, children living at home. Some demographic surveys even report who owns pet fish.

Don't be fooled: when it comes to advertising-driven media you, the reader, aren't the customer. The advertiser is. The media company needs you, but only as something to sell.

Understanding audience as the real product of the media also helped Connye and I understand and debunk one of the great myths about the media: objectivity. Many people believe that the media can be, should be, and generally are objective in their coverage. Objective in this case means free from any particular slant or bias, whether personal on the part of the reporter or corporate on the part of the media ownership. Not only is this false, as people were starting to see with blatantly biased coverage like the Fox News Channel on cable TV and Air America radio, it is also fundamentally impossible.

The content that a media outlet presents and how it presents it are, at least in a broad sense, determined not by truth or reality or public good, but by the need to generate a desirable audience that the company can sell. Media outlets ideally want their audience to be unique, so that they can charge premium prices. To build a unique audience, a media outlet must have a unique message or content. This doesn't mean that editors and producers routinely storm into the offices of their staff and tell them what to say in a particular story, although some do just that. However, it does mean that a publication or station will decide what topics to cover and how to cover them with the main goal of building a particular audience that they can sell.

Objectivity also falls victim to human fallibility. People write, photograph, design, and present media content; people are by nature biased. They all have preferences and quirks that will influence how they gather, choose, and present stories. This can be as simple as whether a reporter is left-handed or nearsighted. Both traits can influence the physical vantage point that they choose for observing the events that they will report on. Standing on the opposite end of a crowd, for instance, changes what a reporter sees and the people at hand to be interviewed. On a broader scale, the people who, in general, generate media content have a demographically driven bias. As a group, they tend to be college educated in the arts and social sciences: journalism, literature, history, political science, theater, design, anthropology. They tend to be Caucasian, upper-middle class, and socially moderate to liberal. Most the front-line reporters tend to be between 25 and 39. This group has its own perspective on the world. As a thought experiment, try to imagine the majority of American news as reported by African-Americans with advanced degrees in science, or the majority of editorials being composed by Latinos over the age of 40 with only a high-school diploma. This doesn't mean that reporters lie or deceive to reach their audience. It does mean that they naturally gravitate towards topics and viewpoints common to their own demographic group. They must work harder to understand the demographic of their target audience, what topics might interest them, and what presentations will keep their attention. But it's all still a non-objective quest for audience to sell.

With *The Local Planet*, the audience that we wanted to build was young, technologically and politically savvy, at least 50% male, and unconventional in their psychological outlook. This shaped what features we ran. All our writers were Caucasian, college educated, and raised west of the Mississippi. We aimed to be accurate and fair, but we accepted subjectivity, embraced it, articulated it, made fun of it, and pointed it out in other media. When business owners questioned what we printed and why, because to them it didn't seem objective, we explained our audience and the nature of bias in the media. Our candor probably shocked and probably confused them. Many businesses seemed to distrust us because we were so open about this. Surely, we must not know what we were doing, if we candidly talked about practices that other editorial outlets pretended didn't happen. I think we made them fear a new fear: the biases that they were already supporting.

As an industry, American media was consolidating into fewer and fewer companies hoping to control increasingly larger portions of advertising spending. These companies included Disney, Viacom, News Corp., General Electric, and Time-Warner. For instance, in television Disney owned ABC, Disney Channel, ESPN, ESPN2, ABC Family, TOON Disney, and SOAPNet. Viacom owned CBS, MTV, BET, Showtime, UPN, Spike, TVLand, VH1, and Nickelodeon. News Corp. owned Fox, Fox Sports, Fox News, Fox Movie Channel, FX, Speed, and the National Geographic channel. General Electric, through its Universal business line, owned NBC, MSNBC, CNBC, Bravo, USA Network, Sci-Fi Channel, and Telemundo. Time-Warner owned CNN, CNN Headline News, Turner Classic Movies, HBO, TBS, TNT, Cartoon Network, CNNfn, and the WB television network. These four companies and their channels comprised the majority of television viewing by Americans.

If corporate concentration in television wasn't daunting enough, these companies also owned the major movie studios and numerous publishing ventures including magazines, books, newspapers, and Internet sites. Nearly half of the most popular sites on the Internet were controlled by just 10 of the largest media companies, including these large television companies. The largest media company in terms of revenue, Time-Warner, owned four of the top Internet sites—CNN, AOL, Netscape, and Time Magazine. Plus, don't forget radio. Most of these media conglomerates owned radio subsidiaries, although they don't come close to rivaling the Frankenstein's monster of the radio industry, Clear Channel. The 1996 Telecomm Act, passed the year that I moved to Spokane, greatly increased media concentration in America. It inflated the limits on how much media, and how much media reach, one company could control. In the wake of the Act, tiny Clear Channel Communications out of San Antonio, Texas grew from 43 radio stations in 1995 to more than 1,200 stations in 2000. Clear Channel also owned SFX, one of the largest concert promotion houses, and hundreds of thousands of outdoor advertising displays.

In Spokane, audience building and media concentration played out on the local level. The Cowles family owned Spokane's daily paper, the NBC television affiliate, the Associated Press wire service office, and shopper magazines for real estate and cars--not to mention a video production company, a newsprint paper mill, a life insurance agency, ten percent of downtown Spokane real estate, and hundreds of acres of county land. Luckily, Cowles Publishing hadn't figured out how to sell one-stop advertising shopping. As far as Connye and I could tell, they didn't offer packages such as combined print classified / online search / television time to businesses like car dealers or real estate companies. It wasn't that they didn't have all the pieces. They just hadn't figure out to put them all together. Still, media concentration in Spokane helped warp the civic culture and dialog in favor of the powerful such as the Cowles.

In the early 1990s, Wanda Cowles (aunt of newspaper publisher William Stacey Cowles) sought to bring a branch of Seattle's Pacific Science Center to Spokane. The Spokane branch of the science center would occupy the heart of Riverfront Park, the downtown park created to house Spokane's world's fair in 1974. Without public comment or debate, the city council voted to lease core parkland to the science center for $1. Steve Corker, a downtown business owner whose marketing and advertising agency carried the Riverfront Park account, questioned the lack of public process in this decision. He led the drive for a public vote on the issue. Despite gaining editorial endorsements in *The Spokesman-Review* and outspending Corker's group by more than 30 to 1, the science center proponents lost the referendum by 200 votes. The Pacific Science Center dropped all interest in Spokane. Soon after the vote, all of Corker's major clients left his agency. They said that they couldn't be seen doing business with him since he had opposed the Cowles. He closed his doors. He was also asked to leave the boards of four non-profit organizations that he served.

In 1997, with many secret meetings and little public input or scrutiny, the city council approved a public-private partnership with the Cowles real estate companies to remodel the family's downtown mall, River Park Square. Much of the money would go into expanding the mall's parking garage. In the deal, the city would own the garage for 20 years, but would have to rent the land under the garage from the family at inflated rates. Part of that land included a street right-of-way that the city agreed to vacate for the project. The Cowles refused to put up collateral for the deal, so the city pledged both its federal grants for community development and monies collected from its parking meters. The projections of the garage's financial performance were based on deliberately skewed figures regarding hourly parking prices, occupancy projections, and the appraisal of the garage's overall worth.

In 2000, a subsequent city council featuring Steve Corker from the science center debate refused to loan the parking meter revenues to the garage, arguing that the garage had no chance of ever paying back the money. The Cowles newspaper often printed biased stories promoting the family's real estate project. The IRS repeatedly ruled that the entire bond transaction to finance the project was not tax-exempt, even though it had been sold to investors as such. By 2003, the mall was entangled in lawsuits and countersuits between the city, the developer, the bond issuers, the bondholders, and several law firms involved in vetting the deal. The millions of dollars spent on the legal fight cut into city services and threatened to bankrupt Spokane. (Mayor Jim West essentially settled the case out of court in 2004 and 2005.)

In 2002 and 2003, the Cowles's newspaper strongly editorialized for spending $70 million in public money to renovate and expand Spokane's downtown convention center. The money came from a special law written by then state senate majority leader Jim West to allow municipalities to retain state tax funds to build special event facilities. Because of this law, six other Washington cities were also expanding their convention facilities.

The paper argued in the opinion pages that convention tourism was a form of economic export, since you're selling to people from outside the local market. At *The Local Planet*, we found urban tourism an illogical goal for a city that's not quite large enough to make the list of America's 100 largest cities. The Convention Center, River Park Square, and the Veteran's Memorial Coliseum (another publicly-funded project) formed what I called the "Tourism Triangle." In the heart of the triangle lay Riverfront Park and the Spokane River. From 1993 to 2003, the city spent $250 million dollars to refurbish the three points of the triangle, in hopes of bolstering tourism. This tourism triangle had been in place since 1975, and in that time Spokane's economy had slid from being on a par with the nation to being considerably below the national average.

Those are all big-dollar examples, but the influence of Cowles's media concentration played out on much smaller scales as well. Once, I approached the head of a successful downtown financial services firm about investing in *The Local Planet*. Several people I knew had worked for or with him and thought that he might be supportive of our paper. He responded that he did, in general, support what we were trying to do. However, he also was involved with several charitable efforts in town and felt that he couldn't afford to be seen doing business with us for fear of losing the support of the Cowles and their peers. (Eventually, I managed to convince him to spend $10,000 with our paper for a series of ads.) In another instance, I approached the manager of a downtown Birkenstock store regarding their advertising. He explained that, as a downtown retail business, he received advertising money from the Downtown Spokane Partnership. The partnership was supported by public funds. The manager told me that the person who handed him his advertising funds also said, "We sure hope that you'll consider spending this money with *The*

Spokesman-Review." He felt the implication was clear, and that's where the money went. It didn't matter that the Birkenstock crowd read *The Local Planet* and not the daily paper. He claimed that other downtown business owners were told the same thing.

An entire book could be written on the Cowles and their influence over the development of Spokane. (In fact, one legendary tome around town was *The Fancher Report*, a doctoral dissertation on exactly this topic. Other journalists in town did write books investigating various Cowles transactions, especially River Park Square.) However, this isn't that book. *The Local Planet* wasn't that book, either, although some wanted to paint our editorial stance as solely anti-Cowles. And most dysfunction in Spokane didn't flow directly from the Cowles family. Much of it came from how others perceived their reliance on the Cowles or their friends, and thus gauged their behavior to at least not displease them. The Cowles had no direct involvement in this behavior self-modification. Still, city politics and business suffered from a dynamic that people variously described as paternalist or feudalistic.

Such was the national and local media climate in which Connye and I worked to build a profitable newspaper.

Initially I held the title of Director of Operations, because Mitch wanted the title of Publisher. Making sure the phones and computers worked, the bills got paid, and the taxes filed became my job. Plenty of people are enamored with the idea of being business owners, masters of their own destinies, with nobody else telling them what to do. They envision doing what they want, when they want. Those who have owned a business, especially those who start a new business, often say it's the toughest job they've ever had.

As a business owner, I felt responsible for everything, so I wanted to participate in everything. In addition to business management, I felt like I could offer a little extra something for whatever department needed a boost at the time. If editorial needed a story edited or an additional short article written, I was there. On Tuesdays, production nights, I laid out pages and help decide on the final cover design. For sales, I developed promotional ideas and tactical directions, gave the staff a longer view of upcoming stories and trends they could use, and coached them through proposals and negotiations with specific customers. I even managed to bring in about a third of all sales. In the end, though, being a business owner put me at the back of the line. I was the last one to get paid, after all the other bills are met, which meant I didn't get paid. At night, I was often the last one in the office. When it came time to clean the break room or take out the trash or vacuum the office, I was the last one to whom the chores fell. I hired employees for their specific skills at specific jobs. I wanted to get the most value out of them, so I picked up the rest of the work. Compared to finishing two college degrees and working for 11 years at Microsoft, a company notorious for tough work, being my own boss was certainly my hardest job.

As first-time business owners, Connye and I made our share of mistakes. I'd always heard and read that new businesses often overspend at first, and then struggle for cash later. At the start, I thought that we struck a good balance between being frugal and treating our employees well. We started with the best of intentions on both ends of the balance. When we finally settled into permanent offices, we gave as many employees as possible individual offices with a closing door and a window. But we did it at an annual cost per square foot which was half of what other people around us in downtown Spokane were paying. We gave people the minimum two weeks of vacation, but also told employees that we'd cash out unused vacation hours when they left the company. Connye insisted that we provide health insurance, so we paid 75% of the premium for participating employees, because that's what the plan required. However, our plan delivered good coverage for about 25% less than other companies were paying. We bought new, birch veneer desks at a downtown Danish furniture store, but only from the bargain basement or the cheapest product line.

Despite our bargain hunting, we still spent too much money. Being a Microsoft refugee meant that I overdid some of our technology. Our in-house email system could have handled ten times more employees than we had and contained features that we never used. It required more, and more expert, maintenance than we could afford or I could provide on my own. We spent $20,000 cash and thousands more in trade advertising for a custom-written, database driven website with archives and other special features. We drew a lot more web traffic than many other local Spokane news sites, but never managed to turn that traffic into revenue. I later learned that we could have leased a comparable website for about $250 a month.

The same went for our phones, once we got rid of U.S. Worst. We leased our own PBX system with a computer that ran the voicemail system. Doing that was cheaper than buying voicemail, but it still meant we paid over $600 a month just for office phones and voicemail. In the beginning, I also agreed to pay for cell phones for sales reps. They needed to stay in touch while being out of the office, I reasoned. They were an outside sales force, after all. When the cellular bill crossed $1,000 a month for fewer than half a dozen people, I lowered the minutes on the calling plans and told users that they'd have to pay for their overages. One rep, when hit with $200 worth of extra charges, angrily said to me "I knew this was going to happen." Credit cards also got us into trouble. Coming from a larger-corporation background, I knew that managers often had company credit cards for expenses. I wanted to trust my managers and have them work as efficiently as possible. But the balances on the cards quickly maxed out and I revoked them. It was my fault. I didn't make people turn in expense reports with receipts.

In the early days, we paid freelance writers seven to 10 cents a word for articles. Connye started the former editorial cartoonist of *The Spokesman-Review* at more than $100 a drawing. At one point, a team of investigative journalists wanted us to pay them $1 per word for an article. I flatly rejected that idea—from my own freelancing I knew that only airline magazines and glossy monthlies like *The Atlantic* paid those sorts of rates. After that, I scrutinized our editorial costs. Connye didn't like having her budget reined in and then totally corralled, but she took it professionally when she understood the bigger financial picture. By our second year we were paying no more than $10 a week for cartoons, $20 a week for horoscopes and movie reviews, and nothing for freelance editorial content.

You'd be surprised at how much editorial content is given to a publication for free. We joked about putting the "free" in freelancing. Some writers love the notion of their names and words in print. Some people are simply passionate about a topic; they care more about getting their message out than getting money in their wallet. Other writers are looking for printed samples of their work that they can later use in applying for real writing jobs. Editors know all these motivations and use them to build as much good content for as little as possible. Good editors do, at least. But we also got what we paid for. People who write for free are also free to turn in stories that are bad, or late. Sometimes they don't submit a story at all. What's an editor to do? Without money, we had very little leverage over volunteers. We couldn't fire them or dock their pay. Good people who work for free don't usually stay for long.

Our biggest sin was carrying too large of a payroll. We had inherited a staff when we bought the paper and had left them in place. I left them too long. Connye wanted to pay people what they were worth. Often that was more than we could afford or justify. In addition, we thought we needed to expand our staff to expand our publication schedule from every-other-week to every week. We grew to 16 employees at one point, including five editorial staffers. Our payroll wasn't larger than other weeklies, but we didn't have the revenues to support that many people. Since payroll and the accompanying taxes, fees, and insurance policies account for at least half of a newspaper's budget, employing too many people was a very costly mistake that had only one immediate remedy: firing people.

By early 2001, it was clear for several reasons that the newspaper staff needed restructuring. Firing people is hard work. We had to decide how to do it, and how whatever work that person performed would be done after they are gone. We had to decide whom to fire, although some employees make that decision rather obvious. First, I fired Byran, the tattooed former car salesman in charge of marketing the newspaper, after his second drunken fight in a bar that advertised with us. I should have felt outraged at Byran's behavior, or his lack of results or even motivation. Instead, when it came time to let him go, my hands trembled and my voice quivered. I'd never fired anyone before. How would he support his family? Didn't I have an obligation to him? I did, but he also had an obligation to me and all the others that relied on the newspaper for a living.

For the last two months of 2000, I paid the salary for our distribution manager while she lay in the hospital recovering from surgery. In hindsight, I should have investigated whether some sort of disability insurance could have covered her pay. When she returned in January 2001, I told her that she needed to increase our distribution network immediately from 16,000 copies to 23,000 copies. She started screaming at me, loud enough for the entire office to hear. I walked away without saying a word, part of my too-stoic personality. She stormed out of the office a few minutes later. The next morning, I fired her without feeling nervous or anxious. I managed distribution for three months, until we hired Connye's sister Dayna for the job.

Next came the sales department. Our sales were not where they needed to be. We'd sold about $90,000 worth of advertising for 30 issues in 2000. Our commission rate was too high, and checks were paid when ads were sold instead of when ad payments were collected. Phil, Mitch's best friend and the sales manager, showed horrible judgment. He admitted to drinking at a promotional event that he was running for the newspaper. He exceeded his company cell phone minutes and his credit card limit. He took for his personal use goods and services that we received in payment for advertising. His wife was suffering from clinical depression, so he hired an incredibly attractive hairdresser for his sales force so he could sleep with her. Mitch fired the hairdresser when her sales plummeted to zero. She was a nice person who got herself in a bad situation. Throughout all of this, I kept giving Phil warnings and written reprimands.

After I demoted Phil from sales management to simply sales, neither Mitch nor I proved to be effective sales managers. We were too busy with other responsibilities to handle the job, and it wasn't really our skill set. Connye and I asked around and advertised for a sales manager. After several interviews, it became clear to us that we should hire Bonnie, who came recommended by one of her former employers. Bonnie was nearly 50 years old, which made her twice as old as some of the staff. She had sales management experience, an overly positive disposition, and community connections through her position as president of the Spokane Parks Board. Mitch and Phil complained that we hired Bonnie without consulting them. They saw her as a community activist without any media experience. They wanted to hire as sales manager a guy named Bill, a former media salesperson who, at the time, was running the hot dog shack at Home Depot.

During Bonnie's first day on the job, I told her that I thought Phil and Barb, another salesperson, both needed to be fired. Bonnie asked that I give her a week to assess the existing team. On Friday she let Phil and Barb go. She hired Home Depot Bill, but he didn't last two months. Eventually, we fired all of the existing sales staff for various reasons.

With Bonnie managing the sales force, Connye and I could focus on the editorial staff. Switching from every-other-week to weekly publication proved an efficiency gain, instead of an additional burden. The schedule of events and stories was easier to manage. All the while, we were improving our writing and production processes. We didn't need all the editorial staff that we had hired. In addition, Connye felt that she couldn't continue the stressful work of editing the paper while trying to shepherd Brad through coming out, care for Walt with his seizures and problems reading, and make sure Christian wasn't neglected. She knew that there'd come a time for her to leave.

I was stressed, as well. Once, I felt so frustrated that I went into the utility room and smashed a chair to pieces. This particular chair matched the chairs encircling our large conference room table. It was already missing one leg; I just hadn't thrown it out yet. Quietly, I closed the door and picked up a hammer. I thought no one would hear me pulverizing the wooden frame into splinters. I clenched my teeth and grunted as I swung the hammer.

Connye met me as I came left the utility room. She peered past me and saw the shards of wood on the linoleum floor. "What happened here?"

"Just taking out my aggressions."

"That's not good."

I thought that an odd thing to say. "Sure it is," I said, catching my breath a bit. "I feel better."

Later, I realized that she wasn't concerned about me releasing my frustrations, but about the frustrations themselves. Mr. Even Keel felt the need to bludgeon. With better emotional schooling, maybe I would have realized that getting so frustrated wasn't healthy, that things needed to change. Instead, I contented myself with just the release of emotion, without addressing the source of that emotion.

One day Connye received a story from Tom Grant, a reporter for the local ABC television affiliate. Tom had a reputation as the best reporter in town but also a bulldog, not necessarily the easiest person to have on staff. He was built like a bulldog, too: 5'8" but broad enough to fill a doorway, with a big round face that was always grinning or laughing. In high school he had been an outstanding heavyweight wrestler, as well as a swimmer and runner. He had won a dozen national awards in his career in both print and broadcast journalism, including the Columbia duPont Silver Baton, which many consider the Pulitzer of broadcast news. His stories helped release innocent people from jail, convict killers, and uncover multimillion-dollar frauds. Tom sent us the story of Owen McDonald, a very poor man who froze to death in a trailer in a little town north of Spokane. Tom made Owen the focal point for failures in the social services system of rural Washington. Originally Tom offered the story to his TV employer, who would not run it. Connye asked me to edit the story. I was a little intimidated working on Tom's material. He had a Masters in Journalism from Columbia and had been a Mike Wallace journalism fellow at the University of Michigan; I had no journalism experience. Luckily, I found only one thing that needed any serious comment. The story ended on a sentence hoping that, in death, Owen had finally found "a warmer place." To me, that seemed like an unintentional reference to going to Hell. Tom chuckled at the observation and rewrote the ending.

When Ted McGregor, publisher of *The Inlander*, saw that we had published Tom's story, he complained to the ABC affiliate. Ted's paper and the ABC station had something of a partnership, and Ted insisted that Tom must offer them any stories that he wrote. Tom's boss pressed this issue. Tom explained that *The Inlander* had never wanted anything he'd offered them in the past, and besides he thought *The Local Planet* was a better paper. Tom's boss told him that if he felt that he had to write news stories, he must submit them to *The Inlander*. This episode was the last in a line of complaints that Tom had with the ABC station. He called up Connye and asked if we could meet.

We met Tom and his wife, Mary Ann, at an Indian buffet for lunch. Although we were conducting a preliminary interview with Tom, Mary Ann did much of the talking. She told nearly as good a story as Tom, although her tales were more sarcastic. Tom wanted to return to writing. All he needed was for us to match his current salary. Although it was nearly 50% more than we were paying anyone at the time, it was shockingly low for someone with Tom's experience and credentials. After a second interview, Connye wanted to hire Tom. She felt that he could eventually replace her as editor of the paper. I wondered how we could afford yet another person on the payroll, no matter how good.

I didn't have to wonder long. One of our current staffers, Paulette, thought that she should be made the editor. She had been there from the first issue, she argued, and written our first cover story. We should promote from within, and she deserved the job. Connye and I disagreed. This was her first writing job. Her stories needed a lot of work. She didn't have the writing chops or the personality to manage staff or set the editorial direction and tone of the paper. When Tom's hiring as News Editor became official, Paulette sent Connye and me a long and angry piece of email denouncing our decision and resigning her job. Our web site programmer was dating Paulette, and he resigned as well. One staff writer had already resigned because he didn't like Paulette. Another writer found a better paying job editing copy for the advertising agency next door.

Like Bonnie, Tom was pushing 50. He also turned out to be about the most "alternative" person working at our alternative newspaper. One of the writers he worked with, Jeremy, was the son of the president of the Spokane Regional Chamber of Commerce. On a sunny spring weekend, Jeremy's parents and 13-year-old sister came up to our offices to find Jeremy. As they stepped off the elevators, they were blasted by loud and profane rap music. Jeremy's mom immediately covered her daughter's ears and steered her into a nearby conference room. Jeremy's dad went to find who was blaring the music. It was Tom, grinning away while he unpacked his books and files in his new office. After more than twenty years in journalism, it was the first real office he'd ever had. He apologized with a chuckle and turned down the tunes.

Once the paper's cost of sales and content were reorganized, it was time to look at management. Mitch was nominally publisher and owner of 20% of the paper. He hadn't made a dent as acting sales manager. We now had an art director, so he wasn't doing as much design. He couldn't write and he didn't want any part of the administration of the paper. Plus, Mitch felt angry that Connye and I systematically dismantled the staff that he had assembled. He thought that I was incredibly unfair to his friend Phil. He didn't agree with us hiring of Bonnie. Exactly why were we continuing to pay him? To me, it was time to for Mitch to go. Not that Mitch didn't have a reason to leave. His wife was a nurse who wanted to attend medical school in Seattle.

Legal and financial liabilities and ramifications make forcing out a partner harder than firing an employee. If we wanted Mitch to go, we had to honor his investment. By this time, a year after the purchase, the paper was in such a state that his 20% was arguably worth less than nothing. As partner, he was partly responsibly for all the debts and commitments of the paper. I eventually agreed to pay him $1,000 for his 20%, and to hold him harmless from all liabilities arising from the paper. Legally that was incredibly generous, but realistically I knew that he couldn't afford to help pay debts anyway. Paying him $1,000 would help him move. I even offered to buy his old laser printer, which we used for bookkeeping, for $700. That would give him additional moving money and save me from finding another printer. He wouldn't sell the printer, and I found the same model used on the Internet for $300.

While Connye and I made rookie mistakes in running a business, we also had our successes.

One measure of success was our first awards banquet. Every year, regional chapters of the Society for Professional Journalists (SPJ) present awards for writing, page design, photography, and video news. Winners are selected from entries judged by another region's journalists (Spokane traded entries with Riverside, California.) In 2001, our SPJ chapter gathered in the Benevolent Order of Friends hall, an old, white stone building on the edge of downtown with the raised interstate running right behind it. The main floor held small businesses, like a hair salon run by twin sisters whom we never succeeded in getting to advertise. One of our distribution racks stood in the lobby. A group of businessmen in the 1920s started the BOF as a social club and it became the first legal casino in Spokane. The top floor was the BOF headquarters. The lodge still claimed a few active, if elderly, members. The barrel-vaulted ceiling was painted blue, with white stars that floated over the linoleum tile dance floor rimmed with old folding tables. In one corner of the meeting hall stood panels displaying the photography and page design entries. Our table slumped across the room from the display, while the rival *Inlander* staff sat closer to the displays, at tables directly across the dance floor from the podium.

We arrived at the awards banquet as the scrappy, scruffy, and witty new kid on the block. We'd published only 30 slim issues the previous year, compared to *The Inlander*'s 52 fat ones. A few of their "special" issues had more than 100 pages. We Planeteers pooled our money, called over a waitress, and told her that we wanted to buy a round of drinks for *The Inlander* staff. Their rank-and-file folks gladly went along. Their managers balked. Ted, the publisher, spent the whole night sitting with his back turned towards us, even though it meant he stared into the back corner of the room. In the final tally, we won more awards, and more first place awards, even though we printed only one-third the number of pages. But they still had all the advertisers.

On a Wednesday afternoon not long after our success with the SPJ awards, we held a rowdy staff meeting in our newly painted conference room. We were preparing for Connye's and my upcoming trip to the annual convention of the Association of Alternative Newsweeklies (AAN). The papers we looked up to— *The Stranger* in Seattle, *Willamette Week* in Portland, *The Village Voice* in New York City—all belonged to the AAN. Membership meant credibility plus access to industry-specific information and benefits shared only with members. Entry into AAN was selective. We applied, and current association members would vote on whether we measured up. Some papers published for more than 10 years before applying to the AAN. Many papers that apply were never accepted, and often members applied several times before finally getting in. Membership elections were part of the convention, but so were the usual convention activities of conferences, vendor displays, and social functions.

One convention activity was the Promo Item Swap Meet. Papers could give out their leftover promo items—t-shirts, pens, CDs, bumper stickers—and get promotional ideas from other papers. We didn't have any promo items yet, but we could get free condoms from the local Planned Parenthood office and cheap labels to feed through our laser printer. The entire staff brainstormed around our cherry veneer conference table, purchased used, in our hydrangea blue chairs, also purchased used. On the table stood miniature bottles of rum and vodka, the kind of bottles used on airplanes. Littering the table were two-packs of condoms. The alcohol fueled our sloganeering. By the end of the meeting, we had condoms with stickers featuring our logo and sayings like "Get It Weekly," "Buy It By The Inch" (newspaper ads are measured in column inches), and "Every Reader A Wanted Reader" (a nod to Planned Parenthood's slogan of "Every Child A Wanted Child").

Brad stuck out his lower lip and slumped his shoulders when he learned we wouldn't take him to New Orleans with us. A trip would have rewarded his recent bad behavior. Some of it was typical teenage attitude: parents are stupid, chores are stupid, school is stupid, why can't I just do what I want? But Brad had also been sneaking out at night and driving the station wagon. At first, he denied taking the car. But in the mornings, I would find the driver's seat pushed too far back for me reach the pedals, the steering wheel tilted all the way down, and the radio set way too loud on a Top 40 station I never listen to. Connye and I knew that it was either Brad or his cousin Michael. They were the only ones who could get the keys easily and would need to move the driver's seat. And Michael had alibis. During a parental conference in my office, Connye and I told Brad to stop taking the car because he wasn't very good at it. "If you're going to get into mischief," I told him, "at least give us the courtesy of not getting caught."

There's only one reason to have a convention in New Orleans in July—cheap hotel rooms during the muggy season. Connye and I had a long flight from Spokane to New Orleans, including the customary layover in Seattle. Ted and Jer McGregor, the Brothers *Inlander*, rode the same flight. They sat a couple rows ahead of us, on the other side of the center aisle. I hated having to look at them for hours. When we finally opened our hotel room door, sweaty at the end of a long day, we found a large vase of flowers waiting for us, with a card from our staff. We had forgotten that it was our first wedding anniversary, but we were too exhausted for anything more than a hug before sleeping.

Connye participated in the editorial track of conference sessions and loathed seeing Ted in many of her meetings. I took the publishing track, with a couple distribution sessions added in. Somehow, I managed to miss Jer. Every morning the association staff published a small newspaper about the convention featuring events of the day, interviews from the previous days, and news from the industry. On the next to last morning, the convention newsletter included the membership committee's recommendations regarding the newspapers applying for membership. Twenty-two papers applied that year (including two others with "Planet" in their titles). Connye and I skimmed through the blurbs to find ours:

> "**Local Planet**, Spokane, Washington. The line between editorial and advertorial is blurred. One main feature was a softball profile of some local communications company, and some pieces were little more than public-service announcements. Clever and thoughtful in some longer pieces but filled with daily-style puffery in shorter stories. Assignments are good, writing is fair, but editing, which could make it better, lets everyone down. And they have to kill the boosterism impulse. Still, these guys are doing a lot of local news in 32 pages — some of it pretty creatively. It hits on most, if not all, cylinders. (6 yes; 5 no) The committee recommends to admit."

Ouch. This critique seemed ironic to us, because back home people asked us why we hated Spokane. And the issues that we submitted for membership review had been written months earlier and didn't feature Tom's work. We felt that we were much better than this. We were one of the seven recommended for admission, but by such a slim margin that Connye and I wondered if we'd make it.

Connye sought out the executive editor of the *San Francisco Bay Guardian*, one of the granddaddy newspapers of alternative journalism. Tim's graying beard and easy demeanor certainly matched his job as an alternative editor in America's most alternative city. He bought us a drink in the hotel bar. As a member of the association's membership committee, he assured us that the discussion about our paper wasn't nearly as negative as that one published paragraph made it sound. Tim had championed our paper and knew an amazing amount about Spokane simply by reading our stories. So, why the negative write up? Tim said that Clif, the admissions chair, wasn't as sold on our paper. Plus, he said that Ted recently sent an email to all the admissions committee accusing *The Local Planet* of being the mouthpiece for a conservative high-tech businessman in Spokane. Connye and I were angry, but also bemused. The businessman in question had purchased just two pages of advertising from us, barely enough to pay the office rent for a month. I personally had never met the man.

When we left the bar, Connye and I encountered Clif, the admissions committee chair. He confirmed that he'd received Ted's allegations in email. Clif said that he asked Ted for any proof to back his claims, but Ted never produced any. We asked if we could see the email; Clif doubted that he still had it.

The social function that night was called "Party with Your Kind." Tables in the restaurant were labeled with different job titles: Publisher, Editor, Writer, Sales, Distribution. Connye spotted Ted and wanted to confront him. "What's the point?" I asked. It's my standard evaluation of emotionally charged situations. "Even if he admits it, what are we supposed to do?"

"I want him to know that we know," Connye said, and marched across the room.

I hung back and watched. Connye stood about chest-high to Ted. I could see her look him in the face. She didn't flail her arms or poke him in the chest with her finger, but she did stand toe-to-toe and ask him questions.

After about a minute, she came back. "So?" I asked.

"He admitted it."

That surprised me. Judging from the wishy-washy articles in his newspaper, I figured Ted would deny the whole thing. "Did he say why?"

"He said it was a point of pride. They didn't get accepted on their first try, and they didn't want to see us get in."

I shook my head, baffled by such unethical and silly behavior motivated by such flimsy emotion.

It wasn't the only crappy behavior we'd get from Ted and his crew. We caught them presenting their prospective advertisers with stats comparing their current audience demographics to ours from a previous year. We filed a compliant with the independent demographics bureau that both papers used. I heard that they were told to use the data accurately and ethically. We caught them copying our stories. There was a pattern of them publishing stories on topics identical to ours within a couple weeks of our stories. My writers drew up a timeline and documentation and took to the *Inlander's* offices. They denied anything was wrong. So, we published our research and timeline and let the readers decide.

Connye went off to talk with someone she'd met in an editorial session. I gazed at the table reserved for publishers. Gathered around it were four tall, trim guys in suits. I recognized them as publishers of newspapers owned by the New Times chain of weekly papers, the 800-pound gorilla of the association. Intellectually, I knew that I should introduce myself. But I felt intimidated. What did I have to say to them, or ask them? I knew I wanted to be like them, successful publishers of profitable papers. Part of me wanted to have obscene amounts of publishing money like the Cowles. That was one reason why I was sinking money into a business. Power corrupts, but I thought it wouldn't corrupt me. I remained a wallflower.

On the last afternoon of the convention, the membership and applicants gathered in a hotel ballroom to vote on new members and transact business. To our relief, the membership voted to admit *The Local Planet*. We became the youngest paper in memory to gain admission. I'm sure Ted wasn't happy. We didn't get accepted into the Alternative Weekly Network (AWN), a group of weekly papers that banded together to sell national advertising. I figured membership in AWN would have meant at least $30,000 a year in ad revenue. We could certainly use the money. However, *The Inlander* was a charter member of AWN, which effectively scuttled our chances. Once again, we had the recognition, but they had the advertisers and the money.

BRIGHT BLOSSOMS
OF FLAME

On Tuesday morning, September 11, 2001, I awoke before 5:45
a.m. I usually woke up early and spontaneously. The heat and
glare of Spokane's summer was fading quickly, with mornings once
again dim and crisp. With a gentle flick, I turned off the alarm
before it could erupt at six. Connye had been fighting something
like the flu for nearly two weeks, so I tried not to disturb her. In the
kitchen I made tea in the coffee maker that I consecrated to tea
and prepped the other coffee maker for Connye. It would be a long
day. Tuesdays at the newspaper we assembled the week's stories
and pictures and ads into digital pages and uploaded them to our
printer across the state line in Idaho. We could be at work for 16
hours that day, or more.

I sat at the dining room table waiting for my tea to brew and
for Henry to go piddle in the back yard. I switched on the little
television atop the old cabinet sewing machine that Connye had
once used for her business handcrafting dolls. I wasn't a fan of
TV, but I ran a newspaper and was expected to follow politics and
events even if they wouldn't appear in my local pages.

CNN carried live footage of smoke curling up from the
World Trade Center in New York City. I used the remote to thumb

through the news channels. So did MSNBC and Headline News and all the local morning new shows. Dan Rather announced that a plane had crashed into the north tower. Typical sensationalist TV news, I thought, all image and no substance. So what if a plane—I thought a small prop plane or maybe an executive jet— had crashed into a building? The pilot might have been drunk, or suicidal, or experiencing a heart attack or stroke. Surely this story didn't warrant preemptive, live national coverage.

Then, just after 6 a.m. a second plane, what appeared to be a big commercial jetliner flying low over the skyline, banked its wings counterclockwise and slammed into the south tower. CNN showed footage shot from street level looking north towards the flames and ash-colored smoke rising from the north tower. n the background the whining roar of engines built. The camera pulled back a bit and revealed more of the bright blue September sky, part of the Manhattan skyline, and the still-green top of a nearby tree. The plane entered the frame. When shown amongst the buildings, the magnitude and speed of the plane became large and real. It disappeared into the south tower, replaced by bright blossoms of flame.

Normally I would have hesitated about waking Connye early when she wasn't feeling well, but my instinct told me this wasn't just another accident reported as news. I went into our darkened bedroom and gently shook her awake. "You need to come see this. It's like Pearl Harbor out there." Back in the kitchen, I switched on the coffee maker.

Connye got up quickly, put on a robe, and sat at the dining room table. I told her what I knew, about one plane and then another, then puttered through the kitchen quickly pouring her a mug of coffee.

"Oh my God," she said. We watched the repeated video clips of planes missling into buildings and exploding. "Is this real?" she asked. The plume of smoke from the first tower grew into a thick gray column. I mentioned something about people, years earlier, trying to bring down the World Trade Towers with a bomb built in a rental truck. The pace and volume of commentator chatter quickly increased as the top of the north tower collapsed downward, a burnt soufflé falling in on itself. The weight of the upper floors compacted one lower floor after another after another. It was clear the entire building would collapse story by story.

"We have to throw out the cover," Connye said, "and maybe the entire paper." That week we planned to publish our first sex issue. Connye believed that Spokane was a town that needed to get laid, so we scheduled an annual sex issue right around the time that college students returned to school. Our planned cover image featured a black plastic female mannequin, naked, PhotoShopped to look like it was attacking the Spokane skyline. Clearly that would have to change.

I said that I'd grab a quick breakfast, then shower and catch a bus downtown to the office. She'd get the boys up and then join me as soon as she dropped Walt and Christian at school. When I returned to the dining room showered and dressed, reports were coming in of a plane plowing into the Pentagon in Washington, D.C. We watched the second tower collapse like the first. My cousin's husband worked as the head of the computer science department at NYU and probably commuted near the towers on his way to work. I hoped he was safe but didn't know how to find out. The phone lines were most likely jammed. I gathered my cell phone and papers into my black messenger bag. The television reported another plane crashing in Pennsylvania.

Connye picked up the phone.

"Who are you calling?" I asked.

"Freelancers," she said with a cough. "We have to redo our entire issue. Tell any editorial folks you see that we're meeting at 9:15."

The editorial meeting looked like a living history of *The Local Planet*'s young life. Practically every freelancer who'd written a news story for us attended. Connye ran the meeting. The focus of the issue we'd write that day, the story we could and should tell, was our community's reaction to events. We weren't a paper of record. We weren't a big paper, or daily. Our work had to remain compelling eight days later, after a week in which events and facts would appear, shift and vanish repeatedly. Connye and Cory, our art director, would search for another cover image. Our news editor Tom would monitor events in New York and Washington and write a summary late that night. Save a space near the front of the paper for him. One freelancer would cover the schools and talk about how young parents, our readers, could handle and discuss these events with their children. Another would attend the quickly organized interfaith meeting announced for noon at the base of the clock tower in Riverfront Park.

"What about *The Inlander*?" someone asked.

"I doubt that they'll do anything at all," I said. "This week is their big Fall Arts issue. It's probably close to 100 pages. They've already had to start printing sections of it. They can't postpone that issue."

I left the meeting oddly energized. In less than a morning our little weekly newspaper had temporarily transformed itself into a daily newsroom. This would be our 81st issue. We'd been a weekly publication for only a year. Yet, we had the confidence in our mission and in our skills to create an entire issue from scratch in roughly 12 hours.

Village Voice Media, one of the major companies in the alternative newspaper business, provided a lot of help to fellow papers that day. One of their publishers was flying into New York that morning for a meeting at his paper's corporate headquarters. His flight was directly behind the second plane that hit the towers. He wrote a commentary and provided it free of charge to other papers in the Association of Alternative Newsweeklies. A Village Voice photographer was near the towers that morning and snapped photos of the attack. We used one of his photos as our cover.

As Tuesday September 11 rolled over to Wednesday September 12, we neared completion of our new issue. Our new pages wouldn't win any design awards. We had too much text on many pages, and the flow from page to page was rough. It certainly looked like a last-minute issue. But on Thursday morning when the Spokane weekly papers hit the stands, our competitor's mammoth arts issue sat on their racks, not moving. By Friday, they managed to squeeze out a 12-page circular in response to events. Its layout looked worse than ours. Nearly all their copy came from national and international syndicates and wire services, hardly anything local, and was outdated by the time it was printed. Looking back, it seems catty to view events of that week as a business competition, but that's exactly what occurred. We saw it as proof that we were more responsive, more in tune with our community and with our role in it. Of course, our continual hope and plan was that, by being a better paper for our community, we'd also become an integral and profitable business in our community. That remained to be seen. But it felt good to be the new publisher scooping the competition.

A week later, our September 20, 2001 cover story, "Seven Days at Ground Zero," afforded us a more considered look at the events of 9/11. It opened:

Tuesday, September 11

At dawn, with the sun just beginning to rise over
Manhattan, the steel and glass of the World Trade
Center offered no reflection. During the day the towers
act like a giant mirror, shooting the sun's light back at
anyone trying to view them. But without the glare the
towers were beautiful.

Offices on Lower Broadway were empty, lit only by bank-
er's lamps that glowed over desks. Few people were out.
Two building maintenance workers hosed down the sidewalk. They stood under scaffolding, smoking cigarettes,
spraying the water from side to side. Five Hispanic limo
drivers were huddled on the curb, smoking cigarettes
and talking, having just dropped off their employers. At
Nassau and Liberty streets, four firemen sat on the back
of their truck.

Matthew Cole

Just before the first plane hit it made the heavy rasp-
ing common to most machines that travel at very high
velocities. Millions of documents floated down in the sky.
Sirens sounded almost immediately. Fist-sized chunks of
concrete and long strips of steel and tiny pieces of glass
were hitting the ground. "Jesus Christ. Oh, Jesus Christ,"
someone said. I saw two bodies fall and I saw four on the
ground. I saw one fall on the opposite edge of the square,
arms out and legs straight. I heard it tear through the
roof of a bandstand and heard it hit the ground. Closer
to me I saw one actually hit. Both times I heard a sound
that, had I not seen the impact, I would have taken for
an explosion.

The second plane hit at nine. I heard the glass tinkling around me and soothing music coming from speakers above me. Air conditioning ducts were dropping but the falling glass abated. "We need triage now!" someone shouted. There were women in tears. I saw raw flesh on the side of a woman's face. I saw people dripping blood.

Nick Spangler

The day after the attacks, Tom had contacted his Journalism professors at Columbia University in New York City, where he'd earned his Masters. He asked if the graduate students there would write a collaborative piece about the week in New York following the attacks. The professors agreed and collected stories from 17 students. Tom and his old professors edited the student stories into alternating vignettes of the week following the attack on the World Trade Center. The resulting story went on to win the AAN's Alternative Weekly national award for best feature story of 2001 for papers with circulation less than 50,000.

Winning an AAN Award is a big deal. Judges come from the ranks of Pulitzer Prize winners, J-school professors, major publication editors, and others who know a thing or two. AAN member papers compete many years before winner a national award. Many never do. We won two in our first year of competition.

Connye continued feeling under the weather throughout September. She went to her primary care doctor, who diagnosed a sinus infection. He prescribed cephlex, an antibiotic. Connye added this to her regime of nortriptyline, a standard anti-depressant; lactulose, a sugary syrup used to treat constipation; and OrthoCycline birth control pills. She'd been using all three prescriptions for years. It seemed unusual that an otherwise healthy 35-year-old woman, who exercised regularly, ate her vegetables and drank quarts of water, relied on daily doses of laxative. Normally, lactulose aids the bowels of elderly, bed-ridden patients and those in comas. Thanks to the cephlex, her condition morphed into a systemic yeast infection as the antibiotic killed off beneficial organisms along with her sinus infection. Strange clouds of black and gray drifted under her skin. Brad was also taking cephlex. He had contracted pink eye from the other kids when he returned to school. Then Connye got that as well.

Illness, job stress, and the adjustment of children going back to school all combined to start Connye and I grousing at each other. At times, Connye thought that we should just close the paper. It was bleeding us dry, she said. Spokane businesses didn't care about supporting us. One mid-September morning in our cramped bathroom we jostled to get dressed for the day. The morning rush increased our tension.

"I'm fed up with the newspaper. I want to leave. The boys need me."

"If you need to leave, then leave," I huffed. I was confident in my plans, especially now that we had fired most of the old guard and hired Tom and Bonnie.

I wasn't ready for her second bathroom pronouncement a few days later.

Connye stood in front of the mirror blow-drying her hair, a yellow towel wrapped around her torso. I worked around her to brush my teeth before catching the bus to the office. After rinsing the toothpaste from my mouth, I straightened up from the sink and stood behind her. She turned off the blow dryer, lowered her arms, and looked straight ahead at me in the mirror. Her complexion was paler than usual. Dark circles shadowed her eyes. "I'm going to get sick again," she said, "and this time it's going to be bad."

I froze, unable to locate my feelings. After a moment, I held Connye's shoulders and kissed her warm, moist neck. "We'll be alright," I said and left for work.

In email to the newspaper staff a few days later, I announced a quarterly review meeting for the last Friday of the month, September 28. That was partially true—I did want to review the quarter—but the smart staffers understood that we didn't normally review the quarter. I knew that we needed serious changes. The paper was still losing money. Plenty of people had told me to expect that a new publication would lose money for three years. I went to work every day expecting to make money. Events of 9/11 would make profitability even harder to reach and maintain. I finally felt forced to make necessary emotional decisions that I had avoided until now.

In the meeting, I passed out graphs of our sales for the quarter and for the year-to-date. Our summer revenues bucked the normal media lull. We were on track to sell more than $300,000 worth of ads for the year. That was more than twice the previous year's total. But we still weren't profitable. Due to our financial situation and the anticipated impact of the recent attacks, I felt that we needed to reduce our costs. Because payroll and printing were variable costs that accounted for 75% of our expenses, those were the areas that I had to reduce for the paper to continue moving towards profitability in tighter times.

Towards that end, Connye would be leaving the newspaper. She and I had already discussed this. I would temporarily assume the title of editor and take over writing our editorials. Tom would continue as News Editor and Jeremy as Culture Editor. Chris, the current Culture Editor, had independently decided that morning to leave the paper and move to Seattle. In light of fewer staff and potentially tighter revenues, we could no longer print 32 unprofitable pages each week. I capped the size of our weekly issues at 28 pages. If need be, we'd print 24 pages. It was time to be serious about making money with an even balance of editorial and paying ads.

I also eliminated the separate position of distribution manager, which meant that Connye's sister Dayna would also leave the paper. I would take on the task of managing circulation. This seemed reasonable, since I had built our distribution tracking system in Microsoft Excel and trained Dayna in it. In six months, she'd grown our distribution network to roughly 400 locations where we dropped more than 20,000 papers each week. We wouldn't need to expand our network for the foreseeable future. We would end distribution in Kettle Falls, Sandpoint, Bonners Ferry, or any city north of the Spokane Indian tribal casino in Chewelah. Readers in those small northern towns weren't measured in our demographic surveys; businesses there didn't buy ads.

After the meeting, I asked Tom and Jeremy separately to accept a temporary 10 percent reduction in salary. I would raise it again as soon as I could, but for the next few months it would make a difference. They both agreed, although reluctantly. Tom later came to me and asked me for the title of Editor. With Connye gone and him doing even more editorial work, he argued that it was fair. Also, if this paper didn't survive the recent turn of world events, he wanted the title of Editor on his resume. I agreed and happily ceded more editorial work to him, although I kept writing editorials.

Jeremy said that it was already tough for him to get by on his salary before any pay cut. I offered him one of the paper's distribution routes. He could spend Thursday mornings delivering papers. I had budget there and preferred it go to full-time staff. He accepted. I gave him the route serving part of Spokane's downtown core. That way he'd be close to his home and our office, so delivery wouldn't be too much of an impact on his time. But being close to home meant that Jeremy ran into friends and sources throughout his route. He'd stop and talk, eat lunch, research stories. The route that I could finish in three hours took him all day. Within six months, I raised his salary back to normal and gave his route to a contract employee. Still, I was glad that Jeremy had his experience in distribution. We had initially hired him as a salesperson—he had a degree in marketing and good graphic design skills—although he really wanted to write. He turned out to be one of our best revenue producers. After he hit his sales target of $3,000 per issue, we made a spot for him as Music Editor. Serving a stint in distribution meant that he had experienced three of the four major areas for the newspaper. Administration was the last remaining area. If I ever needed a replacement, Jeremy might be it.

For a few weeks, my changes worked. We began to break even financially on issues. We ended October with $1000 dollars left in the bank. My heart rode two ribs higher in my chest. Instead of losing money for three years, as many people had predicted, we were breaking even after less than two years of total operations and just one year of weekly publication. But I doubted this would last. Several large companies heeded the "business as usual" and "don't let the terrorists win" messages government and civic leaders pumped out after 9/11. Their patriotism showed in several big advertising buys for the month. None of those buys turned into long-term contracts, though. Our financial luck probably wouldn't hold into the coming year.

A LIMO TO
ANOTHER HOTEL

In October 2001, a month into Brad's sophomore year at the remodeled and reopened Lewis and Clark High School, Connye and I found ourselves sitting with Brad in the vice principal's office. The school security officer discovered Brad skipping class and smoking on school grounds. His grades had slipped very quickly, starting the first week of school. We noticed changes at home, too. He wasn't his cheerful, overly social self. He'd grown quiet and more anxious than usual. The tips of his fingers were scabbed where he chewed his fingernails.

Personally, I didn't like the vice principal simply because he was a vice principal. From stories we'd done at *The Local Planet,* I knew that this guy sat in his new office in his new $40 million school making about $90,000 a year. That alone was enough to stir my schoolyard rebel. His office was bigger than our living room and lined with polished wood furniture that radiated the autumn sunlight. It resembled a photo in the IKEA catalog. I've never liked school authority figures. I may have settled down to be a placid teenager, but as a pre-teen I'd been banished to the principal's office on several occasions for disrespecting the authority of gym teachers, playground monitors, and school crossing guards.

Principals and their fellow travelers have struck me as smiling snakes since the time I hid behind a rotating wire rack of drug store greeting cards and watched my elementary school principal buy a copy of *Playboy*. I wasn't prudish then and I'm not now, but it seemed me a symptom of hypocrisy. Admittedly, my dislike of school authority is its own hypocrisy, considering that my mom's father was a school district superintendent for many years, my sister and her husband are both teachers, and I came within two courses of earning a teaching certificate.

The vice principal began the meeting by asking Brad about his grades. I don't think Brad completed a sentence before Connye jumped in. "My son says he's being harassed in your school, and I want to know what you intend to do about it."

Brad seemed a little embarrassed by his mom's vehemence. He was also embarrassed about being harassed. When pressed, he described how a group of juniors would insult, taunt, and intimidate him at his locker, in the halls, and on the school grounds.

"Who are these kids?" the vice principal asked.

Brad said that he didn't know their names.

I had a bright idea. "Can we go through the yearbook, and you can pick them out?"

Brad said he didn't want to. "If I tell on them, what's going to stop them from getting their friends to just keep doing it?"

I thought that if the punishment were severe enough, like total expulsion from the school, no one else would try. The vice principal seemed open to my idea. His agreement bothered me.

Connye sided with Brad. "What can you do to keep my kid safe here at school?"

The vice principal insisted that the school had done and was doing all it could. He said teachers patrolled the hallways during passing times. Brad named teachers who had witnessed him being harassed and silently passed by. The school conducted anti-discrimination and anti-harassment presentations in homerooms. The vice principal pulled a binder from his birch-and-chrome shelving system and pointed to a day on a calendar when such presentations were supposedly made. Brad said he was at school that day and didn't remember any such presentation in his homeroom. We hit an impasse. If Brad refused to identify his harassers, then there wasn't much more to be done. Connye believed that Brad didn't and wouldn't feel safe anymore at Lewis and Clark.

She decided to enroll Brad in an alternative program called Real. A former middle school building on the near north side of town housed several alternative programs, like ones for teenaged mothers or students just released from juvenile detention and drug rehab. Real was the program for college-bound kids who didn't fit in with the regular student body. It occupied two large rooms and a gymnasium at the back of the building, with work areas instead of rows of desks. One teacher supervised each room. Maybe this was where a bright gay kid could survive high school, surrounded by other kids who didn't fit.

Brad perked up after seeing Real and meeting the teachers. The flamboyant, aspiring celebrity part of Brad liked to feel special, exotic, somehow apart from the normal sleepwalking riffraff. The separateness and nonconformity of Real appealed to that part. Within a few days of our meeting at Lewis & Clark, Brad transferred to the alternative program and settled into a routine of riding the city bus past his old school on the way to and from his new one.

After work on Friday night, October 19, Connye and I were trying to reclaim some normalcy of life. Walt and Christian were spending the weekend at their dad's house; Brad was hanging out at the mall downtown. Without the pressure of working at *The Local Planet*, Connye seemed relieved. She had invited Alan and Sherie for dinner. It was probably the first time Connye and I had done anything fun, social, and leisurely for just us since our wedding more a year prior. Alan hosted the morning show on Spokane's alternative rock station and frequently put me on the air to promote the newspaper. They arrived a little before six. We all had a glass of red wine to sip while Connye finished cooking dinner. She didn't normally cook, but I think making dinner and entertaining was her way of taking back her life.

Just as we sat to eat, the phone rang. Knowing our mood that evening, someone joked about telemarketers calling at mealtime. I got up and answered the phone. It wasn't a telemarketer; it was a paramedic asking if I was Brad's parent. He told me that he and his crew were with Brad at the bus stop under the interstate right by Lewis & Clark High School.

I told Connye that Brad wasn't feeling well and I was going to pick him up. "Stay, enjoy yourselves," I told our guests. "I'll be right back."

When I arrived in the station wagon, Brad was sitting on a low brick wall, wrapped in a blanket. The paramedics flanked him. His complexion was white and his eyes seemed sleepy and a little glassy. He said he had a huge headache, he felt dizzy, and his right leg hurt. During his bus ride home from downtown, he began feeling sick. He managed to stagger to the front of the moving bus and tell the driver that he needed to get off, that he felt ill. Brad must have looked awful, because the driver stopped the bus and called for assistance.

"Just take me home," he told me quietly.

I supported at least half his weight in helping him to the car. As I flogged the big station wagon up the hill to home, Brad winced and huffed and clenched his fists and teeth. His right leg looked like it was starting to spasm. When we reached the house, I parked the car on the street, got out, and circled around to help Brad. He couldn't get out of the car seat by himself. Once I had him out and standing up, his whole body crumpled. I caught him by the armpits before he hit the grass.

Connye came out the front door onto the porch. "What's wrong?"

I knew that this was more than something simple like the flu or food poisioning. Trying to be gentle but quick, I dumped Brad back in the car. "I'm taking him to the emergency room."

"I'll follow you," Connye called and headed for the garage. Alan and Sherie graciously put away our dinner then locked the house on their way out.

At the emergency room where Walt got his wrist stitched up, an orderly helped me lower Brad into a wheelchair. The triage nurse asked Brad some standard admission questions. He whispered his answers through clenched teeth. By now, his muscles were clearly seizing. His back arched like a bridge and his chin jutted upwards and out. His fingers looked like claws, and his right leg was tense and lifted off the seat of the wheelchair. The staff moved him into one of the semi-private rooms in the emergency room and laid him on a gurney. There, we waited. Friday night in emergency rooms is normally busy. We watched police teams bring in car accident victims.

Connye and I hovered about our little room. Brad squirmed on the gurney. The muscles across his back continued to seize, forcing his chest to arch. He could still talk and told us he was in pain. A doctor finally came to interview us: Brad had no history of seizures (but his brother had them), no head trauma, no known drug use. He passed a drug test. Eventually the doctor pulled us aside and said that this was not like any classic seizure. With no history of illness, trauma or drug use, she suspected that his seizure might be psychogenic. In other words, she thought it was all in Brad's mind. He was clearly anxious and agitated.

Of course he was, we replied. He's in pain. He's having a seizure. Sure, life had been a little stressful lately. He just switched schools because of harassment. His mom was changing jobs. His brother had seizures. But we just didn't believe that Brad's stress had risen to the point of psychogenic seizures.

The doctor gave Brad a shot of Ativan, a mild sedative used to reduce anxiety. She also ordered a CT scan of his head to check for any abnormalities. After another wait, an orderly came and rolled Brad to his test through double doors at the back of the ER.

Need I say that time goes slowly for parents in an ER? Every visit lasts at least a couple of hours but can feel like an entire night. Connye and I waited, fretted, speculated. Maybe the drug test missed something. Maybe this was related to Walt's condition. We avoided the more ominous possibilities that the scan might reveal, such as a brain tumor. We'd been at the ER for three hours. None of us had eaten dinner. New patients continued to stream in.

A half hour later, when his gurney rolled back in through the double doors, Brad clearly felt better. His seizure had abated and he looked comfortable. By now our private little room held another patient, so the orderly parked Brad in an open examination area. Three or four gurneys could have idled there side by side, but we were the only one.

Connye leaned over and stroked Brad's hair back from his forehead. "How are you feeling?"

"Okay," Brad said calmly. He smiled a little smile, and Connye brightened. He turned his head away and up, like he was trying to look back over his shoulder while lying down. He smiled again and almost giggled.

"What?" Connye asked with a half chuckle.

"There are people laughing back there." Brad gestured with his chin towards the wall behind him. "Is there a comedy club back there?"

Connye and I looked at each other. There was no laughter in the emergency room that night. Neither of us knew what to make of this. "No honey, you're at the hospital."

"It sounds like people are laughing."

"Do you think they're laughing at you?" I asked. I wondered if the Ativan had somehow made him paranoid.

"They just sound like they're having a good time. Can I go back there?"

"No Brad, you need to stay here for now."

"Oh, okay." He was content to lie on the gurney and listen to the laughter.

We tried to get the attention of our doctor. It wasn't easy, given the number of patients. As we waited, Brad continued to smile and look back towards the wall. After a while he said he wanted to sit up. Then with his design sense, he somehow managed to transform his hospital smock into a cute little tunic.

The doctor returned and said that the scan results were normal. She couldn't think of any other explanation for his seizure at this time. We explained that Brad was now hearing things and didn't seem to understand that he was in the hospital.

The doctor asked Brad some general orienting questions: What day is it? He didn't know. Where are you? He thought he was in a hotel. Who are these people? Connye and I were his staff, part of his entourage. This was Brad's aspiring celebrity side. He told the doctor that we were all waiting for a limousine to arrive to take him to another, better hotel. This one was all right, he said, to not hurt the kind lady's feelings, but he was going to a better one.

"Can I get up and walk around?" he asked.

"Sure, but stay right around here," the doctor said. "You don't want to miss your limo." The doctor looked at me and Connye. We kept an eye on him, so he didn't wander away. Brad sashayed around the ER in his tunic, absently inspecting some of the equipment. He peered past the entrance guards to see if his ride had arrived.

We didn't know what was going on. The doctor doubted that the Ativan could make Brad hallucinate. She'd injected a small dose, especially for someone weighing 180 pounds. Connye and I didn't believe the psychogenic seizure theory, but we had no other good explanation. The doctor suggested calling the mental health professional (MHP). We agreed. We needed another chance at some answers.

Another wait, and then the MHP arrived. He was a stocky, bearded man wearing khaki shorts and carrying a clipboard. At first I thought he was a gym teacher, and thus a little suspect to my inner schoolyard rebel. His interview with Brad yielded the same story about changing hotels. The MHP conferred with the doctor, read over the ER notes and confessed that he had no answers, either. "Brad doesn't seem to be in any danger at the moment, but he's also clearly not oriented. We can send him home with you if you think that you can keep him under supervision, or we can admit him to the child psych ward at Sacred Heart."

Connye had been on the adult psych ward at Sacred Heart Hospital during her depression in '94 and '95. She knew what it was like. She turned to me for a plan.

"You probably don't want to do this," I said, "but I think he should go to the ward. You've been sick and I'm exhausted. We haven't eaten in 12 hours. We don't have an answer to his condition. Neither one of us can stay up with him all night, especially if he turns angry or hostile. And he could have another seizure, which means that he'd be back at the hospital anyway."

Reluctantly, Connye agreed. The staff called for an ambulance to transport Brad a few blocks east to Sacred Heart. He was happy to see his limo arrive. He climbed in on his own and laid down on the gurney. We followed the ambulance to Sacred Heart so that Connye could complete his admissions paperwork there.

Connye and I arrived home past midnight, after more than six hours at two different hospitals. Henry sprang from the couch, yipping nervously after being left alone for so long. Connye made it to the dining table before she collapsed against me and let out a mournful, hollow sob. Henry jumped up on us, begging attention. "I can't lose him. Oh God Matt. What if he has schizophrenia, or he's bipolar?"

I held her and stroked her hair. I didn't know any more than Connye what we'd do. "It'll be okay. We'll handle whatever comes."

"People die of those things."

We numbly brushed our teeth, undressed and got into bed. I dropped immediately in the dreamless sleep of fatigue. I didn't hear the phone ring at 1:30 in the morning. Connye picked it up. "Mom, mom, you have to get me out of here. Get me out of here." Then she heard the phone slam down. Worry gnawed on her the rest of the night.

In the morning, we visited the ward. Connye directed me which parking area was best, which elevator to take, which way to turn in the maze of long, gray hospital hallways. She had traced these same paths many times in 1995 while undergoing electroconvulsive therapy to treat her depression. Eventually we turned a corner and came to a double set of security doors. Connye picked up the phone next to the doors and asked the nurse to let us in. Once past the first set of doors, we answered more questions from the nurse inside the glassed-in nurse's station before being buzzed through to the day room, a kind of a lobby for the ward.

Like many hospital areas, this room had that stuck-in-the-1970s décor: linoleum tile floors, angular vinyl couches, dark wood end tables with dated magazines. As we waited for the nurse, a slight boy perhaps 12 years old crossed from our right to our left, moving from one wing of the ward to the other. He smiled silently at us. He wasn't any bigger than Walt. We later found out that this boy had credibly threatened to kill his mother.

The nurse sat down with us and told us the rules of the ward. Access to phones, radios, CD players, and the like was virtually non-existent for the first three days on the ward. Gaining privileges on the ward was linked to participation in therapeutic activities and completion of various assignments. She took the toiletries and treats Connye brought, to inspect and dole out according to the rules and Brad's standing on the ward.

Brad's room was surprisingly large. A closet and bed stood against the left and right walls. Picture windows at the far end of the room overlooked the interstate, downtown Spokane, and suburbs stretching north to the county line. Because Sacred Heart is built on the slope of Spokane's South Hill, the window was a few stories off the ground. No bars obstructed the view. A condo in this very spot could command a hefty price. Between the hospital and the interstate stood a neighborhood of smaller establishments that typically cluster around a major hospital: medical offices, law firms, and florists. The sign for the Ball and Dodd funeral home stood above the low structures, right at eye level with motorists on the section of elevated interstate.

Brad moved around a lot, fussing with his clothes and magazines, pacing the floor, sitting on the corner of his bed. He was agitated and angry, but not in any way that I'd seen before. One minute he would not talk to us. The next minute he sat leaning forward with his legs tightly crossed, elbow on knee and chin resting on the tip of his index finger. He tried to draw us into a Socratic debate about our flawed reasoning for admitting him. Clearly, we were idiots for sending him to the ward. In another minute, he would cry inconsolably. I was baffled. This wasn't the Brad I knew. Not just his attitude, but also his mannerisms, his speech, his thinking.

As we left, Connye recounted how Brad's moods were cycling. She had always been more emotionally observant than I was and was more schooled in psychology as well. Her assessment seemed surprisingly clinical to me, especially compared to her grieving the previous evening.

Saturday stretched into Sunday. Spokane County didn't conduct mental health commitment hearings on weekends. This was an issue that Connye had tackled while working for the mental health watchdog committee, before working at the newspaper. She knew Brad's case might not be reviewed until Tuesday or Wednesday.

By our visit on Monday, Brad had calmed down and felt better. He was still angry with us. Group therapy was pointless, the other kids were younger and really messed up, and obviously we were stupid and unloving.

The staff reviewed Brad's case on Tuesday. Everyone involved gathered in a small room outside the double doors to the ward. The conference table was too large for the room and left barely enough space around the edges for chairs. Connye and I squeezed into the room along with nurses, the MHP, and the psychiatrist Dr. E. I was only 38, but to me Dr. E looked impossibly young, with smooth skin and wavy hair the color of dark sand. He could have been 25 years old, although it's nearly impossible to finish psychiatry training before age 30. His bowtie seemed to me more like a prank than a preference, but I didn't sense any irony from Dr. E.

Discussion of Brad's case progressed around the table. No one offered a definitive diagnosis for sudden seizure, hallucinations, and personality shift. The patient seemed better. He mostly followed the rules of the ward, although he was clearly unhappy about being there. The team agreed that Brad should be released, prescribed Depakote for the headache and seizure, and placed under the outpatient care of Dr. E.

In the car on the way home, Brad leaned forward from the back seat and asked, "Can I go hang out with some friends from school?"

"You just got out of the hospital," Connye answered.

"I feel fine."

"No, I want you to stay home for now."

Brad sat back and exhaled loudly. I could tell he was perturbed. I dropped them off at home and went back to work. It was Tuesday, after all, time again to assemble another issue and deliver it to the printer.

THE LITTLE IMITATOR

Just before Halloween 2001, Connye started work as a marketing assistant for Planned Parenthood of the Inland Northwest. She would help them with fundraising and media relations. In the past, she had volunteered for Planned Parenthood. She understood the organization and believed in its mission. Her stress level seemed to keep dropping. Now she had a job that used her skills, appreciated her dedication, and paid her acceptable wages and benefits. However, flu-like symptoms continued to nag her. She stayed home ill one day one week, then three days the next. She couldn't get well. After she used all her sick leave within a few weeks and wasn't getting better, the executive director suggested that she use Planned Parenthood's short-term disability insurance. That's why they paid the premiums, she urged. By early December, Connye was completely off work and missed the office holiday party held at a bakery just a mile from our house. I attended without her, to pass along her regrets and wish everyone a merry Christmas.

Connye's general practitioner couldn't find a cause for her constant fatigue, nausea, constipation, pain, fever and chills. The results for any tests he ran came back negative. He referred her to an infectious disease specialist in the hope that someone more specialized could discover the root of her problems. The specialist,

Dr. G, interviewed Connye at length and ran numerous blood tests. For nearly every appointment I rushed out of work, drove south up the hill, and picked up Connye to accompany her. I wanted to know what was going on. When she fell ill in '94 and '95, Sam and his family told her that it was all in her head. I couldn't deny the sweat or goose bumps on her skin, the pallor of her complexion or her obvious weakness. When Dr. G finished his barrage of infection tests without finding any diseases, he mentioned that sometimes steroids cleared up fevers and complaints of unknown origins. Connye and I agreed to try. After two months of illness, we wanted to find something that helped even if it only addressed the symptoms.

After a few days of slowly increasing doses of steroids, Connye started to feel better. She was comfortable, mobile, even happy. In mid-December, she accompanied the boys and me to the newspaper holiday party, held at Bonnie's house. The staff was happy to see her again after working three months without her. She smiled at being out among friends again. At one point the conversation turned to the subject of tattoos. Connye mentioned that she had one, which surprised a lot of people. She stood up from the large easy chair in the corner, turned around, bent over, and pulled down the waistband of her pants about six inches to show the green sea turtle drawn across the small of her back. Everyone laughed and cheered.

I knew the story of the turtle that I had nicknamed Baxter as a pun. Connye had him drawn after she recovered from her illness in 1995. She wanted to put a positive mark on her body to contrast the negative scar across her left wrist. Sea turtles were a totemic animal for her. She taped a postcard of one to the upper left corner of our bathroom mirror. A blue decorative pot shaped like one stood at one end of our bungalow's mantle. Sea turtle rings, necklaces, and earrings filled her jewelry box.

Her moment of turtle bonding had come while scuba diving, when she gazed into the eyes of a sea turtle that hovered in the water to examine her. Their eyes met and, she said, she felt an undiscovered wisdom and compassion and strength. She liked to compare her journey to that of the sea turtles that are born as small as coins and nearly helpless, but who grow large enough to swim thousands of miles and fend off sharks. Once she told me that my green eyes, with the small smile lines at the corners, reminded her of the turtle.

Although the steroids seemed to help Connye, we still didn't have a diagnosis. The infection specialist suggested a whole-body scan with radioactive gallium. Gallium concentrates at sites of infection or thyroid malfunction. Scanning for glowing spots of gallium pinpoints any hidden problems. On the morning of Christmas Eve, 2001, I accompanied Connye into the nuclear medicine department of Deaconess Hospital. The technician gave her the gallium to drink and then made her wait about an hour. When I saw the results of the scan, they looked like a Connye-shaped country at night as seen from a commercial flight. Glowing green dots and lines populated the land. But no urban centers of hidden infection shone in the darkness. The specialist said that he was out of ideas. He referred us to a rheumatologist.

The steroids brought back Connye's interest in sex. With the stress of the newspaper, job changes, and illness, neither one of us had had the time, energy, or even interest in making love. Whatever time we got in bed was zealously reserved for sleep. One night in early January, Connye gave me more than the usual goodnight kiss. Soon she was on top of me and hanging on to the headboard. This wasn't her normal position. I didn't remember her on top since our first summer together during our picnic at Lake Roosevelt. Afterwards she smiled, half contentment and half victory, and sighed, "I think we've found a new position."

The boost from the steroids was short-lived. Two weeks later Connye awoke in the middle of the night, screaming in pain and clutching her knees. I turned on the lights and threw back the covers. Nothing appeared visibly wrong.

"What is it?"

"My bones," she hissed through clenched teeth. "It feels like they're grinding together."

In another two weeks, she could barely walk. We purchased a walker, metal tubing with wheels, handbrake, seat and basket. "It's only temporary," I assured her while I loaded the walker into the station wagon. "Plus, the insurance will cover the cost." The steroids were starting to make her face round and puffy.

Despite her pain and symptoms, Connye managed the medical insurance paperwork as if it was her job. We cheered when she received the letter granting her short-term disability coverage. With her off work, we'd had no money coming in. Walt or Christian must have said something to Sam about our celebration. Sam called Planned Parenthood to claim that Connye wasn't really disabled, that she was defrauding insurance, and that through *The Local Planet* she was worth millions of dollars. I had to smirk a little. If only he knew how much money I'd already poured into the paper. I'd seen Sam pull nasty stuff related to the kids and divorce, but he had mostly behaved himself for two years. This, however, had nothing to do with him. He wasn't even inconvenienced with taking care of the boys more often. His actions seemed like nothing but spite. Inspired by a nickname generator printed in *The Spokesman-Review*'s Sunday comics, I'd named this side of Sam's personality Captain Blowdick. I wrote the Captain a letter stating that Connye had a disabling condition. His actions could be considered criminal harassment under the Americans with Disabilities Act. Connye later told me that Sam apologized to her during a phone call. She forgave and forgot. I remained baffled and disgusted.

Dr. B, our new rheumatologist, showed no sense of urgency about healing. I think he caught that from his patients. Elderly couples with chronic arthritis rusted in his waiting room. Connye and I always arrived late in the day, during the cold dark of February. Evenings were the only times that Dr. B could fit us into his schedule. Connye had recently turned 36, yet she sat slumped in a wheelchair in Dr. B's office. Fatigue and constant pain in her hips and joints cut her mobility. She had shaved her head because showering and shampooing were difficult. Her hair, which was normally a dirty blonde if she didn't dye it, was growing back reddish-brown. She wore a purple velvet cap to stay warm and to hide her hair. She looked like a cancer patient on chemotherapy.

Although slow, Dr. B was always polite and kind. He was weaning Connye from steroids, because they didn't seem to help any more. He also prescribed OxyContin, a time-released opiate, to help control her pain. News reports referred to OxyContin as Hillbilly Heroin, due to the theft and abuse of the drug that was first widely noticed in the Southeast. Users soak or rub the time-release coating off the pills before taking them, thereby getting the 12-hour dose all at once. The high is supposedly intense, but the sickness afterwards can last for days. The pills also come stamped with their milligram dosage, so addicts and dealers use them as a type of currency.

None of the standard rheumatological tests or conditions explained Connye's illness. Unlike the general practitioner and infection specialist, though, Dr. B didn't pass us on. He wanted to find what was wrong. He wondered if Connye had a neurological condition such as multiple sclerosis (MS); Spokane was a worldwide hotspot for MS. He ordered an MRI scan of Connye's head and spine. The results showed a couple bright white spots of nerve demylinization, but nothing conclusive of MS. Next, he thought that she might have pancreatic cancer. Connye always complained of stabbing pains in the middle of her back, like a knife being twisted between her ribs. For a CT scan of her abdomen, she had to choke down through her nausea a gallon of white metallic contrast. Initially, the CT technician thought the tip of Connye's pancreas showed some cancerous activity, but neither the radiologist nor internist confirmed that speculation. Dr. B browsed through medical books and found a heart condition that could explain many of Connye's symptoms. Sometimes a dome-shaped growth forms in one chamber of the heart. He ordered a trans-esophageal echocardiogram. We went to the heart institute, where doctors placed a cable down her windpipe to position a sonar transmitter next to Connye's heart. This let them get a very clear picture. No growths, no valve damage, no infection—just a healthy heart lub-dubbing along.

Dr. B reviewed Connye's medical records again. He wondered why she had been taking lactulose daily for years and ordered a colonoscopy. I held her hand while she lay on a gurney parked alongside four other patients but wasn't allowed to accompany her during the actual procedure. Normally, patients need little or no sedation or pain control for the procedure. Connye, though, told me afterwards that she was screaming in pain during hers. The assisting nurse told her to shut up, that the doctor was trying to work. I was furious. The next day, I called the head partner of the GI practice to complain about Connye's barbaric treatment. The notes from the procedure said only that Connye's colon was brittle, like that of someone twice her age or more. No explanation, no possible causes—nothing.

Easter was nearly here and Dr. B was running out of theories. He still thought Connye's problem seemed neurological. He tried to get us a neurology appointment in Spokane but said that nothing was available for three months.

"So, we're supposed to wait another three months?" I asked. "Connye's been sick for four months already, and she's not getting better."

Dr. B assured me that three months was the best he could do in Spokane. If we wanted to go outside our medical insurance network, we could. Connye and I agreed that we weren't going to wait. We'd get the help we needed and argue with our insurance company later. Dr. B gave us a referral to neurology at Virginia Mason Medical Center in Seattle. We scheduled an appointment for the week of spring break.

In the meantime, Connye decided to try smoking marijuana to help her symptoms. OxyContin couldn't always control her pain. Plus, she had severe nausea. Like plenty of teenagers of the 1980s, Connye occasionally smoked pot in high school. It had been a while, though. I'd never seen her do it. Personally, I'd never smoked. Friends and teammates did it, but it never interested me. (Once shortly after college, I ate a pot-laced brownie on the last day of a group camping trip because it was the only food left and I was hungry, which now seems an ironic twist on the munchies. The scenery on the car ride home looked particularly nice.)

Connye scored some pot at first from a friend of her sister. She also scored through connections from the newspaper's staff; after all, we were the true alternative newspaper in town. Our cover story the week before 9/11 was called "The New Pot Economy." Our music writer Jeremy won awards for his profile of a local man who ran a small growing room in his attic. The grower sold almost exclusively to family, friends, and friends of friends. Certainly a small time operator, but he made over $20,000 a year from his hobby.

Connye smoked in our upstairs bathroom, with a towel across the bottom of the door and the exhaust fan running. Sometimes her nausea was so bad that even the smell of the resin on the leaves, or just the thought of the smoke, made her gag. But, after a couple of puffs she could relax and eat a little ice cream. Pot cut through the nausea and the pain more quickly and effectively than the cancer-related drugs she was prescribed. It helped her get to where she could keep down her oral medications.

Brad was envious. He didn't understand why his mom could smoke pot and he couldn't. All the explanations—that she wasn't getting high, that she was in a lot of pain, that it helped with the nausea—he just shrugged off. He was still getting into trouble, although he had stopped sneaking off at night with the station wagon. After his seizure episode, we told him that if he had a seizure while driving and crashed, he could kill himself or someone else. If he was caught, there was a chance that he would never be licensed to drive. We also told him that if he did it again, we would report the car as stolen and turn him over to the police.

After Brad came home drunk and threw up in the bathtub, Connye asked if he needed some counseling. To our surprise, Brad said yes.

The outpatient counselor Connye found at Deaconess Hospital acted a little gruff but seemed to connect with Brad. Because I was working so much and Connye was sick, Brad rode the bus to his appointments on his own. Part of the program was random drug tests. Brad's results showed some alcohol and pot, but nothing more serious. He seemed to be making progress and maybe even enjoying the counseling. Then, after only six weeks of appointments, Deaconess announced that it was closing the entire outpatient drug-counseling program as part of cost reductions.

Connye soon noticed her OxyContin pills were disappearing. We immediately suspected Brad. It wouldn't be the first time he got into trouble—but stealing opiates was worse than drinking or taking the car. After double-checking our facts, recounting the pills and searching the house, we knew the culprit was Brad, although we had no hard evidence. Walt and Christian wouldn't take the pills, because they had no idea what they really were or their value. Neither would their friends. Connye wasn't taking too many. I wasn't taking them. The only other people who had access to the house were Brad and any of his friends who came over.

Brad vehemently denied our logic. So, we asked him for the name and phone numbers of his friends, because they were the next suspects. Brad protested this, as well. We hadn't actually found pills in his possession or seen him high on them, so there wasn't much more to do.

I installed a locking doorknob on our bedroom door, but pills kept disappearing. It was too much to expect Connye to run a security facility while she was sick. She spent most of her days in pajamas that didn't have pockets for keys. I screwed a clasp on our bedroom closet door and secured it with a padlock. Pills still disappeared. I figured that Brad was unscrewing the lock hardware from the wall. But, since we didn't have any proof and never saw Brad high, we couldn't do anything other than take precautions and ignore the lies. I bought a small safe for all the drugs and any extra house and car keys.

Connye and I decided to take a short vacation in Seattle around her neurology appointment. Between Tom and Bonnie, the paper would be just fine for a few days. Walt and Christian spent the week with Sam. We again left Brad in Spokane, not wanting to reward his behavior. Frankly, we needed a break from him nearly as much as we needed a diagnosis for Connye. He had the option of staying the week with his dad in Las Vegas, but he decided to stay home alone with surveillance from his aunt.

We spent our short vacation during spring break 2002 housesitting in my friend Christopher's home in Seattle's Greenlake neighborhood. Christopher had been my office mate at Microsoft, and the only Seattle friend with whom I kept in regular contact. His large bungalow, older than ours with box beam ceilings and push-button light switches, would fit perfectly in our Spokane neighborhood. Connye and I enjoyed the quiet days with no kids, no work, no chores, and nothing scheduled aside from one doctor's appointment. We shopped at Whole Foods, an urban luxury that hadn't yet arrived in Spokane, and watched DVDs on the mammoth TV in Christopher's basement media room. Connye still had a hard time walking, which made getting down into the basement tough. Usually within 20 minutes of a movie's opening credits, she'd be asleep with her head in my lap. I stroked her short reddish hair, watched the movie, and tried to recover a little from my exhaustion.

On the day of her appointment, Connye used her walker to negotiate the hallways and elevators of Virginia Mason Medical Center. It was a sunny March day in Seattle, something of an oddity. The towers of the city gleamed. Light streamed in the lobby windows of the neurology floor. I felt like we had graduated to the medical big leagues, the place where real researchers worked. People waited in couples or small family units. They sat quietly, not even browsing through magazines. I felt their eyes on us as Connye and I walked from the check-in desk towards the lobby chairs. I realized that Connye was the worst looking person in the room: hair like a chemo patient, ghostly complexion, pushing a walker.

In contrast to Virginia Mason's big city setting, the actual examination room was sparse, almost utilitarian. By now I was a connoisseur of medical facilities. This room appeared large compared to other rooms I'd seen. The sturdy, square examination table resembled a workbench. It looked left over from a much older, prior facility. No art or medical posters hung on the walls.

Dr. S, the neurologist, was thin, quiet, and bespectacled. I'd hoped for a more dramatic persona for this specialist, for two reasons. One, I really thought that we'd get a diagnosis from this doctor, this visit. Two, for a long time I held a Walter Mitty fantasy of being a famous neurologist. Not a brain surgeon, but someone who knew the intricacies and mysteries of the brain. Oliver Sacks was my hero. Once, I read Isaac Asimov's guide to the brain just for fun.

In his quiet voice, Dr. S asked Connye to tell him more about her symptoms. He'd read the information sent over by Dr. B, but he wanted to hear from her. He wrote notes as he listened. He then performed what I took as a standard neurological exam, testing Connye's reflexes, senses, strength, muscle tone, coordination and the like. Some of it was hard work for Connye, who was fatigued in general and already worn out by just traveling to the appointment. At the end of the examination, Dr. S told us that he didn't believe that Connye's symptoms were "a classically neurological problem." He made more notes in her chart, and we left.

When we returned to Spokane, Dr. B suggested Connye be tested for porphyria. I wasn't sure whether Dr. B had discovered something while we were in Seattle, or if Dr. S suggested the test. We picked up the big brown plastic jug from the pharmacy—the test requires a 24-hour urine collection—and dutifully followed the instructions about starting and stopping the collection on time, keeping the jug cool and away from light, and turning in the completed sample as soon as possible.

At our next appointment, Dr. B began in his usual slow and kind manner, asking Connye about her symptoms and how she was doing. She felt a little better. With the steroids out of her system, she was losing her puffiness. She could get around without her walker, although I still held her arm as we walked.

As Dr. B's questioning went on, I grew impatient. "What about the test results?" I interrupted.

"Results? Oh, those. They're here somewhere. Upstairs, I think. I can get them later and call you."

"No, we're here now and we'd like the results."

"I'll have to go get them. It'll be a few minutes."

I looked at Connye. "We can wait." Once Dr. B left the room, I started to rant. "What is he thinking? We've been sick for six months now; waiting for test results shouldn't be a big deal? I want to know. I'm sure you want to know. We're not like his arthritis patients."

When Dr. B returned with a few new sheets of paper, he looked puzzled. "Well, what do you know? The test is positive." I peered over his shoulder at the report. "Still, this might not be anything. Porphyria is very rare. This could be just a lab error. We should wait a month and do the test again."

Wait a month—really. I lost my patience. When I do that, I become dismissive. "Okay, just give us the paperwork and we'll do the test before we see you again." As Connye and I walked out of Dr. B's office, I turned to her and said, "A month—is he nuts? We're doing that test this weekend."

Same test, same results: her levels of coproporphyrin were four times higher than normal. This confirmed that she had a variant known as hereditary coproporphyria (HCP). Connye hadn't heard of porphyria, but I had. The play and movie *The Madness of King George* recounts the bizarre behavior of England's King George III and postulates that it stemmed from porphyria. Isabel Allende framed her memoir *Paula* around her daughter's fight against the disease.

Here's how I explained the mechanics of porphyria to those who asked. I would gauge what people needed to know and give them the short, medium, or long description. It's a habit left over from my days as a technical writer.

Short description: Porphyria is an enzyme deficiency that damages the nervous system.

Medium description: Porphyria is a genetic enzyme deficiency that causes byproducts of blood production to accumulate in the bloodstream. The byproducts attack the nervous system, causing a variety of symptoms. There are several kinds of porphyria that vary in symptoms and severity. There is no cure for porphyria, but there are several therapeutic, dietary, and behavioral ways to lessen the severity of symptoms.

Long description: Your body uses a substance called heme to transport oxygen through the bloodstream. For instance, heme is part of hemoglobin, a blood component familiar to many people. The chemical process of producing heme takes eight steps. Each step normally includes an enzyme to process the by-products of that step. Those by-products are called porphyrins. When you're missing one of these enzymes, the porphyrins from the botched heme production accumulate in your blood. Plus, because the heme production process is incomplete, your body doesn't get the signal that there's enough heme. The system keeps working to make more heme, but instead makes more and more porphyrins. In sufficient quantities, usually about four times the normal levels or more, porphyrins can start acting as a neurotoxin, attacking any voluntary or involuntary nervous system. Porphyrins can thus disrupt any bodily function controlled by nerves. Common symptoms include nerve pain like that experienced by burn victims and a host of abdominal problems such as nausea, vomiting, constipation, and incontinence. Porphyria can generate other neurological problems such as anxiety, depression, hallucination, heart palpitation, tremors, seizure, blindness, paralysis, brain damage, stroke, heart attack and respiratory failure. Porphyrins can also be sensitive to sunlight. Patients with some types of porphyria experience radiation-like burns when exposed to even indirect sunlight. For some, repeated burning of the skin can lead to disfigurement in the hands and face. Some symptoms happen more frequently than others, but the range of symptoms for porphyria is broad and unpredictable. This range of symptoms led some researchers to nickname the disease "The Little Imitator." Because there are eight steps and eight enzymes involved in heme production, there are eight identified types of porphyria. The porphyrias range in severity from nuisance to lethal.

Some medical researchers and scholars erroneously speculated, or even announced at scientific conferences, that porphyria is the root of the vampire myth. Think about it: avoidance of sunlight, disfigured face, strange behavior, and a need for new blood. Of course this is total bunk. But in 1946 a Romanian shoemaker was executed because he was believed to be a vampire. His head was decapitated and buried separately. In 1996, his widow won a lawsuit giving her the right to have her husband's head exhumed and buried with his body. She proved that he was not a vampire but had suffered from porphyria.

No matter how I described the disease, there was only one way that I even came close to understanding the everyday experience of living with hereditary coproporphyria. Think back to when you last had a rotavirus, otherwise known as the stomach flu. You had a fever but felt chilled. A tight queasiness squeezed your gut, like a fist pushing upward on your diaphragm, trying to escape. Your hips hurt, and so did your head. The best you could do was form a fetal ball under a thick comforter and watch daytime TV until the ibuprofen and Pepto-Bismol kicked in, or you threw up—whichever came first. Your misery lasted a day, maybe two, and then you felt nearly normal again.

For porphyria, magnify that rotavirus experience. Your temperature courses up and down throughout the day. You are so nauseated that you need intravenous injections of anti-nausea drugs normally given to chemotherapy patients. Stabbing, aching, and throbbing pains wrack your body with enough force that you require more morphine than is usually given to the battlefield wounded. These symptoms don't go away in a couple days, like with rotavirus. Porphyria symptoms can come and go or remain for weeks, months, or years at a time.

Dr. B referred us to Dr. Q, our fourth specialist but one who was supposedly experienced in handling porphyria. He was tall and beefy, with a fair complexion and thinning light brown hair. He seemed fairly young, younger than me but maybe Connye's age. His casual air said former athlete, maybe even frat boy. He specialized in hematology and oncology. Hematologists (blood doctors) are one type of specialist who cares for patients with porphyria; others are heptologists (liver doctors), gastrointerologists (digestive doctors), and dermatologists (skin doctors).

Connye was very anxious during her first appointment with Dr. Q. Anxiety can be a symptom of porphyria, but the situation also made her nervous. We were seeing another specialist, but for completely different reasons. Now we had a diagnosis, and it wasn't a promising one. This particular exam room was unremarkable other than it was small and painted yet another variation of that burnt umber color that the medical world supposes is warm and soothing.

Dr. Q began the appointment with the now-familiar patient interview and exam. When he asked how she was, Connye confessed that she was scared. She'd been sick for months, couldn't work, couldn't drive, and felt constant pain and nausea. She had three boys to raise, her husband needed her, and she felt horrible, useless, and guilty. She'd read enough since her diagnosis to know that her condition was chronic, and that HCP could have very serious symptoms. She started to cry.

Dr. Q frowned and pushed his eyebrows together. He seemed uncomfortable with a first-time patient behaving this way. "It sounds like you have more problems than just porphyria."

Even through her tears, I could see Connye's sapphire eyes flash and focus on Dr. Q's face. She had survived cervical cancer, sexual assault, depression, electroshock therapy and attempted suicide. She fully meant to survive this, too, and she didn't need some frat boy's commentary. "What the hell does that mean?" she asked.

"Just that you have other things in your life contributing to your condition."

"You don't think that porphyria is a big part of why my life is like this?" she shot back.

He confessed that he had treated only one porphyria patient before, and it was someone who more appropriately should have been seen by a dermatologist. He stepped out of the exam room for a while, and then returned to hand us a chapter photocopied from a hematology textbook. It described porphyria and included a table of complications and their frequencies. The list contained some awful entries: seizure, blindness, stroke, respiratory failure, heart attack. The likelihood that any of these might occur ranged up to 10 percent. I had to acknowledge that Connye's disease had a statistical chance of killing her. On the other hand, the odds seemed low, her spirit was strong, and she was actively seeking treatment and health. I choose to focus on the greater than 90 percent chance that nothing on the list would happen to her.

A standard treatment, Dr. Q told us, was administering hematin, which is basically concentrated heme from donated blood. Injecting heme could help shut down the body's own heme production cycle, which in turn would slow down the production of nerve-damaging porphyrins.

Hematin sounded like a plan to us. "When can we start?" Connye asked.

Dr. Q didn't think that Connye was sick enough to warrant the treatment. He didn't want to risk administering a blood product. Infusing blood products carried a risk of infection or disease transmission. Connye and I left the appointment astounded, bewildered, and tired.

During the next few appointments, it became clear that Dr. Q would not take any new steps to address Connye's disease or her symptoms. We asked if there was another porphyria expert in Spokane that we could see. Dr. Q didn't know of any.

We again went outside of our medical system, this time to Portland. And again we left Brad in Spokane. In my Internet research about porphyria, I discovered that a porphyria researcher taught at Oregon Health Sciences University in Portland. We set out early on a Wednesday morning in May, just a few hours after sending the week's issue to the printer, for the six-hour drive.

Connye lay in the back seat of the Volkswagen, curled under a blanket. She slept most of the trip. I drove straight to the Portland clinic for our afternoon appointment.

Dr. L was a short, stocky, balding, energetic man. His hospital Internet page showed him running up a mountain road. His examination room was the smallest yet, barely large enough for the three of us to sit. He interviewed us, gave Connye the standard exam, and left the room with the papers we brought from Spokane. After a while he returned and told Connye that yes, she did have porphyria. Furthermore, he thought they could help. Was she willing to be admitted to the hospital?

Connye started crying. These tears probably came from a mixture of emotions. In part, she was frightened because by now, after three specialists confirming her diagnosis, she knew there was a quantifiable chance that her disease could kill her. In part, it was relief over finally having good confirmation about all the symptoms she suffered. She was happy that someone actually believed her and was willing to help. Maybe she wasn't just crazy back in '94 when she was writhing on the floor in pain, when she saw the bloody bodies of her boys stacked in her bathroom, when she felt like she should kill herself. All of those symptoms could have come from porphyria, and the stress of being raped could have precipitated her symptoms. And in part she felt sorrow, because the name of her illness contained the word "hereditary." Her boys might suffer through the hell she had known. After waiting for nurses and clerks to shuffle forms and obtain signatures, we walked across the street and checked Connye into a room. By then it was late in the day. She wanted to sleep. I still needed to find my hotel.

The next morning, I returned to spend the day with Connye. This was the first time she would actually be treated for her condition. I wanted to watch and learn. For all the scale of the medical school and teaching hospital, with its posh lobby and city vistas, the wards were drab. The rooms in Connye's wing probably hadn't been remodeled in her lifetime. An IV therapist visited Connye and inserted a PICC, a sort of super IV line, in her upper arm. The doctor kept Connye on oral OxyContin for pain and also started her on intravenous 20% dextrose and hematin for the porphyria. The dextrose was basically sugar water; carbohydrates can help metabolize porphyrins. Hematin came stored in powdered form and was mixed in a small, clear glass jar slightly smaller than the little milk cartons sold with school lunches. When mixed, it's thick and black like motor oil. Dr. L also treated Connye's other symptoms aggressively. He prescribed phenergin for nausea, and ducasate and senna for constipation.

After months of illness and uncertainty, Connye and I felt hopeful now that she would actually receive treatment. Getting all the orders, equipment, and medications delivered to her room was a slow process. "You don't have to stay all the time," she told me.

"Are you sure?"

"I've got the staff here, I'll be okay. Plus they're taking forever. Go out for a while."

I hadn't planned on free time during this trip. But it would be nice to actually have some easy hours to myself. Plus, I wanted to find a few things to decorate her room.

Downhill from the hospital waited Portland State University. I needed to find an Internet café to check my email and send in a story for the newspaper. After dispensing with those chores, I strolled through the university district and wandered into to the PSU bookstore. Back when I had time for pleasure reading, bookstores had been my favorite haunts. They were among the places that I missed when I left Seattle. I browsed through the literary journals and cast an eye at the blank books. Connye was forever buying blank books and then abandoning them after filling just 10 or 20 pages. I felt guilty that Connye was in the hospital while I was reconnecting with a world of art and books and classes that seemed gone, or at least far away. It felt like an eternity since we'd been graduate students. I bought postcards with photos of flowers on them. I figured those would be easier in the hospital than ones that needed a vase. I also bought her a couple of magazines and the first book by Margaret Cho, a comic we both liked.

On the weekend, the pace at the hospital slowed down. The nurses measured everything that went in and came out of Connye, including collecting urine for another porphyrin test. For a teaching hospital with a porphyria researcher on staff, the nurses didn't seem very familiar with the disease. A few med school students came by, mostly without Dr. L, to interview Connye and learn more about her symptoms and diagnosis. If I were in the room, sometimes they asked me questions as well, or I filled in things that Connye had forgotten. As we told them about our lives and Connye's condition, we realized that we were becoming more informed about this disease than most medical professionals that we encountered.

By coincidence, Tom and Mary Ann Grant were in Portland that weekend as well. One of Mary Ann's sons lived in town and they'd come down to visit their granddaughter. Tom invited me to join their family and friends for a dinner party. We met at a steak house just west of downtown. We filled a large booth with 10 people. Normally I'm not a steak house kind of guy, nor do I enjoy being alone in an unknown social setting. I felt strange, socializing without Connye. We'd been married not even two years, but I felt like she'd always been by my side. The different surroundings, new people, and plain fun of a Saturday night out didn't mask my stress. In the morning I'd be leaving Portland, leaving behind my wife with a debilitating disease. (Connye's parents were already in Spokane for the summer; they were driving to Portland to bring her home so that I could get back to the paper.) I'd drive back past the spot where Walt had his seizure on Christmas Day and up the same hills that had been shrouded in fog. At home waited one son turning delinquent, another with unexplained seizures, a third who was gifted and ignored, and a business that demanded all my time and energy and money.

If I were emotionally smarter then, I would have returned to Spokane and closed the paper. But I still believed that I could solve it all.

MAKING A
SMALL FORTUNE

How do you make a small fortune?

Use your slightly larger fortune to start a newspaper.

I could crack jokes around office once again, after I admitted that I chose my struggles. I chose to keep the paper open. I chose to keep working my plans, keep selling investments to cover payroll, keep waiting for our sales effort to turn the corner.

Money is an enabler. It enables you to do things and buy things but, more importantly, it enables you to be who you are. If you're a wild show-off or a raging asshole or a paranoid freak, money will help you buy the biggest, fanciest car or handgun or security system you can imagine. Money enabled me to be stubborn. I could keep publishing because I could pay to keep publishing. Was I making a profit from making a difference? Not yet, but it wasn't for lack of trying. Life was tough, but somehow it didn't yet seem time to walk away from a business investment of several hundred thousand dollars. I still believed that there were things in my control that could make the paper successful.

Shortly after we bought *The Local Planet* from the spineless one, the stupid one, and the drug addict, I gave the staff a letter of introduction. Until then I was merely a freelancer, living with the editor, helping out where I could. Once I became the main owner, I felt that I should tell the staff who I was and how much I was worth. They deserved assurance during the transition. At the time, April of 2000, I was worth $1.2 million on paper. Over the years, as I funded our operations, I would cross Riverside Avenue from our offices to my stockbroker's office and sell shares of stock that I owned. The proceeds went to support the paper, and our household. Some months required less funding than others. But by the summer of 2002, money was becoming a real concern. If sales didn't improve soon, I'd be forced to close the paper.

Connye and I scrambled for any drop of cash that we could make flow towards us, instead of away. Even through her illness, Connye handled all the paperwork in fighting for long-term disability under Planned Parenthood's insurance. She marshaled all the forms and records. She coordinated with her doctors and the insurance clerks. I made some phone calls to the insurance company on her behalf, but that was getting harder to do. The looming implementation of healthcare privacy standards pushed doctors and insurers towards stricter procedures. Some topics I couldn't discuss with doctors or insurers anymore unless Connye signed a waiver allowing me to represent her.

The insurance company turned down Connye's initial application for long-term disability coverage. They cited her treatment for a sinus infection in September 2001 as proof that her porphyria symptoms existed prior to her enrolling in Planned Parenthood's medical plan. This assertion was pure insanity. The sinus infection was unrelated in origin or scope to her porphyria. I suspected that denial was just standard operating procedure, a way to control costs. Deny everyone, legitimate or not; every quitter becomes profit. Connye spent three months appealing the ruling and eventually won. The payments didn't amount to much, about $1,000 tax-free per month, but at least one of us was bringing in some cash. Combined with the child support from Jim and Sam, it covered nearly all our basic expenses. Thankfully we had no house payment, and just one car payment and one student loan payment.

Did I want my money and freedom back? Definitely. And what would I do with a restored pile of money? Not blow it on another quixotic adventure. Of course, I'd like to see Italy again and work on my own schedule, but still work. I got bored when I wasn't working. That's part of what got me into my predicament. Maybe I could take music lessons. But travel and flexibility and music were all things I could enjoy without a seven-figure net worth. I was never motivated by money purely for money's sake. I lived the same lifestyle, big fortune or small.

Spokane grew from a mining boom. In 1900, 15 millionaires lived there. They grew rich extracting silver and lead from northern Idaho, and from selling liquor and dry goods and rooms to the miners. Their mansions stand as the landmarks of the city. Spokane remained prosperous through the mid-1970s. The high-water mark came in 1974, when the town became the smallest city to successfully host a World's Fair. City leaders focused their energy into remaking the polluted rail yards downtown along the river into an urban park. President Jimmy Carter opened the fair and introduced its environmental theme. He said that it was time to move beyond dependence on oil to an unpolluted future of green hills and solar power. With a reclaimed downtown, Spokane would prosper from the clean industry of tourism.

In the years after the World's Fair, Spokane's per capita income declined to 20% below the national average. By 2000, employers there said that they pay "Spokane wages" because the cost of living was lower. Any measure of local prices I found showed that, in Spokane, housing cost about 10% less than the national average, and utilities about 30% less. Every other expense hovered at or above the national average. Yet wages here fell significantly below average. Spokane was the home of the $10-an-hour job and hence impoverished neighborhoods like West Central and East Central and Hillyard.

In February 2002, I drove to a press conference at the West Central Community Center. The media advisory emailed from Marlene at city hall said the conference would explain the "One Spokane" banners hanging from downtown light poles for the last few weeks. Approaching the West Central Community Center by driving west on Boone Street from Division Street, Spokane's main north-south arterial, I mapped the city's economic divide. Near Boone and Division loomed the RockPointe office complex, the cash cow for the Worthy family who also purchased and renovated the historic Davenport Hotel in the heart of downtown. Then I passed Veteran's Memorial Arena, home of the Spokane Chiefs minor league hockey team, owned by the Brett brothers of baseball fame. The Bretts also owned the local minor league hockey and soccer teams. Near the arena stood Spokane Civic Theater, one of the best and best-funded civic theaters in the nation. Across from the arena sat KXLY television and radio, Tom Grant's former employer. Along this northern edge of downtown, the first sign of economic struggle was the Value Village thrift store. The busiest commercial establishment in the area was the one selling used T-shirts for 99 cents. Heading west across Monroe Street, the REI outdoor gear store marked the end of economic vitality. Along the north side of Boone slouched old houses in need of repair.

Many were rentals. The city's bus barn occupied the south side of the street.

Continuing west across Maple Street felt like crossing into the Deep South of the 1950s. Maple Street marked the eastern edge of the West Central neighborhood, persistently one of the poorest areas in Washington state. The cars there were older, rusty American models, Impalas and Escorts and K cars. A few cared-for homes contrasted with the dilapidated rentals left untended by absentee landlords. Weeds drowned shrubs. Porches sagged.

From Boone in the heart of West Central, I drove north four blocks to reach the community center. The center was chartered in 1980 to "provide social, health, education and recreational services" to neighborhood residents. It offered everything from Head Start and computer labs to summer day camp and kendo lessons. After 20 years, though, the center hadn't made an economic dent on the area. Political insiders mocked the center as "City Hall West." Real clout in Spokane rested in a network of non-profit boards of directors, with the West Central board at its center. Boards established status, enforced hierarchy, dolled out favors, and trained the next generation of political yes-men. At the time of the press conference, none of the West Central Community Center directors lived in the neighborhood. Some didn't even live within the city limits. But they were the same white, wealthy, educated, socially networked people that I encountered at other press conferences, board meetings, fundraisers, political rallies and civic events.

By the time I arrived for the press conference, the crowd was standing-room-only. Banners and posters proclaiming "One Spokane" hung throughout the multi-purpose room. Mayor John Powers announced One Spokane as his new anti-poverty initiative. Powers was a bankruptcy attorney by trade. I thought he missed his true vocation as a minister. One Spokane was, in his words, the way to put a stake in the ground and draw a line in the sand and finally do something about poverty in Spokane. Powers announced his goal to raise the city's per-capita income back to the national average over the next 20 years. I yawned.

In my editorial the following week, I praised the idea of reducing poverty, but labeled One Spokane as a public relations effort with little potential. The Mayor didn't like that. He sounded angry the moment I answered his phone call.

"What have you got against One Spokane?" he demanded.

"I don't think that raising our income to average over 20 years is much of a goal," I said. "I've seen what can happen in a city in five or 10 years."

The mayor huffed, "I didn't say it would take 20 years."

"John, I stood in the press conference and heard you say your goal was to raise per-capita income to the national average within 20 years."

He didn't have a comeback. "What's wrong with that?"

"Twenty years is another generation raised in poverty. I don't want that, and I don't think that you want that, either"

"I don't."

"Then why don't you do something about it?"

No answer.

One Spokane formally started at the end of May with an evening gathering in the auditorium of Lewis & Clark High School. A comedy troupe, The Montana Logging & Ballet Company, performed songs and skits about getting by in Spokane. The governor attended along with both of the state's U.S. senators. Senator Patty Murray spoke quite personally about her own economic hard times growing up north of Seattle. She grew up as one of seven children whose father developed multiple sclerosis. Her family relied on food stamps for several months while her mother figured out how to raise the kids, care for her sick husband, pay medical bills, and go back to community college in an effort to get a better job. The family ultimately made the transition to a working mom with a better job. Those seven kids became, in Murray's words, a firefighter, a lawyer, a computer programmer, a sportswriter, a homemaker, a junior high school teacher, and a United States Senator—a great return on a school loan and a few months of food stamps.

One Spokane continued the next day at Whitworth College. I joined a couple hundred invited delegates for an all-day workshop on ways to address poverty. During the opening remarks, the moderator challenged us to "come without any agenda or pre-conceived notions." While walking to the refreshments immediately after that comment, I passed a 4' x 12' plan of a proposed new Spokane Science Center. Wanda Cowles's idea from the early 1990s, the one that torpedoed Steve Corker's business, hadn't died. So much for no agendas.

The rest of the morning consisted of playing a game based around resources. At each table, everyone was dealt a hand of resources such as education, employment, transportation, or savings. Each player then moved through the game board, gaining or losing resources in response to life's challenges. Experience a car accident; lose transportation and two month's work. In the afternoon, we danced the standard workshop waltz: break into small groups and identify strengths, weaknesses, opportunities, and threats related to our economy. Some folks were busy remaking Division Street into the Champs d'Alysees while others wondered how we could increase affordable day care for single parents.

Over the summer, with participation again from the Pacific Science Center, the notion of a downtown science center returned to Spokane's civic debate. The center was positioned as an economic revitalization project. It would stand on the north bank of the river, adjacent to Riverfront Park, on land purchased three years earlier through public vote and public funds. All sides in the debate, however, conceded that every science center in America consistently lost money. The parks board voted to give the center a favorable 100-year lease not only for their building, but also for land north of the site that they could then sublet to cover their operating losses. Center advocates insisted that they would not agree to any public vote this time, and none was held. The lease was supposedly contingent upon the group presenting a business and financing plan within 12 months. And the person leading the science center effort? The same person who moderated the One Spokane workshops and exhorted us to abandon our agendas.

The story of One Spokane was tailored to *The Local Planet*. Pocketbook issues had always been among our most popular stories. I wrote editorials and short news articles. Tom researched the costs and benefits of building a science center. Rob, a freelancer, wrote cover stories about local people making the transition out of poverty. Although I thought Mayor Powers didn't have a prayer of improving anything other than his own image, covering the anti-poverty story made real sense to me. My family was in the resource game—and losing. Spouse develops rare disease—lose one income. Receive disability insurance—gain half an income. Terrorist attack causes nationwide recession—sell retirement fund to keep family business open. If we kept playing much longer, we would soon be in poverty.

In June 2002, *The Local Planet* received our first copy of the financial standards from the Association of Alternative Newsweeklies. These benchmarks of financial performance were my main reason for wanting association membership and worth ten times the price of admission. Each spring, member papers completed a 15-page financial survey on their business. The questions covered everything: sales and pricing, payroll and taxes, printing and distribution, administration and overhead. Dena, our business manager, and I spent an afternoon completing our survey. An independent CPA in New York then aggregated all the surveys and customized a report for each individual paper. The results provided averages for each statistic, organized by groups of papers separated by amount of annual revenue: less than $1 million, $1-2 million, $3-4 million, and so on. The report also placed an individual paper's survey responses in the context of the group averages. Since I first learned about the existence of the standards, I had begged several fellow publishers for copies. They all said that they would give them to me, but none did. I still wonder why. Without this type of information, it's easy for start-up papers to waste scarce dollars.

According to the standards, we were doing well but had room for improvement. Our salaried, hourly, and contract payroll fell in line with our revenue group. Our printing costs were some of the lowest in the country. This was good news, because payroll and printing account for 70% or more of a newspaper's budget. Our rent per square foot was half of what others were paying, but we had twice as much space as other papers our size. Our distribution costs and circulation-per-distribution-spot were dead on average. However, we fell down in sales. Sales per salesperson were extremely low, and our cost of sales was much higher than average. Even before receiving the financial standards, I had discussed this several times with my sales staff. In comparing the compensation they received to the revenue they generated, they were my most costly employees. I went over the numbers with them and presented them with a choice of compensation plans that would be fairer to the entire staff in the present, but in the future paid them more than their current plans would as their sales grew. No one accepted any of my choices. Based on this data, I fired two of our three remaining sales staff. My heart no longer pounded when I dismissed someone from the company, although it always sank low enough to make me nauseous.

After letting these two people go, just Bonnie and one salesperson remained. The paper finally required no more money from me. People had said it would take three years to break even. We'd touched the break-even point for the second time in less than three years, with a major national calamity and stock market meltdown weighing on the economy. I knew that I was invested in *The Local Planet* for a lot of money. I knew that Connye was sick and wouldn't be able to earn much for quite a while. But our plan all along had been to invest several hundred thousand dollars in establishing *The Local Planet*. Maybe there was hope. I believed that I could do it all. Still, it was a mixed financial picture. Cash flow was far better than it had been but wasn't what it needed to be. I still received no pay. We always seemed one lucky break, one good salesperson, one big contract, away from turning the corner and making money. My job was to keep us close, pray for more time, and think of yet another plan. I could see how we might make it, but I could also see my fortune quickly growing smaller.

DOWN THERE
IN SPOKANE

Connye described Spokane by saying, "This town needs to get laid." To her, our willingness to discuss sexual material in *The Local Planet* provided release to a town that desperately needed it. At first, I thought Connye's quote merely funny. Then I started to notice Spokane's sexual dysfunction.

Testosterone levels rise in people during stressful situations, such as combat. Testosterone also fuels sex drive. People under stress can get quite horny. Given a healthy outlet, that increased sex drive shouldn't pose a problem. With the decline in Spokane wages, stress was bound to rise, and sex drive along with it. Spokane is also a predominantly Catholic town. Maybe some of Spokane's sexual dysfunction sprang from being a town of economically stressed, religiously repressed people suffering from a sublimated and contorted sex drive. This Catholic connection might seem like a stretch, but the diocese of Spokane contained more than 10 priests who were either accused, sued, or convicted of sexual abuse or who settled out of court. They were a leading example of the clergy sexual abuse scandal early in the 21st century. The costs related to these accusations and suits drove local church leaders to seek Chapter 11 bankruptcy reorganization.

Pedophile priests weren't the only sexual controversy in Spokane while we were publishing the newspaper.

In May 2000, city police finally captured serial killer Robert Yates, Jr. On the day of the Yates's arrest, Spokane police swarmed past Walt's soccer practice to converge on Yates's house just a block away from the fields. Yates had killed for many years. In the late 1970s he worked as a prison guard in Walla Walla, about two hours south of Spokane. While there, he landed on the suspect list regarding the shotgun murder of a couple while they picnicked along a creek in the nearby Blue Mountains. Police questioned him at the time but released him. Yates later confessed to killing 15 women in Spokane as part of a plea bargain for information about other victims. He also confessed to killing the Walla Walla couple. Eventually he was convicted for previously unsolved murders in the Tacoma area.

One detail from Yates's plea bargain will always haunt me. The Yates family lived in a split-level home. Robert and his wife Linda shared a bedroom on the lower level of the house. The head of their bed stood under the room's ground-level window. During his confessions, Yates led police officers to the body of the final missing Spokane victim. She lay buried under his bedroom window; only the foundation wall separated her body from Yates and his wife as they fell asleep each night. Linda Yates never knew any of this—especially this—until her husband confessed.

In the days following Yates's arrest, Connye rushed to finish a story she had been developing about his victims. She believed the local media labeled the victims as merely prostitutes or addicts, instead of depicting them as real women and sisters and daughters and mothers. I wrote a short editorial against trying Yates in the press. If he was guilty, I wanted a rock-solid trial that would result in imprisonment for life. I didn't want any undue media hype skewing the trial or polluting the jury pool. *60 Minutes* might have passed on doing a story about the effect of media concentration on Spokane, but *48 Hours* reported on the Yates case. Such is the press that Spokane garnered.

Spokane County received more sexual offenders out of the state prison system than it put in. Many offenders from Washington state's more populous King County (home to Seattle) chose to be released in Spokane County once they completed their sentences. They hoped for anonymity in a new community that was large enough to offer the support and monitoring services that they required. *The Local Planet* published an interview with one released offender. Star Xanadu (as far as I could tell, that was his legal name) served time for child molestation. His M.O. was befriending boys around 10 or 11 years old on the playgrounds of Manito Park, Spokane's premier city park located just down the street from our house. Often, he sought boys whose fathers were absent because of divorce or frequent work-related travel, boys like Brad and Walt and Christian. Xanadu reported establishing friendships with dozens of boys. He convinced them that he loved them more than their father ever did or could. Once this transference was complete, he could sexually express his caring.

We published the interview with Xanadu because we wanted parents to hear firsthand the thinking of someone who took advantage of young children. We felt it was a public service that other media were not brave enough to offer. Connye, who as a child had been molested by her grandfather, was the one who greenlighted the story. Of course, many people complained that we should never give a public platform to such a sick person as Xanadu. Part of me knew that Xanadu hoped the interview would help "explain" his side of the story. I didn't care about his motivations for participating in the story. Part of me admired

Xanadu's courage for putting his face on what the community considered a very heinous problem. We printed his picture in the paper. A vigilante could easily spot Xanadu and decide to beat him senseless. Occasionally I spotted Xanadu walking through downtown. He seemed like just another economically stressed, middle-aged man. No one assaulted him that I knew of.

As the real alternative newspaper in town, we didn't shy away from sex-related advertising, either. Alternative newspapers are known for advertising such businesses as escort services, lingerie stores, strip clubs, and sex shops. I'd heard that one publisher of alternative newspapers from San Diego claimed a real alternative paper wouldn't work in Spokane because there wasn't enough sex-related advertising.

At work one afternoon, a staff member jogged into my office and said that Mark Fuhrman was on the radio trashing our newspaper, again. Yes, that Mark Fuhrman, the former L.A. detective who gained fame, or infamy, during the O. J. Simpson murder trial. He lived in northern Idaho and hosted a local talk radio show. I'd learned about his first harangue against our paper only after the fact. He hadn't had the decency to even call me. After hearing two minutes of his current rant, I called the radio station and talked to his producer, Rebecca. She and Connye were good acquaintances. Their boys played soccer together. Rebecca quickly put me on the air.

"Why do you accept escort advertising?" Fuhrman asked.

Several reasons. One, they paid premium rates on time, in cash. Two, they ran a form of business sanctioned by the county. Three, they accepted restrictions on the type of language and graphics that they could use in their ads.

But why let escorts advertise in our paper?

Because they already advertised in every home in the area through the 70 escort listings in the phone book.

Fine, but did we *have to* let them advertise?

Yes, because I believed that legal businesses had a First Amendment right to advertise. I told Fuhrman a story. Once a church-going woman called and offered to reimburse me the money we received from escort advertising if we removed it from our paper. I declined. I didn't believe that she could raise that sort of money every week. I asked how she would feel if the daily paper made a similar deal with an atheist who wanted all advertising of organized religion removed from the Saturday culture section. She quietly hung up and never called back.

Did we realize what went on with escorts? Fuhrman asked.

I said that escorts were supposed to be licensed as entertainers. How they and their clients decided to be entertained was between two consenting adults. And in fact, we had previously published interviews with several escort service owners. They told us some of the good, bad, and sad stories about the trade. For example, while interviewing a potential escort, one service owner realized that the applicant had been a girl in the Blue Bird troop that she once led—except that now the young lady was missing most of her teeth.

But escorts will get a man into a hotel room, Fuhrman claimed, and then triple their price using the threat of alleging rape. What did I think about that?

I thought that constituted extortion and should be prosecuted as such. But it had little to do with whether a legal form of business that already placed print advertising in the community should be able to advertise in my publication.

Fuhrman resorted to the "Broken Window" argument. An urban reformer had recently posited that one broken window in a building led to more broken windows, to physical deterioration, to social apathy, to general decay. Fixing small problems early prevented decay later.

I knew the "Broken Window" argument and had even used it in writing an editorial on urban blight in downtown Spokane. I doubted that our printing and distributing legal and established advertising constituted a broken window. If Fuhrman wanted to change the status quo, then he should take up the licensing of escorts with the county. Once our community decided to no longer accept these businesses, then escort services would become a matter for the police. And they would stop advertising. But until then, he shouldn't squelch the free speech rights of sanctioned businesses.

Did we check their business licenses? he asked.

No, we did not check any advertiser's business license. Should we ask every bar, dentist office, and acupuncturist for all their necessary and valid licenses? Code enforcement was not a job for my sales department.

For 40 minutes I dismantled all of Fuhrman's objections to our sex-related advertising. He gave up when we reached the end of his airtime. I hung up the phone. The first radio commercial at the end of his show pitched penis enlargement pills.

Sex in Spokane wasn't all gloom; some people tried using humor.

In 2001, we sponsored a presentation of the play, *The Vagina Monologues*. It was a fundraiser for a rape-prevention group that Connye and Dayna joined. We donated advertising for the show and loaned the cast our conference room for rehearsals. The production nearly sold out the historic, 750-seat Metropolitan

Theater in downtown. The amateur cast absolutely killed. I hadn't laughed or thought so hard in a long time.

In 2002, a women's studies group at Gonzaga University wanted to stage another production of *The Vagina Monologues* on campus. For a couple weeks the word "vagina" stirred debate on campus and in the media. The Jesuit fathers who ran the school asked why the play couldn't be renamed *The Down-There Monologues*. The priests finally decided to permit students to participate in such a show, and that the show could take place with the Gonzaga University women's alliance listed as one of the sponsors. However, the production could not run on school grounds. Plenty of liberal-minded people complained to me about Gonzaga's decision. I just shrugged. Gonzaga was a private, religious organization. The Jesuits could make nearly any decision that they wanted within the bounds of law. I thought that they had struck a balance between academic freedom and religious mission. The liberal complainers thought me weird, or a traitor to their cause.

Another group also staged a production of *The Vagina Monologues* in Spokane. A Clear Channel radio station aimed squarely at the 25-45 year old female demographic aired spots for the show. The ads mentioned the word "vagina" only twice in 30 seconds. That's not easy, with the word appearing in the title of the play. After a couple of women called Clear Channel to complain, the station pulled the ads. Tom Grant wrote a story descrying the station's decision. Clear Channel was free to run their station how they want, but it seemed silly to me to pull a tasteful radio ad that barely mentioned the human body part that defined the station's target audience. Would they pull an ad mentioning breast augmentation? There were 3 billion human vaginas on the planet, give or take, but in Spokane you couldn't mention them on the radio. (Unless, of course, you're a rival rap station who tries to attract an audience of 18-29 year old women by playing songs calling the listeners bitches and hos.)

We also advertised an Australian comedy show, *Puppetry of the Penis*, when it came to town. The show was subtitled, *The Ancient Art of Genital Origami*. This was the creator's terminology for twisting male genitalia into the shape of a hamburger, the Eiffel Tower, the Lock Ness monster, and about 60 other objects. This comedy show had played around the world for several years and overcome censors and community objections in many other countries. One of our interns and I went to the press conference, which featured a sample performance of some of their "installations." Comedy is all about timing, and the timing of this demonstration felt all wrong. Outside, summer sun glared down on Spokane. It was too early in the afternoon to drink respectfully, let alone see live, full frontal, male nudity. The press introduction and Q&A session prior to the actor's short performance did nothing to warm up the meager media crowd. Without laughter, the patter between the two performers sounded stilted. I found the whole thing odd, not offensive or lewd, but not very entertaining, either. None of the paper's staff attended the show.

We received complaints about advertising this show, as well. One man wrote to rail that if women put on a companion show it would be labeled lewd and shut down. (Wasn't that part of the point of *The Vagina Monologues*?) Even a year after the show played, one married woman complained to me about the penis puppetry ads. Although I held my tongue, I was tempted to express my sorrow that she did not enjoy penises.

The link between stress, testosterone, and sex certainly applied to a startup business like *The Local Planet*. The office often seemed like the set of a romantic soap opera. I called it "As the *Planet* Turns."

Two newspaper staffers ended up marrying each other.
In the early days of the paper at the Holley-Mason building, all
the editorial staff shared one large room. Folding tables lined the
walls. Paulette, who wrote our first cover story, sat in one corner
of the room. Next to her worked Joe, our first and only employee
dedicated solely to our website. On the other side of Joe sat Greg,
another writer. Joe ganged up with Greg to pick on Paulette. Greg
was tall and sarcastic, Joe short and sardonic. They were the Mutt
and Jeff of office harassment. Greg really loathed Paulette, and
loosed his mean streak on her: pranks, puns, innuendo, personal
digs buried in the articles he wrote. Joe, on the other hand, was
smitten with Paulette and used the teasing to get her attention.
Greg left the paper early in 2001, frustrated with the business
struggles and bored with baiting Paulette. Without Greg around,
Joe and Paulette seemed to relax. Paulette left the paper after we
hired Tom Grant. Joe followed her out the door. They married a
couple years later.

Not every office romance worked out. Our first sales
manager, Phil, was a friend of Mitch's with a black crew cut and
the stocky swagger of a former athlete. His wife, Sadie, exuded
clinical depression. She walked with slumped shoulders and
downcast eyes. Her long, flat brown hair hid her face. Her whole
demeanor could have been the "before" picture in a Prozac ad.
Life wasn't rosy around Phil's house. He and Sadie were getting
divorced. Phil decided to hire Sara from a local salon to work on
his sales team. I could see why: bouncy blonde curls, sapphire eyes,
and hips that could make any man bite his lip (including me). Sadie
suspected Phil was sleeping with Sara, so Sadie took their daughter
back to her family on the central Oregon coast. This distraction
didn't help Phil's already poor performance as sales manager. As
the saga developed, I demoted and reprimanded Phil several times.
My disciplining of Phil pissed off Mitch, who told me that Phil had,

in fact, slept with Sara. In the great staff shakeup of 2001, Mitch fired Sara, and then I let Phil go.

I was not immune to the heightened testosterone effect. By the summer of 2002, Connye and I hadn't made love in at least six months. She was too ill. Talk about vicious cycles: feeling a heightened sex drive because of the stress induced by the illness of my lover. And then to be surrounded by young, attractive, single women in the place where I was the boss and therefore bound by law, decorum, and investment to not have anything to do with them. Some of our staff was nearly young enough to be my daughter, and I was pushing 40, flabby, frazzled, and in charge. Of course nothing was going to happen. But like Spokane, I needed to get laid.

THE FLIP OF A COIN

The Local Planet was draining away my health and money, but at least the office had a fast Internet connection. In the summer of 2002, I used the paper's computers for personal research. My brother told me about a new global positioning system (GPS) wristwatch with built-in cellular phone. The company marketed this device to parents worried about the safety of their pre-teen children. The images on the product website showed kids just old enough to ride a bicycle more than a block, wearing helmets and these watches. With the watch, parents could locate their children on a map on the Internet. They could establish check-in times and places and be notified if a child did not arrive on time. The cellular phone inside the watch could place a 911 emergency call and transmit the current GPS coordinates. This child accessory trumped anything Dick Tracey wore on his wrist and would cost $400 plus $25 a month, once the product was available.

I thought the company missed their real market: parents of troubled teens. I wanted to put one on Brad. His rude and sneaky behavior was draining Connye and me. I was tired of him sneaking out windows, worn out by checking for him late at night, exhausted by driving around past midnight looking for him. The GPS wristwatch seemed like an answer, but I didn't trust Brad not to strap it onto a city bus, or to simply smash it. We couldn't afford to lose the equivalent of a month's groceries.

Finally, one afternoon Connye and I grilled Brad about his behavior. Connye lay on the living room couch. She spent most of her time there lately, fatigued from porphyria and its treatment. I sat in an armchair. We tried to get him to talk about where he was going and what he was doing when he was sneaking out at night. He wasn't the Brad we knew. What happened to the student body treasurer from middle school?

Brad paced between the living and dining rooms or stood at the back of the couch near the front door. He denied using drugs. He lied about crawling out the small window above his bed, even though we could point to the scuffmarks up the side of the house. He disavowed having strangers in our basement extremely late at night, even though I'd seen and heard them. He blamed Walt and Christian for his own yelling and cussing at them.

Connye told Brad that he absolutely could not use drugs. Not just because they were bad, or wrong, but because of the possibility of porphyria. She had the disease, which meant he had a 25 percent chance of inheriting it. All sorts of drugs—illegal, prescription, over-the-counter—could kick off porphyria. "Believe me," she told him, "you do not want this."

He groused that he hated living in our house, with all the stress and no one ever home.

Connye answered that she was home all the time now but couldn't do much. She needed his help around the house since she was sick, and I was working so hard.

Brad told her, "I don't want to have to come home and care about your fucking life."

Brad couldn't say that without consequences. At that moment I made a very conscious plan to lose control, or at least seem to. I slammed my hands on the chair's armrests, launched out of the seat, and crossed the room faster than either Connye or Brad expected. I thrust out my chest and bumped Brad backward with it. Although he stood a few inches taller than me, I stuck my face in his. "If that's your attitude, you can just leave."

I took a gamble. I brushed past him, pulled opened the front door, and held the glass storm door wide open. "Go on, leave."

"So now you're kicking me out?" Brad huffed.

I felt oddly calm. I had chosen my emotional state. "No. If you can't care about your own sick mother, then you don't really care to be part of this family and you can leave."

"I will." Brad stomped back into his room. I heard him slamming doors and drawers.

My outburst stunned Connye. She'd never seen me like this. "That's not helping, Matt. We don't need him out on the streets."

"I don't think he'll leave. I want him to see that he still needs his family. He needs to know that a roof, a bed, and three meals a day is hard to come by."

Brad came out of his room carrying a small gym bag. He was crying. "I'm leaving. You guys don't love me. You don't care about me."

"You don't care about anybody but yourself right now," I shot back, "and if you're going to treat your mother that way, you might as well leave."

As he approached the open door, Brad walked slower and sobbed harder. He stood on the welcome mat, the storm door pressing on his back. He stayed there with his bag dangling in front of him, his head tilted up, tears rolling down his cheeks. He didn't make it to the first step off the porch. After a moment he came back in and went to his room. At that point I knew that we hadn't completely lost him. My anger, something that I'd always feared to let loose, evaporated. This was my most confrontational moment with Brad, but yet it left no lingering scar or hostility in me. In looking back, it was the moments that I kept silent that nagged at me.

Outdoors, it was summer. Children splashed in public pools and sunsets glowed well past dinnertime. Personally, I hadn't liked summer in a long time. I liked it as a kid, spending long, bright afternoons at the neighborhood swim and tennis club, playing "Marco Polo" and, later, swimming laps on the summer swim team. As an adult, I don't like the heat. My first two marriages ended in the summer. Being an employer and a parent, I grew annoyed with the annual hassle of finding childcare during the months when schools were out. Connye's parents spent summers in Spokane and helped us with childcare—not everyone enjoyed that convenience.

In the summers, Walt and Christian often wanted to sleep on the foldout futon couch in the basement TV room. Connye usually let them. They would stay up late and fall asleep in the glow of Japanese animation. Actually, Walt fell asleep; Christian would stay up all night if we let him. He never needed much sleep. When the younger boys slept in the TV room, Brad slept in Christian's basement room. He claimed it was cooler and quieter than his room upstairs near ours. It was also easier for him to sneak out of the house from that room. The head of the queen-sized bed stood directly below the room's ground-level window.

I would struggle to consciousness around 1 a.m. and check on the boys. Connye now had a medical port implanted in her chest for administering intravenous drugs. Her portable morphine pump whirred as I put on my slippers. Walt would always be asleep. If Christian next to him was still watching cartoons, I told him to turn off the TV and go to sleep. Checking on Brad was a crapshoot. Since we told Brad that we'd call the police if he took the station wagon again, I didn't have to go looking for the car late at night anymore. And yet he often was nowhere in the house. Once, Brad bunched up blankets and other pillows under the covers to make it look like he was sleeping. A Styrofoam head used for storing wigs rested on his pillow. Another time, when I opened the bedroom door I saw the silhouette of Brad's head rise off Christian's pillow. His pupils glowed smoky red in the dark and darted rapidly side-to-side. I closed the door. At least he was home. In the morning, I confronted him about using drugs. He denied using and tried to act offended. I described his eyes and saw his expression freeze with the terror of discovery.

Brad later told me some stories about using. Crystal meth was his drug of choice, although he'd take any upper he could find. With his flare for the glamorous, Brad had learned that the town cars of Spokane's famous and recently restored Davenport Hotel would take him anywhere within a dozen miles for $10. He could ride to his high in style. He also arranged a standing appointment with a driver, Max, from Spokane Cab. Max came to our street around 11:30 each night and picked up Brad if he was waiting. Once, Max asked where Brad went late at night. "Homework," he told him, "studying with some friends." After that, Max would ask about the homework. "Fine," Brad would grin and answer, "just fine."

He used with a girl named, ironically, Crystal. They got high at a house in Browne's Addition, a neighborhood of historic millionaires' mansions on the western edge of downtown. Brad was a huge fan of David Bowie. Late one night when he, Crystal and some other folks were really high, Brad called a radio station to request Bowie's "China Girl." He told the DJ a lie about how he was dating a Japanese girl and he was going to ask her to marry him that night. The lonely DJ bought the story and repeated it as the introduction to the song.

Brad and his drug clique explored old grain elevators on the east side of downtown. They could get into the building, walk the catwalks between the silos, and climb up the ladders to the top and look out. They carried walkie-talkies to communicate with each other. Brad told me about this because the possibility of terrorist attacks. The Palouse Hills south of Spokane are one of the greatest food producing regions in the world. We have biotech school programs, companies and supplies in Spokane. One of the local Muslim community leaders, the guy who sold *The Local Planet* our copier, was deported for helping fund Middle East terrorism. A terrorist attack against the food supply in Spokane was not inconceivable.

In July 2002, Connye received unexpected overdraft charges from our bank. I audited her statements and found mysterious ATM withdrawals for $42 or $62. The transaction address matched our neighborhood 7-11 convenience store. After a few moments, I solved the puzzle. The $40 or $60 dollars was the actual withdrawal; the $2 was the service fee. Connye only used the no-fee ATMs operated by our bank. When we confronted Brad, he confessed to the theft. He had done some shoulder surfing to learn his mom's PIN number, and then took the card. Late at night he and Henry walked through Manito Park to the convenience store. When asked why he took the money, he replied with the typical teenage mumble, but didn't confess anything about drug use.

I installed a padlock on the outside of Brad's bedroom door. We told him that we'd lock him in at night and let him out in the morning. If he had to go to the bathroom, he could pee in a coffee can. Connye wanted me to nail shut the windows, but I was afraid of trapping Brad if we had a house fire. I also gave Brad a project, since he complained that there was nothing to do around the house. From our bookshelves I pulled works like *White Noise* by Don DeLillo, *Slaughterhouse Five* by Kurt Vonnegut, Jr., *The Color Purple* by Alice Walker, and *Money* by Martin Amis. On his assignment sheet I wrote that he needed to figure out what it meant to be an adult, especially if he wanted to petition a court, as he had threatened, to be declared an emancipated minor. Personally, I defined an adult as someone who could meet their own needs, take responsibility for their own actions, and put others before themselves. I wanted him to read all the books and then use at least five to write a five-page paper for me, defining and discussing adulthood.

Brad pushed the brown paper grocery bag of books out of his room and into the hallway. "I don't need your stupid busy work."

Bedroom confinement lasted two nights. On the second morning we unlocked the door and found Brad gone. At first, we raced around. We checked the basement, Christian's bedroom and Walt's, the TV room. We looked out the living room windows—the station wagon was still parked on the street, under the leafed-out maple tree. Without taking a shower, Connye and I grabbed a picture of Brad off the wall in the hallway, got in the Volkswagen and drove to the newspaper office. There we scanned the photo and wrote a flier. At the downtown Greyhound bus station, we asked the ticket clerk to post our flier on the wall behind the counter. Brad probably didn't have enough money for a plane ticket. Besides, after 9/11, it was harder and more suspicious to buy a one-way, walk-up plane ticket for cash.

Then we waited. Connye bit and filed her nails. She focused on the danger Brad could be in, sleeping on the streets, being robbed or worse, being beaten up because he was gay. How would he make money—theft? He'd stolen money and pain pills from his own sick mother. What about prostitution? He was a slender temptation for older gay men looking to enact a fantasy. Practically any means he had of getting money could land him in jail, another dangerous place.

Part of me worried about Brad, but another part felt relieved. We could have some rest and normalcy with him gone. Maybe this was a way for him to realize everything he was giving up or spitting on at home. Maybe he would learn how hard life could be on your own when you're an addicted, unemployed, high school drop out. Let him support his habit. I didn't want to do it anymore. Going to bed that first night Brad was gone felt unusually easy. I didn't worry about the car disappearing, about strange people in our house, about Brad stealing Connye's money, pills, or debit card. I didn't have to perform a bed check at one in the morning.

After two days, Brad telephoned to say that he was in Seattle, staying with friends. Connye wanted to know that he was safe, and she wanted a phone number where she could call him. Brad didn't want to give a number but said that he'd call again. In another two days, he called. Then he called the day after that. Connye said that if he wanted to come home, she could have a bus ticket waiting for him at the Seattle terminal. But the price of moving back was living by the rules. Brad lasted a week on his own before claiming his ticket at the Greyhound counter.

Early on a September Saturday Connye, Brad, and I drove across Washington's central desert and down the Yakima Valley. This was the arid land irrigated by Grand Coulee Dam. Orchards and vineyards quilted the brown fields between low basalt cliffs. This was the first trip Connye and I had taken in months that didn't involve a hospital visit for her. The morning drive helped me relax, with the hum of the tires and the landscape colors starting their turn to autumn. When summer ends in eastern Washington, the light falls more softly from a lower angle. It's a shift I look forward to once Labor Day has passed, just as in the spring I looked for swallows swooping in blue skies after Easter.

Brad sat quietly in the back seat of the Volkswagen. After he came back from Seattle, our money started disappearing again. Connye decided that we could no longer handle him on our own. And she was right. She asked our medical insurance about drug rehabilitation coverage and researched adolescent rehab centers throughout the Northwest. Few options existed for juvenile in-patient treatment. Daybreak and Excelsior in Spokane were full for the moment, as was another center in Oregon. Ryther Child Center in Seattle had an opening but was too far away. I recognized Ryther because I drove past it every day on my way home from Microsoft years before. It seemed like some sort of school for the disabled. Sundown M Ranch in Yakima, where we were headed, had space in their youth program and was closer than Seattle. I thought it a depressing name for a rehab program: sundown, the end of light, the end, darkness. From the state highway, the road descended across the face of a basalt ledge. Below, red roofed buildings nestled on a green grassy plain against the base of the ledge. We turned left, drove under the arch in the split-rail fence, and parked in front of the clinic administrative office. It reminded me of a funeral home: low roofline and a covered pull-through area outside, muted colors and smoked glass relights inside.

After we completed the paperwork and paid a small fee for our overnight stay, the staff divided us. Brad joined the other kids headed to the youth building at the rear of the ranch. Connye and I were escorted to our room. The hallways stood wide and plain. The rooms were clean and basic, like a Midwest motel in the 1960s. In another universe I would have loved to stay here as a writer's retreat, like Connye had done at Hedgebrook on Whidbey Island in what seemed like another lifetime.

Parents and children met up again for orientation. Families participated in these first two days of treatment. Some activities would be done together, others apart. Kids would spend the night on the gender-appropriate wing of the youth building. We'd all tour the facility and talk with the counselors. The kids would complete an initial evaluation to see if they would be accepted for continuing treatment. Sundown M recognized that their program didn't work for everyone and tried to screen for those kids with the best chance for success.

After orientation and a tour, the parents filed into a conference room on the second floor of the youth building for a panel discussion with five kids currently in treatment. One of the counselors moderated. We quickly learned that these were some of the hardened kids. It was not their first time in rehab. For some, it was their second or third visit to Sundown. I wondered how effective their screening process was. The kids talked about when they started using, and what, and maybe why. They told us about running away, committing crimes, spending time on the street or in juvenile detention. One girl talked about prostituting herself. To me she didn't seem old enough to spell the word. Throughout the discussion I felt conflicting feelings. I was horrified and disgusted that this might be the sort of kid that Brad was becoming. I felt skeptical that treatment could help, if these kids were on their

second or third six-month rehab, trying to learn how not to
use, how not to lie and steal and bully. And I felt a little greedy
because here were gripping, gritty stories. Could I use them? It's a
deliciously nasty feeling that writers have, that detached part of the
brain that's always scanning for material.

After the kids' confessions, the parents asked questions. One
father asked how to stop the lies, the rule breaking and disrespect.
One boy answered that you had to be hard. Kids wouldn't like it
and would make it really tough, but that was our job as parents.
When you're addicted, you want to use more than anything else,
more than eating or sleeping or caring about what your parents
said and expected. Another father asked each kid to rate, on a scale
of 1 to 10, their chances of staying sober when they left Sundown.
One meant they'd surely use again; 10 meant they'd absolutely
be clean. Most of the kids on the panel said two, three. The most
optimistic one said, "Five," and shrugged. He wanted to stay clean,
but either he'd do it or he wouldn't, like it was the flip of a coin.

Later in the afternoon, we rejoined Brad and participated
in a boy's group therapy session. These guys weren't as hardened,
it seemed, as the other group. We sat in a circle of molded plastic
chairs. Everyone introduced themselves and said what they wanted
to get out of the session. Connye said that she wanted her son
back. The counselor, tall and lean with a blonde moustache, was
a former user. He remembered that the times his mom thought he
was high was when he wasn't. When he was doped up, complacent
and sated, she didn't suspect a thing. Once he was so frustrated at
not being stoned that he threw his mom's upright vacuum cleaner
through the plate glass window of her living room. That's when she
accused him of using.

Brad was a little older than the other boys. He'd just turned
17, while the others were 14, 15, 16. He seemed smarter than

these kids, not just on that day, but also in the past. The counselor noticed this and commented on it. I thought to myself that none of these kids were even B students; none were members of student government or budding activists. They seemed like the stoners I knew in junior high and high school, except that these guys had gotten out of hand. So, what the hell happened to Brad?

Families ate a simple spaghetti dinner together on picnic tables in the reclining evening light. I ate plates and plates of big, saucy noodles and iceberg lettuce, as if I'd been starved for weeks. Maybe it was the changing season, or the change in scenery, or the fact that this was the first meal I'd been treated to in months. Brad said that he'd met a couple of kids that he liked. After dinner, the kids had more work to do but the parents were dismissed for the evening. Connye and I held hands as we walked back across the fields to our bare little room. We could see residents of the adult treatment program out on their patios, smoking a cigarette or reading a book.

Our room didn't have a television, and we were too tired to read. By 8:30 on a Saturday night away from home, Connye and I were already in bed. It had been a long day for her with the pain and fatigue of porphyria. We had just enough energy left for pillow talk. No stars glowed on the room's ceiling, unlike our bedroom at home. Connye hoped that Brad would be accepted here, that he'd get the help he needed and we'd get a break. At the same time, it would hard to return to Spokane without him. We might not see him for weeks at a time. God only knew how long he'd be in a place like this, if those other kids had been here six months or more. Yakima was too far from Spokane for a convenient day trip. She couldn't make the drive herself, and I couldn't spare much time away from the newspaper. But the treatment schedule didn't leave much time for parental visits, anyway. There was a family work weekend scheduled in the middle of the program, and one towards the end. Sundown M didn't want to treat just kids and then return them to the families and situations that might have contributed to their problem in the first place. Connye and I had a hard time imagining how we were contributing to Brad's problem. Sure, you could look at Jim rejecting him, or him coming out as gay, or go all the way back to Connye getting pregnant in college, but none of that dooms a kid to crystal meth.

On Sunday morning, we ate breakfast with Brad in the small cafeteria inside the youth building. I'd slept like a stone, woken refreshed, and once again ate like a farmhand during harvest. Connye thought my zeal for rehab food was nutty. Then we waited in the lobby to discuss Brad's evaluation with one of the counselors. According to their psychological tests, Brad was aggressive rather than assertive. Kids with that profile didn't do well at Sundown M. Plus, counselors caught Brad smoking cigarettes. Under-aged smoking was illegal in the state and clearly against facility rules. Brad wouldn't be staying. The counselor gave us a packet of evaluation papers, plus a list of other juvenile treatment centers in the region. They were all the same places Connye had already researched.

In the parking lot, Brad scoffed. Other kids were smoking too. I was silent. I think he could sense my discouragement. He changed his patter and swore that he didn't need a treatment center. He would lick this thing himself.

Back in Spokane, we still faced what to do with Brad. He had little structure to his days. For his junior year of high school, he switched from the alternative school to a self-study program. He said that there were too many drugs at the alternative school. He could do his work on his own and attend tutoring sessions once a week. Because the counseling at Deaconess Hospital had once seemed to work, Connye enrolled him in outpatient counseling at Daybreak. We bought Brad a monthly youth pass for the bus system, rather than giving him cash, so he could ride the city bus to and from counseling and tutoring. I couldn't spare time away from the paper. Connye felt she was too medicated to drive.

By mid-October, life with Brad had settled into a more tolerable routine. He didn't sneak out at night. His counselor and tutor verified that he kept his appointments and turned in his work. I gave Brad another chance at working at *The Local Planet*. We didn't have a receptionist, so when he wasn't at counseling or tutoring he could sit at our lobby desk and do his schoolwork and answer the phone. I didn't expect that he'd accomplish a lot of work. Mainly, I needed to keep an eye on him. The newspaper staff wasn't thrilled about this arrangement. The last time Brad had been around the office, he stole spare change from their desks and some of the small liquor bottles left over from when we had brainstormed slogans for promotional condoms.

On a Wednesday morning, I gave him an assignment I thought he would like. I was preparing some training for the sales staff and wanted demographic information on differences between Generation X and their descendants, Generation Y. Social trends, pop culture, reporting, Internet research, it was all what Brad said interested him.

"That sounds cool," he said. "I'll get on it. Can you take me home to get my gym bag? I want to go to the gym at lunch."

"Not right now."

"Then can I go catch the bus?"

"No, get some work done first."

A couple times that morning I walked out into our lobby, headed for the bathroom. "How's it going, Brad?"

"Great," he answered. Each time he asked about his gym bag.

Around 11 o'clock, I asked Brad to show me what he'd found so far. He held out a sheet of white paper with two Internet addresses printed on it. Two lines of black text that were probably copied and pasted into a file, not even typed. "There's a lot of good stuff. I can get more if you need it."

My eyebrows pushed together. Was this all he was capable of after two hours? I smiled quickly to hide my puzzlement. "Thanks." Clearly, I'd have to do this myself. Maybe Brad needed more of my guidance right then, needed more than just babysitting, but I didn't have the time or energy to spare.

Back at my desk in the corner office, I sat down and sighed. I'd have to do the demographic research myself. I started my Internet browser and, purely out of procrastination, decided to check our bank balances online. I logged into the bank website and there, on my screen, were listed several newly cleared checks worth a couple hundred dollars each. Connye couldn't have written all those checks, but I called her to make sure. She hadn't.

My heart started thumping. Brad had stolen more money from us. My breathing grew faster and shallow. No more. I had finally reached the end of my tolerance. Something had to change, and now. I told our business manager that I would be gone for a good part of the afternoon, then grabbed my bag and headed for the elevators. I tried to play it cool. It was nearly lunch time. "Brad," I said as I passed him, "I'm going to go get your mom. The three of us are going out. Meet me out in front of the building in 10 minutes."

I raced up the South Hill to get Connye, then plunged back down the hill and made the left turn onto Riverside Avenue. Brad was standing out in front of the building, smoking a cigarette. He hadn't bolted. I hated him smoking, but that was the least of our problems. I stopped the station wagon at the curb. Brad got in. I pushed the door lock button and pulled away.

"Where are we going?" he asked.

"I found more money missing from our bank accounts." My breathing was still rapid and shallow. Later, Brad told me that he knew from my breathing that he had screwed up, big time. "We told you this had to stop. We're taking you to Daybreak and leaving you there."

"You said they don't have room."

"I don't care."

At the Daybreak offices, we could look up and to the left at the windows of the child psych ward where Brad had been exactly a year before. We told the staff our story and said that we needed to find some way to have Brad admitted immediately.

They currently didn't have a bed available but might in a couple of days.

Not good enough. My rational brain kicked in. I put aside my nervous anger for the moment and focused on solving the problem. I started planning out loud.

"What if we have him arrested?" I asked.

"On what grounds?" Connye asked.

"Forgery. Passing checks. Identity theft. We had the evidence. Where would he go?"

"Juvenile detention," the admission clerk answered.

We'd been there before, behind the county courthouse. It was only temporary. "If he were arrested for drugs, would the police bring him to Daybreak?"

"Sometimes," the clerk said. Depends on if they had room.

"What if there were no beds available?"

There was a small detention area in the Daybreak building. The staff called it SCRC, which stood for something like Secure Community Residential Confinement. Police could hold kids there until a bed opened up.

That was the plan. We'd have the police place Brad in SCRC until a bed was available.

Connye begged me with her eyes. Her mother's heart didn't want to place her son in police custody. But another part of her knew that Brad needed immediate help.

Connye, the office staff, and I spent a long time on hold with the non-emergency desk at the police department. Brad waited in the small lobby of Daybreak. I kept expecting him to dash through the doors and run down the hill, towards the freeway. He stayed.

After an hour, a police officer arrived. We explained our situation, and he agreed that he could place Brad in SCRC. When the officer asked Brad why he took the money, he claimed that he needed it to pay drug dealers. They would kill him if he didn't pay. We pressed him for their names. He wouldn't tell us. Did he want these guys putting other kids through what he was going through? No. Then give us their names. He couldn't tell us their names.

After completing some paperwork, we left Brad in the custody of the officers and the Daybreak staff. We drove home to get him clothes and toiletries. Packing gave us the perfect opportunity to thoroughly search Brad's room (not that we needed an excuse anymore). It was hard to see the hardwood floors for the wall-to-wall mash of art supplies, textbooks, bed sheets, blankets, and clean and dirty clothes. Digging deeper we found gay nude magazines, condoms, lube packets, and the vibrator that he took from Connye. I found the cordless drill that I gave up for lost and had just recently replaced. Brad must have used it to remove the lock on Connye's closet door and steal OxyContin. Why didn't I figure that out before? We found syringes. They were the type diabetics used to inject insulin, thinner and shorter than a new No. 2 pencil. We knew he was using drugs, but not shooting. We found his gym bag. In it was a gray nylon travel wallet. Peeling back the Velcro exposed more syringes and a book of Connye's checks bearing Brad's handwriting.

As Connye and I searched his room, Brad tried to shoot up in the Daybreak lobby bathroom. Somehow the staff stopped him. His syringe carried enough meth for a lethal overdose.

It's hard for me to say much about Brad's experience in rehab. Rehab can be transformational, and such experiences are hard to fit into one conversation or even one book. Daybreak didn't require the same level of parental involvement as Sundown. I liked the name Daybreak. It matched the little hope I felt now that Brad was more effectively locked up and supervised. He'd be in treatment for at least 60 days, which would give Connye and me a rest as well.

After a couple days, Brad moved from SCRC to a regular room. We visited him and toured the facility. We saw only the boys' side: wide, plain hallways just like Sundown M. Brad and a counselor showed us the large room downstairs where they did accredited schoolwork under the supervision of certified teachers. In the common dining room upstairs, where families gathered around veneer tables to visit their children, Brad told us about the schedule of chores and meetings that all kids had to obey.

The group dining room was the only visiting area, and there was no privacy between the tables. It didn't much matter. Each family understood why another was there. Still, families talked quietly and tried to seem polite. I don't remember more than three families visiting their kids at any one time. That surprised me, until I remembered that many families lived three, four, eight hours' drive away. The dining room was where I could notice Brad again. By the time he entered Daybreak, he stood 5'11 and weighed 120 pounds. That's 50 pounds less than skinny. The loss happened gradually, and I hadn't noticed before how it hollowed out his cheeks and made his ribs look like ladder rungs. His complexion turned a pale white. He shaved his head. After his first week there, he showed us the letters "BC" carved into the back of his left hand at the base of his thumb. He talked about getting a prison tattoo, ballpoint ink pushed into skin with a needle.

Connye and I still had a lot of pain and anger about Brad's behavior. On some visits it was hard to not simply yell, "What the hell were you thinking?" But Brad occasionally confessed. He admitted that the story about drug dealers threatening him was a complete lie. He told us that he attended Daybreak's outpatient counseling while high and that the counselor didn't have a clue. Didn't they do drug tests? Sure, but he used urine-cleaning tonics he bought at head shops. Twenty bucks a bottle, but it worked for him.

Connye always brought Brad treats: books, pencils and sketch pads, disposable razors and shaving cream, school supplies, CDs and a CD player after he had earned music privileges. He needed to gain weight, so Connye brought him his favorite candies like Charleston Chews, LemonHeads, Jelly Bellies, Everlasting Gobstoppers, Sour Worms and Ring Pops. She threw in watermelon Jolly Ranchers, which Christian had called "Zolly Ranthers" when he was little, before doing speech therapy like Connye and I had both done as kids. It was autumn, nearing Halloween, which meant the grocery stores carried bags of

Caramel Apple Suckers, green apple suckers dipped in caramel. These were among Connye's favorite treats. She would dole out a few lollipops to each of the boys, but kept the bag stashed in her nightstand. In the Daybreak dining room, Connye would draw the candies and treats from a brown paper grocery bag one by one and hand them to Brad. He thanked her for each one. Sometimes he'd paw through the bag himself before she could start, eager for a candy bar or bottle of lotion he'd been wanting for a week.

On Halloween, Brad ran away from Daybreak with another guy he barely knew. One of them pulled the fire alarm. In the ensuing bustle, they slipped out a window. Once they were away from the building, they walked east towards Spokane Valley. They walked miles poorly clothed against the cold. Spokane often has its first dusting of snow just in time for trick-or-treaters to make their rounds. They had no food, water, cigarettes or cash. Brad watched children his brothers' age walk from house to house collecting free candy in their drugstore costumes. Seventeen years old, no coat, shaved head, gaunt—there was no way he could pull off standing on a porch and asking for candy. He told me that he considered taking a random kid's bag of candy. Mostly, he just wanted a smoke.

After a couple of days on the lam, Brad returned to Daybreak. What choice did he have? He couldn't come home. He'd worn out his welcome with friends in Spokane and Seattle. Soon the police would find him. I still wonder why he wasn't brought up on charges for the false fire alarm. But he seemed more contrite after he returned. In mid-November, he gave Connye and me friendship bracelets that he made. I don't think it was part of some craft class assignment. A black bead marked one end of the knotted twine, and a small loop the other. The bead fit snugly through the loop and held the bracelet around my ankle. I kept mine on for nearly two years until it finally wore through.

A month in rehab, a month of square meals and no meth, returned some color to Brad's complexion and meat to his bones. Still, he complained about headaches, numbness in his right thigh, lack of bladder control, and problems sleeping. He kept asking us to bring more ibuprofen, although he said that it didn't help his pain. The Daybreak doctor suggested we see a neurologist and had no problem finding us an appointment. Much like Connye's neurological exam in Seattle, this doctor interviewed Brad and performed some standard tests of nerve response and reflex. And, just like Connye's exam, the doctor reported no problems of a classically neurological nature. He prescribed depakote, a drug used for both seizures and migraine headaches. All prescription drugs at rehab had to be stored in customized blister packs so that the staff could easily inventory and dispense each patient's medications.

Sometimes after seeing Brad, we attended the Daybreak parents meeting. There we sat with other parents in a circle of mismatched chairs. The meetings lacked structure or therapy. Mostly we just listened to others' stories. The cast changed from week to week, because many families lived in other corners of the Northwest and couldn't afford to visit very often. It's horrible to say but, my god, I thought that our story was awful—other parents shared worse stories about their own addiction, abuse, and abandonment. And sometimes, because one of their kids was getting all the negative attention of rehab and court hearings, another kid would start acting up: shoplifting, fighting, running away, pregnancy, car theft. I would leave those meetings feeling superior about myself and my family. We were screwed up at the moment, but we weren't permanently screwed up like some of these people. Yes, I could be that self-centered and unsympathetic.

While Brad was in Daybreak, Connye was admitted to Holy Family Hospital, Sacred Heart's sister facility on the north side of town. That's where Dr. A, now her porphyria specialist, admitted all his patients. Since her porphyria diagnosis, she had been in the hospital on average one week every other month. She would be admitted for uncontrollable pain or fever and wind up staying to fight an infection. Admission to the hospital felt like turning one corner, and discharge another. Turning so many corners started to feel like we were going in a circle. I didn't want to dwell on the possibility that it might be a downward spiral. To me, the odds were still better than 90 percent that nothing serious would happen to Connye, and that's what I felt I needed to portray to her.

With Connye in the hospital and Brad in rehab, I was left caring for Walt and Christian for half of the week, per Connye and Sam's joint custody plan. The other half of the week I was alone with the three cats and Henry the dog when I wasn't at the newspaper, the clinic, or the hospital. Henry joined me on my patient rounds and learned to be a well-behaved hospital dog. He pranced through the halls on the end of his leash and sat by my feet while we rode the elevator. Connye mused about getting him certified as a therapy dog.

One Saturday, I took Walt and Christian to watch a video with their mom. The oncology ward had a television and VCR on a cart, plus a small library of movies. I plugged the cord from the cart into the outlet and popped in the tape. The boys hugged Connye. Christian climbed in her bed for the first few minutes of the movie. When I asked her if she needed anything like some ice chips or juice, she smiled with rounded cheeks but shook her head no. She grinned a lot but didn't say much. Occasionally, she looked at us and smiled quietly. Something didn't seem right, but I didn't say anything. I chocked up my hesitation to fatigue. It could have been just her increased pain medication. Throughout the movie, she remained pleasantly quiet but somehow detached. When we left, she smiled and lifted a silent little wave.

By the next morning she was not oriented, as they say in the profession. She couldn't answer simple questions like what day it was, even though a big day calendar hung on the wall facing her bed. That weekend Dr. Q, the first hematologist Connye saw after being diagnosed, was covering for his partner Dr. A, whom Q hadn't even known handled porphyria (Connye discovered that on her own in an Internet porphyria support group). Dr. Q ordered Connye off all her medications: lactulose and senna for constipation, warfarin to help keep her chest port working, nortriptalin for depression, phenergin for nausea, morphine and neurontin for pain. His order reduced her immediately from 55 milligrams of intravenous morphine an hour to nothing.

Just 36 hours earlier, she had needed a high dose of narcotics to control her pain. Now it didn't seem to matter. She remained blissfully docile without any medication. But as the staff at Daybreak would testify, you can't just drop someone from such a high and consistent dose of narcotics down to nothing. Early Monday morning I visited the hospital before going to work. I arrived on the ward just as orderlies wheeled her out of her room and down to the ER with withdrawal seizures. The trauma doctors managed to restart her breathing and get her stabilized. By Monday evening Connye regained her speech, her orientation, and her pain. On our next office visit with Dr. A, we asked to never see Dr. Q again. (The last I heard, Dr. Q was fired from the Spokane practice and was working in a Walla Walla hospital.)

By Saturday, December 15, Brad had earned enough privileges at Daybreak that he could leave for a few hours on a pass. Connye remained in the hospital, so I picked up Brad and drove him to the hospital to spend a few hours with his mom. It was a cold, sunny day. We crossed the parking lot with our hands jammed in our coat pockets. Brad stopped and smoked a cigarette outside before walking through the double glass doors. I escorted him up to Connye's room on 3-East, visited for a few minutes, and then left for the office. He and Connye deserved some mother-son time, and I needed to enter and analyze distribution numbers.

When I returned a few hours later, Connye was alone in her room. "Where's Brad?"

"They just wheeled him down to ER. He started having seizures."

I was baffled. "Seizures? Here?" I jogged past the elevators and pattered quickly down two flights stairs to the ER on the first floor. There I found Brad lying on a gurney, his back arched from spasms. He could whisper just enough to say he was in pain.

I told Dr. D, the head of the ER, my suspicion that Brad had hereditary coproporphyria. I wanted an EEG test, I wanted Brad admitted to the hospital for observation, and I wanted a 24-hour urine test started.

Dr. D shook his head. "Porphyria is too rare," he told me.

"You don't understand. His mother is on 3-East right now with it. Brad has a 25 percent chance of having it."

"Still, it's too rare."

"So, what do you think is the problem?"

"His seizures are most likely psychogenic."

Dr. D drew an assumption from Brad's medical records, instead of working up a diagnosis. I was annoyed. It felt like blaming the patient because the doctor didn't have a ready answer. "How do you figure?"

"He's in rehab, his mom's in the hospital, he's under a lot of stress."

"I take it you're not going to admit him?"

"No."

I got sarcastic. "So, you'd rather psychoanalyze him than test him for a condition that he has a 25 percent chance of having?"

After a few more of my barbs, Dr. D finally ordered an emergency EEG and wrote a prescription for a 24-hour urine test for porphyrins. I think he did it just to be rid of me. Time and a mild muscle relaxant eventually calmed Brad's seizures. The EEG proved normal and Dr. D discharged Brad back to Daybreak.

On Sunday morning, Daybreak called me hours before my time to pick up Brad. He was seizing again, and they wanted to know what to do. "Transport him to Holy Family," I said. "They just saw him yesterday for this. Tell Brad and the paramedics that I'll meet them up there."

When I arrived, Brad was again on a gurney, back arched.

"You still think this is psychogenic?" I asked Dr. D.

Hours of Brad in pain on a gurney told me Dr. D's answer. He wasn't backing down from his psychoanalysis. I think he let Brad suffer to spite me. By the early evening, Brad's left side was immobile. He couldn't open his left eye. "Underneath, he's really fine," Dr. D told me. "He's young, his vital signs are good."

I got snide. "Half his body doesn't work, and you think he's fine?"

Eventually Brad's pain subsided, although his immobility remained. Dr. D discharged Brad in a wheelchair, even though he couldn't explain why Brad couldn't walk out of the same hospital doors he had strolled into the day before. Brad returned to Daybreak and completed the 24-hour urine collection that evening. I brought him the blue walker that Connye had used for the first half of the year. He leaned on the walker for a week, and then graduated to a cane.

A week later and 2002 was almost over. Connye returned home from the hospital, and I enjoyed a few days off from the newspaper. Our annual revenues were flat compared to 2001, when they really needed to double. Flat revenues meant we lost money for another year, although my operational changes greatly reduced our loss. We were heading into the first quarter, which was always our lowest quarter for ad revenues, and our cash reserves were much lower than a year ago.

Brad came home for Christmas on a multi-day pass. On the afternoon of December 23, Dr. A's office called with Brad's lab results confirming a diagnosis of hereditary coproporphyria. Connye, Brad and I hugged and cried and talked in the living room. It was a different session from when I invited Brad to leave. Brad called his dad in Las Vegas and told him the diagnosis. I should have wanted to lord the diagnosis over Dr. D, but I was too tired. Doctors are just people, and some people are bad at their jobs. Brad could potentially need as much of my care as Connye did, and I didn't know where I'd get the energy to care for two shut-in patients.

Ten days later, Brad graduated from Daybreak after 78 days of treatment. The staff held graduation in the basement multi-purpose room. All the kids and counselors stood in a large circle. In rehab, they tell kids that they are currently on a path. They're at the first stop, rehab. Unless they turn around, the second stop is jail. The last stop is the grave. Brad had gone to Sundown and flunked out—stop one. Then he was detained by the police and placed into the SCRC—stop two. Throughout rehab, doctors, counselors, and family members repeatedly reminded him that the combination of street drugs and porphyria could easily send him to the last stop. But now, at graduation, it looked like he might avoid that. Brad moved from person to person inside the graduation circle. Each person shared something about Brad with him and the group, a wish or a memory or a challenge. Most of the kids were about as profound as a yearbook signing. "You're cool. Don't ever change." The girls struggled, because they had only seen and talked with Brad during the few common chores or activities that all residents shared. One of the counselors refused to participate in the circle, because she believed that Brad wasn't ready to graduate.

Connye and I stood as part of the circle. When Brad came to me, I took his hands. Brad's lips quivered and his eyes teared up. "You probably don't remember this," I said, "but about five years ago when your mom was taking art therapy classes, she asked you to draw your family. You took your sketchpad and sat in the corner of the kitchen at The Shack and drew. After a while she asked to see what you were doing. You showed her one really detailed face. She asked 'Who's that?' You told her it was someone like your great uncle on your father's side. When she had said 'family,' you thought of everyone: parents, brothers, cousins, aunts, uncles. Everyone. Most kids would have included just their immediate family. I want you to remember that family. You have a lot of people who love you. Rely on them and let them support you."

At the end of the ceremony, Brad received a copper coin about the size of a silver dollar. I've known recovered addicts who carried their coins in their pockets every day of their lives. I hoped that his coin would take on similar meaning for Brad, that it would mark the start of his sobriety.

When Brad came home from Daybreak, Connye wouldn't let him leave the house. He was still grounded. She didn't want him to reach that last stop, especially now that he'd been diagnosed. Brad may have been through a lot, but he was still a teenager, still demanding independence while dropping dirty clothes on the floor. He chaffed at grounding. He had just finished a season in rehab— what more should he have to do? We needed to get to know and trust him again. Having Brad around the house again felt strange. We had forgotten how much space he occupied, how much noise and mess he made. He and Connye spent days together in the calm cold of January. They haggled over the TV upstairs, the one on the rolling sewing machine, especially on the days when Walt and Christian stayed with us. Sometimes they agreed to watch critter shows like *The Pet Psychic* or the home makeover shows like *Trading Spaces*. Each one slept quite a bit. I'd come home from work and find them both asleep in front of a show about wallpaper, Connye moving her arms in her sleep to accompany the actions in her morphine dreams.

After grounding Brad for two weeks, Connye let him go out one afternoon with friends whom she had previously met and thought seemed trustworthy. He had to carry her cell phone with him, leave it on, and answer whenever she called. Not answering meant going back to being grounded. Brad left the house about 4 p.m., before I returned home. Connye called and talked to him at 5 and 6. Before she could call again, our phone rang and I answered. One of Brad's friends told me that Brad had overdosed and that they were driving him to Holy Family Hospital. I relayed the news to Connye, grabbed my coat and keys, and launched out the door. We didn't have time to help her get dressed, down the icy porch steps, and into the car. She could come later.

Dr. D wasn't in the ER that night. Any gloating I could do over Brad's diagnosis would be lost in the mayhem of his overdose. The attending doctor wouldn't let me see Brad right away. As we stood and talked at one end of the nurse's station, I could peer around the doctor and see Brad motionless on a gurney, a sheet pulled up to his shoulders. His chin jutted towards the ceiling, and a large plastic tube coiled out of his mouth. Whether it was a stomach pump or a respirator, I never found out. I answered questions from the doctor as best I could, then turned and interrogated Brad's friend. What happened? What was Brad taking? Why didn't you stop him?

"Everyone told Brad that he needed to stop."

"No, I mean, why didn't you take away the pills, hold him down, throw him in a car and drive him back to our house? Why?" I got no good answers.

Eventually Dayna brought Connye to the hospital. Somehow Connye knew, more than I did, that Brad was near death. Death wasn't in my thoughts at the moment. After a few hours, the doctor let us see Brad. The tube was gone. He was heavily sedated from either the drugs he took or the hospital drugs. The doctor said that they were admitting him to the cardiac care ward on the top floor of the hospital. They needed to monitor his heart function for a few days.

The next day, we visited Brad in the hospital. He had electrical leads glued to his chest and a small, black monitoring device the size of a cigarette pack tucked into the chest pocket of his hospital gown. He was feeling well enough to complain about not being able to smoke.

Connye asked him what happened.

Brad said that he was drinking and taking some pills he had. He just kept taking the pills and then they all hit him at once.

"What were all those months in Daybreak about?" I asked.

"When I left Daybreak, I swore I wouldn't shoot drugs anymore." In his mind, that didn't mean not using.

That one holdout counselor at Daybreak was right. I would have assaulted Brad, heart monitor and all, if I hadn't been simply dumbfounded. "You can't use, Brad," I sighed. "Not now, not ever, nothing."

After he came home from the hospital, Brad was grounded again. He whined a small complaint, but it lacked conviction. He knew he had no basis for his cause. Connye and I were frustrated. We had spent months supporting, teaching, guiding, scolding, worrying, inspecting, and policing, but it didn't seem like we had made much progress. This time Brad just barely avoided the grave, the last stop on the path. His chances for survival seemed like the flip of a coin.

One afternoon a week into Brad's second grounding, we noticed the station wagon missing again. There wasn't even a question in my mind any more: Brad took it.

Connye balked at calling the police. I said that we had to. Brad's behavior was still dangerous to himself and others. Besides, we had to follow through on what we said we would do the next time he took the car. How else would he learn the consequences of his behavior?

The police officer arrived while Brad was gone. We started filling out the paperwork. Halfway through the forms, Brad returned with the car. At first, he gave only vague answers about where he had gone and why. He couldn't believe that the police were there for him. He'd come back with the car undamaged. He was wrong and he was sorry. Why did we need the police?

Because he'd stolen the car and driven without a license. We told him before that this would happen. His history of seizures would not help his case before a judge, either.

Brad pleaded and rationalized. The officer towered behind our decision. He said, "Your parents have made up their minds. They're tired of dealing with your behavior. It's time for you to come with me and give them some rest."

As the officer cuffed Brad's hands behind his back, Brad thrust his chin upward. His lips quivered. Tears rolled down his face. He finally admitted that he'd taken the car to meet a guy for sex. "I haven't had sex in so long." On this one statement, I believed him. It must have been hard and maybe shameful to admit that to both the police and his parents. Still, we had to be firm. Connye had to be firm. I felt sorry for Brad, mostly because he kept making such dumb choices.

After the officer left with Brad, Connye looked up at me and asked, "Are you sure we're doing the right thing?"

I was sure. Turning Brad over to the authorities was getting easier for me, maybe because it was getting more familiar. That's a sad thing to admit. Tom Grant, our editor, always encouraged me to keep the police out of Brad's affairs. That way, a criminal record wouldn't haunt Brad after he got his act together. But if Brad wouldn't agree to our control and was incapable of self-control, then he had to be controlled by someone else or he might not ever get his act together. In the meantime, we had to at least keep him from destroying someone else by driving while high or having a seizure.

Before Brad could be processed through the legal system, his porphyria caught up with him. He went from juvenile detention to the hospital. Within days, Connye joined him there. Their two rooms faced each other from opposites sides of 3-East, with the glassed-in nurse's station between them. Nurses called an emergency code on Brad when sensors showed that his morphine pain relief had nearly stopped his breathing. When the survival of two people is a flip of a coin, the chance of losing someone doubles.

A CLINIC FOR TWO

Connye's purple velvet cap contrasted with the new white minivan in the dealer's showroom. She'd tried dying her hair back to its original auburn color, but for some porphyria reason the dye wouldn't take and now her hair color approximated pomegranate. She shaved her head, hoping her hair would grow back healthy. It remained pomegranate. In the cold of January, she stayed warm with a bright hat like those worn by women undergoing chemotherapy. Her pale complexion approached the magnesium white of the minivan.

We spent almost two hours in the car showroom. It seemed silly and expensive for us to keep both a station wagon that needed constant repair and a VW that was nearly 10 years old. We needed one large, reliable car that could carry our kids and dog and baggage. We knew that Connye wouldn't be driving for quite a while. She freely used the word "disabled" now. Besides, just riding in a car made her anxious. If we passed a mom pushing a baby stroller down the sidewalk, her mind flashed to the car jumping the curb and running over mother and stroller.

I hated trading in my VW. It was paid for. I'd never had a car payment—that was just the way I was raised. Writing a check each month for the van made me clench my teeth. The payment equaled a third of what Connye received in long-term disability. Plus, ad sales always slowed at the start of the year. If we had one regular income for the household, we'd be okay financially. I didn't have time for another second job—in caring for Connye and Brad, I was already running a clinic for two.

At home, I'd converted the low bookcases in our living room into our clinic inventory. The shoebox-sized delivery boxes for medical supplies became labeled trays. Every few days a new delivery arrived from the home health company. I unpacked supplies, compared quantities against packing lists, and stored items in their assigned places. It was the only way to keep it all straight, the 20-gauge syringe needles, the angled needles for accessing chest ports, the IV tubes and line locks and connectors, the alcohol wipes, Betadyne swabs, cloth tape, plastic tape, gauze, elastic bandages, Duraskin, dressing kits, latex gloves, surgical masks, catheter tubes, scissors, tweezers, empty 10 ml syringes, 5 ml Heprin syringes, 5 ml and 20 ml saline syringes, 9 volt and "AA" and "C" cell batteries and instruction manuals for running and configuring and reprogramming various pumps and devices to administer different medications. The home care company also delivered Ziploc bags full of intravenous drugs. These I stored in the refrigerator: morphine for pain, phenergin and compazin for nausea, and occasionally antibiotics and anti-fungals like rocefin, pipperacillin, and Levaquin.

In the morning I'd wake, shower and eat, then tend to Connye before going to work. She sat in bed reading the daily newspaper under her full-spectrum light. Her breakfast was usually coffee and peanut butter toast, the crusts of which she gave to Henry. Many days, she also had a small mug of vanilla ice cream thinned with a little milk. Porphyria patients often eat high carbohydrate diets to help metabolize their excess porphyrins, although some doctors dispute how useful this is on an on-going basis. Just like missing Brad losing weight, I didn't really notice that Connye had put on an additional 30 pounds. That's a lot for a woman normally built like a high school cheerleader, small enough to toss and still accustomed to doing the splits. Brad was a more self-sufficient patient than Connye and slept in later. I'd kiss Connye's forehead and say goodbye as she was taking her pills for the morning.

Because of the nausea, Brad and Connye took many of their carbs in the form of candy and sweets: LemonHeads, Skor bars, Milk Duds, Everlasting Gobstoppers, Sour Worms, Crème Savors, Caramellos, Hershey chocolate bars, Jolly Ranchers, Ring Pops, Carmel Apple Suckers, fruit popsicles, ice cream, sherbet, sorbet. This presented a couple of problems for me. First was the irony of sending me to the store to buy desserts and candy. My lack of a sweet tooth made me an unimaginative shopper. Second, I had to fight to keep Walt and Christian from cleaning out any candy stash they found. I repeatedly explained that Connye and Brad needed these foods. The boys complained that it wasn't fair and snuck candy anyway.

Despite all the nausea drugs and easy food, there were weeks where Connye and Brad couldn't keep down any food. For these times, Dr. A placed them on intravenous feeding called total parenteral nutrition, or TPN. Sarah, our home care nurse, showed me how to mix and connect TPN for Connye and Brad. During her lesson I worked to focus on learning instead of on her long blond hair and snug blue jeans. The TPN mixture looked like milk in a rectangular one- or two-liter plastic bag. The bags had to be refrigerated, as did the two different vials of vitamins that I drew into an empty syringe and then injected into each bag I prepared. Once the TPN bag was vitamin fortified, it went into a black nylon backpack, one for each patient. Tubing connected the TPN to Connye and Brad's chest ports. A small, battery-operated pump, similar to the one they used for morphine, administered TPN during a 12-hour overnight cycle. Disconnecting the packs became another part of my morning routine.

The liquid diet of TPN helped with the constipation, which was a side effect of the morphine. Despite all the senna, lactulose, and ducasate, Connye and Brad both developed painful blockages. Connye joked that she should name her bowel movements because they felt like giving birth. At least in a guy's mind, doing chores can be a sign of love. There's nothing more loving than clearing a toilet blocked with rock-hard waste that won't dissolve after 24 hours in water.

In the evenings I returned from the newspaper, cooked dinner for Walt and Chris, performed my clinic duties, and then finally collapsed into bed. It was getting harder for me to focus on the 90 percent chance of nothing permanently bad coming from porphyria. I had plenty on my mind to keep me awake, but exhaustion and the white noise of medical devices usually dropped me straight to sleep. Connye's oxygen concentrator chugged away in my office. A 30' tube delivered oxygen to her nostrils, while her TPN and morphine pumps each whirred through the night to their own dosage schedules.

My best home care couldn't keep Connye out of the hospital. She spent all of March as an inpatient. The bill for the month: $100,000, nearly all of which was covered by insurance. A good chunk of that went to administering hematin to help break the porphyrin production cycle. Hematin's list price was $5,200 for a bottle about the size of a school cafeteria milk carton. Our preferred provider insurance knocked the price down to nearly $1,000. Thankfully we had coverage. Many Americans didn't.

During this hospital stay, Dr. A again tried giving Connye neurontin for her escalating pain. Brad took the FDA maximum dose of 4500 mg a day, and it seemed to help him. We suspected that it had caused Connye's disorientation to which Dr. Q over-reacted. After she built her dosage to 600 mg a day, she started having the same blissful confusion. This time, though, Dr. A could witness the effects himself. Standing at the foot of her bed, he asked, "Do you know who I am?"

Connye sat in her hospital bed, a hesitant grin on her face as she shook her head. She couldn't find the words to answer.

Dr. A smiled. "That's okay. I'm your doctor. Do you know where you are?"

Connye shook her head again. The pumps and tubes and uniforms and furniture gave her no clue. She looked sad to disappoint the nice man questioning her.

Dr. A pointed to me and asked, "Do you know who this man is?"

Connye turned to me, smiled the warmest smile of trust and contentment, and sighed, "Matt."

Dr. A grinned. "Well, all is not lost." But no more neurontin for Connye.

While Connye lay in the hospital, I also cared for Brad at home and tried to keep tabs on Walt and Christian when they were at our house. Connye's mom Janie came to stay and help me during this time. The situation had to be bad for Janie to visit Spokane in the winter. Her mobility wasn't great walking on the warm flat Texas ground, and she didn't drive in the snow. Walt and Christian never liked her home cooking, but I appreciated her help. My sister spent her winter break from teaching with us, and my brother paid for our ongoing maid service.

When they weren't in the hospital, Connye and Brad received dextrose and hematin infusions a couple times a week at the cancer clinic a few blocks east of Daybreak. The back half of the building was one long room edged with reclining therapy chairs. Above the chairs, TVs hung from the ceiling like IV bags. When I arrived to pick up my patients, usually they'd be asleep while the TV dripped audio into their headphones. Connye might be moving her arms slowly through another morphine dream. On the way to the car, she picked up coupons for nutritional drinks like Boost or Ensure and a handful of the special lemon drops found only at the clinic.

Few people in the treatment room watched the ongoing coverage of President George W. Bush's newly launched war in Iraq. A couple months earlier, I had watched Bush's 2003 State of the Union address in Tom's office on a Tuesday night while helping lay out the newspaper. I walked out of Tom's office that night knowing that we were going to war. When Christian asked me about the war, I told him that if I had to vote like the congressmen did, that I would vote no. I didn't understand why we had to attack. I didn't believe that the country of Iraq had attacked us. The terrorist attacks of September 11th had damaged our economy, and war with Iraq would make it worse. As a small business owner, I needed the economy to improve, not worsen.

If Connye were alone at the clinic, she'd fall asleep to wildlife or pet shows. When Brad joined her, they watched the home decorating shows that had come into vogue. It was during one of these shows that Brad realized "people give stuff to sick kids like me." He wrote to one show's producers and asked for a living room makeover for his sick mom, since they both spent so much time at home. No luck. He applied to the Make-a-Wish Foundation, though, and was accepted. He and Connye lit up when they talked about maybe going back to New York, like the last trip they had taken together when they were healthy. Finally, they had something to look forward to. Brad wanted to go clothes shopping. Brad's dad freaked out when he heard about the Make-a-Wish trip. He withheld his permission for Brad to participate, claimed no one had told him that Brad's condition was serious enough to warrant charity, and demanded more information about porphyria, Make-a-Wish, and the advisability of traveling while sick. I wrote him a curt letter reminding him of the phone calls, emails and copies of the medical records he'd already received about Brad's diagnosis, porphyria in general, and the doctors in Las Vegas qualified to discuss this with him. Dr. A wrote his own letter stating that Jim's denial of Brad's condition could be construed as a form of abuse under the Americans with Disabilities Act.

During these clinical days, Bonnie and Tom separately decided to leave *The Local Planet*. I felt betrayed, although I didn't want to. I knew the paper was stressful. I was stressed out and resented feeling like I couldn't leave. I felt I had a commitment to my employees. Part of me just couldn't understand how my editorial and sales leaders could leave me now, when I needed their help the most. True, I was pushing Bonnie hard. Sales had to increase substantially over 2002. At the current pace, it wouldn't happen. Bonnie told me that she wanted to be a better friend more than a better employee. I replaced Bonnie with Connye's good friend, Wendy, who had years of sales experience as a stockbroker.

Tom left to campaign for mayor of Spokane. He knew that he couldn't do both simultaneously. With that approach, he'd have no credibility at either. I kept the editor title for myself and hired Melissa, one of our long-standing interns, as a staff writer. The difference between her salary and Tom's I divided among the rest of the non-sales staff. It was the first raise I'd been able to give them. I remained unpaid.

Walt and Christian stayed with us for the first weekend in June. It was our early Father's Day weekend, since the boys would be with Sam the following week for the real holiday. Saturday was a big day. Walt had a sleepover scheduled at a friend's house. Christian had an appointment to fulfill his dream of dying his hair blue; with one week of elementary school left before summer, the school dress codes were relaxed for sixth graders like him. But Saturday morning started with Walt and Christian in the basement flinging ugly words and fists over a video game. They were loud enough to be heard throughout the house. I snapped. Maybe it was my flashback to a few weeks earlier, standing in our living room and watching Christian outside literally kicking Walt when he was already down on the pavement, all because of a basketball game. At the time, I didn't intervene. I'd tried intervention before. Part of me remained detached and simply observed, storing the moment away for a later revelation.

I stormed into the basement TV room, turned off the video game and sent the boys to their rooms.

Upstairs, Connye and I sat on our bed and talked. Walt and Christian needed to change their behavior. This was no way for boys 11 and 13 to act. Yes, they were stressed like the rest of us, but they needed to learn acceptable ways to express that stress. I told Connye that I wanted to take away their game and ground them, just for the day. Grounding them for only one day meant we, as parents, wouldn't have to endure a week or two of caged, moping children. It also meant canceling Christian's hair appointment and Walt's sleepover.

Connye agreed, until Walt and Christian started badgering her about how unfair this was.

I stood my ground. "I'd feel like I wasn't doing my job as a parent if I let you get away with this behavior," I explained. "I'd feel dumb driving you guys to your appointment and sleepover, like I was rewarding your fighting."

"But you wouldn't be," Christian cried.

I didn't say that he couldn't ever get his hair dyed. It just wasn't happening that day. Walt and I left the bedroom, but Christian sat at the foot of the bed and kept working on Connye. He was a precocious, verbal kid and could twist his mom around.

When I returned, Connye tried to change my mind. "Please, they've been looking forward to this all week."

"Connye, you and I agreed. We can't waffle now. Being inconsistent is the worst thing we can do."

"But these boys don't have a mom anymore." She fidgeted with the comforter. "I just want them to be happy."

"Connye, we agreed. They can't be happy if they're fighting."

Christian looked up at me. "You act as if a promise between you and my mom means something."

I looked at Connye, and then I stared straight into Christian's eyes. "You better hope it does."

He sat speechless and wide-eyed. I'd gotten through to him on that point.

When Walt figured that I wasn't changing my mind, he went into the back yard and smashed apart one of our plastic patio chairs. Later, he called his friend and explained that he was grounded for the day. He also apologized to me, unprompted, and said that I was right. He just didn't want to hear it. I appreciated his apology—I count it as one of the first truly mature things Walt ever did—but didn't tell him about my own episode of chair-smashing frustration. I showered and went to the office to catch up on some work. Connye and Brad napped. Somehow the boys survived.

The next day, Sunday, we still managed to have a mostly boy's night out. I held eight tickets to a Foo Fighters concert, and I was taking the kids. Concert promoters often paid us for their ads, in part, with tickets. We used the tickets as promotional items, or gifts to other advertisers, or as staff benefits. Rarely did I get tickets. Along with Brad, Walt, and Christian, I took Walt's friend Alex and Christian's crush Helen. When Helen's mom Kate called for more information about the event, I invited her to come along. With a fistful of tickets and a new minivan, I had room for all.

Foo Fighters played a great set in the Spokane Convention Center, a crummy venue for a concert. It's a concrete cube with thick pillars holding up the ceiling and blocking the view. Kate and I stood and watched. Standing on the hard, flat floor killed my back. Walt and Alex roamed through the crowd. Christian and Helen stood a few feet apart, facing forward, staring at the band, not talking

Throughout the first half of the concert I occasionally spotted Brad, looking somehow larger than life, crowd surfing in front of the stage. Waves of arms held him above the dancing heads. The lighting and silhouettes reminded me of shadow puppets. Once he came over and asked if I had watched him. As the show wore on, though, I didn't see him anymore and set out to find him. I zigzagged through the crowd and then headed towards the bathrooms. Brad was sitting at the top of the open concrete staircase that led down to the basement. His face was puffy and pale. "I don't feel good." I draped his arm around my shoulders and helped him down the stairs to the bathroom. His sweaty skin felt clammy on my neck. On the way back up, we rested at each step in both flights of stairs. His right leg could barely hold his weight. We rested again at the top.

"I hate it," he whispered, "people staring at me like I'm on drugs. I'm sick."

I touched his cheek and forehead. Even for the warm June night, he felt feverish. The door to the first aid area stood next to the stairs. I helped him limp over and take a seat with the paramedics. One paramedic I recognized from her testimonial ads for a local credit union—ads that didn't run in my newspaper. Even here, in this moment, I couldn't get away from advertising.

The concert was nearly over. Brad's muscles were starting small spasms. I explained his situation to the paramedics. They gave him some water and watched him while I rounded up Kate and all the kids. Once I tapped a shoulder and explained, "Brad's not feeling well," each one of my concertgoers quietly followed me out of the convention center.

The next Sunday—Father's Day, June 15—started quietly around the house. Walt and Christian were with Sam. For me, Sunday was another morning to go to work. I woke up, showered, ate breakfast, and dressed. Before I left, I did my clinic duties and made sure that Connye was situated with her coffee, peanut butter toast, and Sunday newspaper. I hooked up her Levaquin IV drip and hung the medicine bag from an eyehook screwed into the window trim. She was trying to shake an infection.

I leaned over and kissed her forehead. "I'll be home for lunch."

I planned to work through the morning while Connye and Brad slept in, and then spend the better afternoon hours with them. I parked the minivan in front of the Wells Fargo building, instead of in my usual pay lot, because the downtown parking meters were free and unused on Sunday mornings. Mine was the only car on the block. At least I didn't have to step over a homeless man sleeping in front of the bank lobby to get into the elevators.

Our offices were deserted. Although many of us worked on the weekends, most of my staff were not early risers, especially after staying out late on a Saturday night. I counted on three hours of uninterrupted solitude crunching distribution numbers, printing route sheets, and editing early stories. I didn't listen to music as I worked, even while alone in the office. If the Seattle Mariners baseball game was on the radio, I might turn it on low, but the Mariners were playing at home and the game didn't start until after lunch.

At 10:30 the phone rang. It was Brad. "Dad Dad it's Mom she's not breathing."

In a single moment I stood, grabbed my van keys and bag and asked, "Did you call 911?"

"Yes hurry hurry."

Once in the van I made a squealing U-turn in the middle of Riverside Avenue and ran every red light between downtown and home. The paramedics and ambulance were already at the house. I walked quickly up our front steps and tried not to be annoyed at Brad's stereo cabinet and old albums still on the porch after I'd asked him to move them.

A paramedic with a clipboard stopped me in the living room. "Are you the husband?"

"Yes." I could see a cluster of uniformed men kneeling in the hallway outside our bedroom.

"Your wife is in grave condition at the moment. The men are working on her. I need you to stay here."

"Fine."

"I'll check on her status for you."

Connye lay on her back on the hallway floor, with her arms above her head. The men continued to work. That hallway. It had become Connye's world. Just last week I gave her a rare, standing full-on hug there, between the doors to the bathroom and our bedroom.

The paramedic with the clipboard returned. "She's still in grave condition. Do you want all means taken to help her?"

"Yes."

The paramedics prepared to transport Connye to Sacred Heart emergency room. As they left to get a gurney, I pushed the dining room table and chairs out of the way. Even in a crisis, I was trying to be helpful, rational. Outside on the porch, I picked up the glass door to Brad's stereo cabinet. The safety glass shattered in my hands. Translucent pebbles cascaded down the steps. I swept the glass aside with my foot and propped open the storm door so the gurney could roll in.

The gurney rolled right back out, it seemed, with Connye on it strapped to a backboard. Her arms were still above her head. I expect her to be topless, if the paramedics had been performing CPR, but she still wore her favorite ratty old yellow shirt. I closed the door behind the gurney. "I'll follow you," I told the paramedic.

"Are you okay to drive?"

"Yes."

"I'm coming with you," Brad said.

"I'm going now. Call Dayna and tell her. She can bring you."

About forty minutes later we gathered in the ER family waiting room: Brad, Dayna, her parents and me. A doctor sat with us and talked about how normally he wouldn't have brought Connye in, but he heard her age—37—and thought that there might be a chance.

"So, she didn't make it?" Dayna asked.

"No, she didn't."

Dayna covered her mouth. Brad bolted from the room.

"I'm sorry," the doctor apologized, "I thought you'd been told already."

I excused myself to look for Brad. He didn't go far. I found him just outside the automatic doors, sitting on a bench and smoking a cigarette. I put my arm around him. I don't remember him crying right then. I know that I wasn't. There were people and chores to tend to. I'd have time to cry later.

The doctors eventually let us see Connye. She lay on a gurney in the middle of a trauma room. Her chin pointed up to the ceiling, and a black plastic tube stuck out of her mouth. We gathered around her. Brad stroked her hair and kissed her forehead much like I had done that morning. The color of her hands drained from pink to yellow to white as her circulation retreated.

11 p.m., Father's Day 2003. It was way past my bedtime. I found a t-shirt in our bedroom, gray with a small United States flag and blue lettering that said, "All American Dad." It must have been a present Connye wanted to give me from the boys. Brad was in his room, sleeping, I suppose. Earlier he called Sam's cell phone to

tell Walt and Christian about their mom dying. They were driving back from visiting Sam's parents outside Seattle. When they heard the news, the boys insisted on turning around and returning to their grandparents.

My heart felt painfully squeezed. That 10 percent chance happened. I dreaded trying to sleep, even though I was exhausted. But there was a deadline that only I could meet. I needed to write an obituary, something to go in our page 5 opinion slot, to announce Connye's death. Come the morning there would be lists of things to do: arrangements to make, friends to tell, lawyers and clerks and bankers to contact, forms to sign. I found a picture of Connye for the obituary. She was sitting at a small bistro table in St. Mark's Square, Venice. She was wearing sunglasses, sorting her cards for Gin, and poking the tip of her tongue through her lips at the camera because there was nothing that she can do about me taking her picture.

In a quiet house, under the only glowing light, I wrote.

In Memoriam
By Matthew Spaur

Here's how a traditional newspaper might report the death of my wife:

"Connye Miller passed away on Sunday, June 15 from complications related to porphyria. The 37-year-old mother of three held a Bachelor's and Master's degree from Eastern Washington University and was instrumental in founding *The Local Planet Weekly*, an alternative newspaper in Spokane. Aside from her children, she is survived by her husband, parents, brother, sister, and several nieces and nephews."

But this is not a traditional newspaper. It is Connye's and my newspaper, as well as yours. We always try to do things differently here. I want this to be a different kind of obituary. Yet the traditional newspaper constraint of space forces me to fit this difference, Connye's difference, into just 475 more words. Here goes.

Connye was a survivor. She survived a Texas childhood populated with scorpions and cottonmouths and mosquito trucks. She survived childbirth, cervical cancer, divorce, and single parenting. She survived attending nine different schools just to earn her undergraduate degree. Fondly she'd recount scuba diving with hammerhead sharks as one of her most exhilarating experiences. She risked frostbite from poor circulation just to spend time outdoors in the winter.

404 words left.

Connye was a romantic. She loved irises and babies, paintings and poems. She drew me pictures and wrote me cards. Her Texas childhood she invested with mystery and magic. Our honeymoon to Venice was guided by her life-long dream of seeing the city that rises out of the water. Her passion for justice came from a rebel's romance. She stood 5'4" and weighed 120 pounds, but she'd look anyone in the eye out of compassion or contention. She'd defend any belief she thought was right, no matter how lopsided the odds.

305 words left.

Connye believed in me, in all things, even when I was wrong. She trusted me with her heart after it had been broken. She trusted me with her innermost secrets while we grew as writers together. She trusted me with her children, whom I love. She trusted me with her money and our paper, even though I'd never owned a business or taken a single journalism class. With her cats and her garden and her health and all things, she trusted me.

220 words left.

This list could go on forever, a paragraph for each of her qualities: beauty, humor, intellect, spirit. I loved her, and writers love in paragraphs and poems. But my universe of black dots on white paper can never compare to the universe of moments in her life or the stars in the Montana nights she cherished.

Did I mention Connye loved to travel? She'd been to London and Paris and New York, Mexico and Fiji and Venice.

But I already said Venice.

Only 106 more words.

And so I'm left with approximations of Connye. Memories, mementos, and even her kids are one-off from the real thing. You're left with approximations, too, if you've read this far. And I haven't even told you that her eyes were blue like cornflowers or that her real hair color was light auburn that she dyed blonde for years. I haven't told you that she slipped into pool halls and roadhouses like they were old jeans. I haven't told you that she loved fried okra but couldn't really cook, that she drank the beer in our house, and that she still missed her old dog Greta.

I haven't told you that even in her last days she loved the exoticness of pineapple.

And now I'm out of words.

At the office the next morning, I was all business despite little sleep. Wendy wasn't at her desk as I passed by. I had email waiting for me from our printers. They needed payment of our $20,000 balance before printing another issue.

I picked up the phone. "Hi, Frank? This is Matt at *The Local Planet*. I got your email. My wife, who's been sick, passed away yesterday. But don't worry—we had life insurance. You'll have your payment within two weeks." Then I hung up. I don't think that I let him get a single word in.

Next, I called Wayne, our business insurance agent. When we formed the company to run the newspaper, we had the foresight to buy life insurance on our key members. Connye and I also took out personal life insurance policies. Wayne was as businesslike as I was. He matter-of-factly told me what documentation he needed from me to process the claim against both policies on Connye. I promised to deliver the paperwork to him as quickly as possible.

I walked down to Wendy's office again. She was in. I shut her door, pulled a chair close to hers, and took her hand in mine. I hadn't called her on Sunday because she was with her beau at the lake cabin, and I decided that she'd know soon enough without ruining that time. Then I looked at her and said simply, "Wendy, Connye passed away yesterday."

She froze for a moment, and then let out a wail. "I thought we still had years," she sobbed.

I told the rest of the staff as I encountered them that morning. I let them know that I had written an editorial, that I would figure out the print run and distribution for the coming issue, and then they wouldn't see me for a few days.

Jim flew in from Las Vegas to visit Brad and attend the memorial service. When Jim arrived, he and Brad went to a neighborhood Starbucks for coffee and some time together. Brad didn't want Jim in the house. Before they left, I asked Brad if he felt okay going alone with his dad. I worried that he might feel trapped, like he couldn't leave if the conversation got ugly. He said he'd be fine.

When they returned, the three of us sat in the back yard on the remaining plastic patio chairs. Jim invited Brad to come live in Las Vegas with him and Molly.

Brad said that he wanted to stay, that Spokane felt more like his home. He didn't think that medically he could move to Vegas right now. He was walking with a cane at the moment, he'd been in and out of the hospital over the last few months, and he didn't want to search for a new porphyria specialist in a new town.

Jim reached into his leather portfolio and pulled out a short letter. He signed it and handed it to me: a medical release, so that I could continue overseeing Brad's medical treatment. I pushed down the urge to wad up the paper and yell in Jim's face. He hadn't visited Brad during any of his hospitalizations, hadn't called any of the hematologists in Las Vegas for a second opinion, and hadn't done any reading about porphyria. He'd been completely absent from Brad's medical care. Why was his permission even relevant? But I didn't yell, or mention any of this. I simply accepted the piece of paper, folded it over once, and held on to it. Brad turned 18 in less than two months, so the release was nearly moot.

Jim joined us at Brad's appointment with Dr. A that week. I hoped that if Jim met Dr. A and saw the oncology clinic, then he might start to accept and understand his son's battle with porphyria. On the other hand, I also resented Jim for being there at all, increasing Brad's stress level. The three of us crammed into one of the small examination rooms and somehow found space for both Dr. A and one of clinic nurses.

Dr. A put on his professor's hat—he was an adjunct faculty member of University of Washington School of Medicine—and taught us about the patterns of porphyria. As the son of a nurse, a caregiver, and a frequent patient myself, I found him one of the most personable yet professional doctors I'd met. I sensed that he'd given this lecture before, although it was new to me. He described four major patterns of porphyria activity. Some women experienced frequent monthly attacks related to their menstrual cycle. Patients might have recurring attacks separated by long latency periods lasting months or years. Others might have a single significant outbreak at the end of puberty and then remain asymptomatic for a long while. We hoped this would be the case with Brad, although most patterns were discernible only after the fact. And some patients experienced what is known as a crescendo of attacks, where the outbreaks spiral down with increasing severity. This seemed to be close to what Connye experienced. I saw Dr. A's eyes tear up. He conjectured that Connye might have died of a blood clot breaking loose from her legs and lodging in the junction between her lungs. When that happens, the heart can go into a severely erratic pattern that is extremely hard to break. But, porphyria can also cause sudden stroke and heart attack as well, so it was hard to be definitive. He didn't think there was anything to be gained by performing an autopsy.

After Jim returned to Las Vegas, he stopped paying any child support. This wasn't a large financial loss, though. For years he had paid only one-third of the decreed child support. I understood that Jim might have felt rejected. But by stopping all support, he might as well have given Brad up for adoption.

I asked all three boys if they wanted to go to the funeral home with me to identify Connye's body before cremation. They deserved the chance to see her one last time. Brad said yes, which surprised me. As I expected, both Walt and Christian told me that they didn't want to go. I said I understood. For some Southern reason, Connye's mom Janie thought my body-identification appointment was a "visitation" and insisted on coming. That meant her whole clan would come along, too.

When Brad and I arrived at the funeral home, Brad said, "Oh god, Sam's here with the boys."

Sam shepherded Walt and Christian out of his company car and into the lobby. They told me he forced them to come. We milled in the lobby while the staff made preparations. When I walked down the steps into the basement and towards the viewing room, everyone followed me except Sam. He sat, legs crossed, in the lobby armchair closest to the front door.

I led everyone down the basement hallway to the viewing area and held open the door. Connye laid on a table in a room the size of our living room. She wore the dress she got married in. Stitches sealed her eyes. I donated her corneas to research; they were the only part of her body that was probably usable after the damage from porphyria and infection. Brad entered but briefly. Walt and Christian peered through the doorway and turned away. Janie reached the center of the room before fainting. Once she recovered, she pulled a small pair of scissors from her purse and clipped a bit of Connye's hair.

When everyone was in the room, I backtracked down the hall. I felt annoyed by all these relatives complicating my chore. I just wanted to find the forms that I needed to sign and then leave. Brad, Walt, and Christian followed me, never more than two feet away. As I put my name on the forms, I told the boys, "There are plenty of places in the world where you can still find your mom. This isn't one of them." They automatically murmured in agreement, then followed at my elbow back up the stairs.

Connye's parents arranged the memorial service at the Methodist church where they worshipped when they stayed in Spokane. Flowers arrived in the sanctuary from I don't know where. My next-door neighbor, who owned a picture framing business, enlarged and mounted photos of Connye from our wedding. Despite holding the service on a Wednesday afternoon without sending any invitations, more than 100 people filled the pews.

The regular Methodist minister was on vacation, but she recommended that Pastor Roberts, a retired minister, fill in. We didn't know him from Adam, or he us. Roberts was a gaunt and quiet elderly man who projected surprising authority and comfort in front of a congregation. Listening to him, I sensed that gave his standard funeral sermon. He told a story taken from the letters of movie producer David O. Selznick. One sunny afternoon, Selznick lounged in a rowboat on a lake. He watched a squat, beetle-like creature crawl, wet, onto the rowboat gunwales and proceed to split open lengthwise, down its back. Out of the cracked shell emerged a long, thin dragonfly. It unfurled its green gossamer wings and gently fanned them in the afternoon sun. Once its wings hardened, the dragonfly flew away, leaving behind its shattered former body. If such a transformation awaited the lowliest of grubs in a lake, Selznick thought, imagine what transformation awaited us, those made in God's image?

After Robert's finished speaking, I took the pulpit to speak. When I looked down, I was startled to see Sam sitting in the front pew. For some reason, I didn't expect to see him there with Walt and Christian. Next to him sat his girlfriend. It was the first time I'd considered the four of them as a formal family unit. I worried about how he might take some of my planned comments about his ex-wife. Then I thought, *Screw him*. That was probably not the best thought to have while standing at a pulpit, but he was the one who abandoned her when she needed him.

I moved my lips and tried to comment on the synchronicity between Pastor Robert's story and the time when Connye and I watched a blessing of dragonflies during a Tiepolo evening. My mind's eye saw them perfectly—dangling jewels of ebony and crystal, little flying tubes of joy—but my choked-up voice couldn't paint the picture for the congregation.

"Can you hear me?" I asked. A few people shook their heads.

I apologized, promised to speak up, and took out my planned reading. I explained that a few years ago Connye and I shared a duplex that we called The Shack. We weren't even living together, but Connye wanted to make sure our relationship would last. She asked if we could work through a marriage-counseling book that she owned. Together, we read the chapters out loud and completed the exercises. When we were finished, one of the products of our work was a written vision of our relationship. I typed it up, printed it on thick, beige paper, and hung it in our bedroom. I wanted to read this as an example of what we had shared and hoped to share:

Our Relationship Vision

We share emotional intimacy by

Believing in each other

Trusting one another

Accepting one another fully

Valuing each other as individuals

Making each other feel loved and important

Communicating openly and honestly

Honoring our spiritual lives

Seeking personal growth

Helping each other with individual goals and dreams

We enjoy each other's company by
Trying new things together
Sharing a community of friends and colleagues
Celebrating good news together
Improvising, telling jokes, making up songs and stories
Playing games, laughing together, and having fun
Reading together in bed
Traveling together
Watching movies and plays
Exercising outdoors together

We share the hots for each other by
Enjoying our lovemaking
Caring for each other's physical health
Cuddling
Taking baths together

We conduct ourselves with respect and mindfulness by
Sharing responsibilities
Asking for favors from each other
Making sacrifices for each other
Discussing plans, decisions, goals
Approaching problems as a team
Presenting a united front to the world
Recognizing each other's need for private time and space
Supporting each other in parenting effectively and lovingly
Being generous with our time and resources

After the service, we held a memorial reception in the bagel
bakery in the lobby of the Holley-Mason building, the same
building where we once had the paper's offices, the building where

Brad had started high school. I asked the bakery staff to run a tab and I'd pay it when we were done. Normally I'm not good at working a room, but I did my best mingling ever that afternoon. Tending to other people was a task that I could focus on, a chore I could do. I didn't see Sam at the reception, but he told Wendy that he would immediately wean the boys from me. With Dayna he was more blunt: Walt and Christian would never sleep in my house again.

At the end of the week, I drove the white minivan through the Spokane Valley's maze of suburban streets and cul-de-sacs looking for the house of Wayne, our insurance agent. The life insurance checks had arrived by overnight delivery. When he handed me the envelope, Wayne said that in 30 years of selling insurance, this was the fastest payout he'd ever seen for a quarter-million dollars. The comment seemed callous, almost gloating, and odd coming from someone who faced death as part of his business. I'd like to say that I felt pangs about profiting from Connye's death, but I didn't think about it in those terms. I hadn't won the lottery. The $250,000 in benefits would certainly help with the bills related to the newspaper and Connye's estate, like $20,000 to our printer just to keep the paper open.

GRIEF LIKE A FEVER

Our Metro bus sat stuck in Seattle traffic. I was trying to get the boys and I to a Mariners baseball game without driving our rental car from one end of downtown to the other. We were quite a crew: Brad was weak from porphyria symptoms, I winced with back spasms, Walt limped on his sprained toe, and all of us grieved for Connye. The bus was packed with people. Everyone was hot and sullen. Then the rude woman boarded the bus.

After Connye died, Brad called the Make-a-Wish foundation and changed his plan. He wished he could just get out of town for a while. Over dinner at Spokane's only Moroccan restaurant, our Make-a-Wish rep gave us a package of information for our trip to Seattle: plane tickets, a room at the Westin, rental car, baseball tickets, harbor tour passes, dinner reservations at the Space Needle, spending money. Brad would go on a shopping spree in downtown. I'd take Walt and Christian to the giant, two-story video arcade. This would be my first and probably only family trip as a single parent. I felt too exhausted to make this a fun trip for them. Connye always handled this level of parenting. She had no problem traveling with the boys. She took them to Sandpoint, Idaho for spring break in 2000; they flew to Palm Springs in 2001. After that, she had been too sick.

Two stops after we boarded the bus, a woman with blond spiky hair and designer mosaic eyeglasses stepped aboard and made her way down the aisle. Her equally trendy male companion followed her. I couldn't tell whether they were spouses, friends, or siblings. They stopped when they reached the articulated part of the bus, which was where we sat.

"There's two empty seats further back," a fellow passenger told her. She declined the invitation, and instead stood in the aisle next to me holding onto a pole for support. Normally, I would have offered her my seat, but she had already been refused an offer and chosen to stand. My clenched back welcomed her choice. She started talking rather loudly with her male companion.

I overheard her comment about how all these young men should offer her a seat. I tried to tune out her words. I was hot, in pain, and grieving. Then she raised her voice and started editorializing about how rude children were today.

Brad glanced at me. She was talking about us.

Why she singled us out, I don't know. Plenty of other young, healthy people could have given her a seat. She looked younger than me, certainly seemed capable of standing, and had already refused a seat. I didn't want to make a scene. That didn't seem like the right example to set for the boys. I kept ignoring her. I'd read that people shun the widowed as failures. After all, widows failed to keep their spouse alive. The widowed certainly can feel shunned, but it seems a weird reaction for others to project onto them. I wondered if it's not a primal response, something tribal. Maybe it was something this woman instinctively sensed about me.

She progressed to speculating that parents today must be awful at teaching their kids to respect their elders. Maybe she thought that we couldn't hear her. I don't know why—everyone within ten feet could hear her above the rumbling engines and honking horns. Those passengers looked at us. All three boys glared at me. I realized that I'd crossed the line from being socially gracious to becoming a doormat. The scene I wanted to avoid was already being made.

Finally, I slowly turned my head to the right and up, as much as my back would allow. I gave her my best sideways glare. "You were offered a seat and you declined."

She immediately shut up. She and her compatriot walked towards the front of the bus and got off at the next stop.

Later, I spotted her a few rows behind us at the baseball game. My mind played the fantasy scene of marching up to her and informing her that there's more happening in people's lives than meets her stylish, selfish eye. I decided instead that I probably wouldn't change her. Besides, she'd intruded enough into our trip.

The Make-a-Wish trip was the last time I spent parenting Walt and Christian. After learning Sam's comment about weaning the boys from me, I decided that I wouldn't fight over them. They needed decent parenting and I thought that Sam could provide that. I wasn't sure that I could. There was still Brad and the newspaper to look after, plus settling Connye's estate. I felt the boys needed peace in their lives more than my divided attention. Between divorce, split custody, an addicted brother, and losing their mom, they'd had several turbulent years. They stood a better chance of having peace if they had a more settled routine: one house, one family. Of course, they wouldn't see much of Brad. However, Brad wasn't great company while he was sick, and Walt and Christian didn't have much trust or rapport with him after his atrocious behavior while using meth. After our trip, Christian occasionally came back to my house, mostly because he could cook ramen noodles to his liking on our stove and not his dad's. Walt rarely came near, even when he was playing with friends next door to me. If he did come in the house, he wouldn't go anywhere near the master bedroom or the hallway.

Through the summer, my delayed grief became a fever. It hazed over every moment. It weighed down my shoulders and made my chest ache. I felt hot but chilled and couldn't keep warm, no matter how many blankets I hid under. Sleep was fitful, uncomfortable, if it came at all. Showering took so much energy I didn't want to bother. I couldn't eat. Nausea waxed and waned. My taste buds switched off, so food became just mushy pulp rolling around in my mouth. Forget housework. Laundry wasn't a problem, because I hardly changed out of my pajamas. Even talking on the phone was labor. Talking at all was work. And yet somehow I managed to pay the bills and make it to work most days to keep *The Local Planet* publishing.

Often, there was nothing to be done but watch bad TV. Fever and grief seem the only plausible explanations for most of what's on television. I balled under blankets, motionless except for an occasional shudder from chills. Commercials for nausea medicines didn't help. Neither did the pitches of personal injury lawyers. But Henry and the cats were happy. I was home, warm, horizontal, and immobile: the perfect napping platform. As I lay in a fetal position, a cat perched on top of my hip while Henry curled in the fortress of my legs.

A moment eventually came when grief weakened. It started before I fully noticed. Sleep came a bit more easily. An apple tasted tart and wet again. Some inspired producer managed to get an original, funny moment onto TV and made me laugh a small laugh. For that brief moment it felt good. I felt good. I hadn't laughed in weeks. A song finally found some space in my head and I whistled along. When was the last time I whistled? Had I really gotten that bad? I started to notice the weather outside and

saw that it was sunny. I hid my greasy hair under a baseball cap
and took Henry for a short walk. We used to go for walks, Connye
and I. For the moment I tried not to think that thought. The sun
felt good on my cheeks. I'd taken walks alone before, too. Not too
far from home I stopped, sighed, and turn around. Henry looked
at me, confused, ready to trot many more blocks. Home seemed
a long way back. I'd make it, but I need a nap later. The purring
of a cat and drone of commercials would help me sleep. The
ache was still there. I felt weak, nauseous and flush. My appetite
barely registered. But the haze was slowly lifting. I noticed a little
more than yesterday, or the day before. A shower finally sounded
like a good idea, and fresh sheets on the bed would help. There
were things to do again, plans and chores and obligations but also
pleasures, small pleasures. I could begin to look back on how bad
I felt, but also farther back to how good I'd felt once upon a time.
Feeling good seemed possible again. At least I wanted to try.

Brad wished for a lot of things that summer. He asked for
trips to the grocery store. It was an excuse for him to leave the
house and see someone other than Henry and me. He wanted to
pick out his favorite sherbet (raspberry) or browse at the candy
display. Lottery tickets were another favorite. He bought ones
that involved a lot of scratching and matching, and we'd sit at the
dining room table comparing numbers. Other times, he asked if
we could go to the movies. The multiplex in River Park Square
mall downtown played all the summer blockbusters marketed to
teenaged boys. Brad slept through most of them. Something about
the cinema and his medicines made him conk out before the first
reel was done.

Often, Brad stood on our back porch and smoked while
Henry relieved himself in the yard. Sometimes I'd join him outside,
to talk with him and nag him about quitting smoking. Occasionally

he fumed at his father's side of the family. They did nothing for him: no visits, no child support, no get-well cards. Occasionally, they telephoned. They expected him to travel to them, when many days he could barely make it out of bed or out of the hospital. They made no attempt to understand his diagnosis. They told him, "You come down here to Texas. Five days of good food and we'll have you up and around."

Several times Brad asked, "Is it okay if I stay here?" Of course it was, but he needed the reassurance. He asked if he could move into the basement since Walt and Christian weren't living with us anymore. Personally, I was happy to stop sharing the upstairs bathroom with him. He could prowl around in the basement all night, obeying his weird sleep schedule, and I could finally get some rest. I told Brad that we'd treat it like the home design shows he watched with his mom. We could remove a closet to join Christian's former bedroom and the basement TV room into a single suite. I gave him a budget of $1,500. From that we'd pay for carpentry, painting, electrical, furniture, accessories and supplies. I could do most of the structural changes required and then contract out the rest. He could choose how to spend any money left over from construction.

I'd come home from the newspaper and sob on my bed nearly every day after work. Brad found me once sitting on the edge of the bed crying and put his arm around me. I think it helped him to see someone else grieving. After a little dinner, we'd stand on the back porch and talk. Then I set to work in the basement, removing the closet and, later, executing Brad's six-color palette of painting. I found some neighborhood kids to help move Connye's desk into Brad's suite. He picked out some Danish modern furniture: a couch, two side chairs, round red pillows the shape of hatboxes. Red velvet curtains hung in front of his sitting room windows. He fashioned tiebacks out of chain. In the end, Brad had a basement suite that looked like a spread from some imaginary magazine called *Gay Teen*, and I had chores to concentrate on in those summer evenings alone.

Sam waited an almost-decent couple of months before emailing me a request for all of Connye's medical records. He offered to have the records delivered directly to his brother Greg, who was an attorney and whom Connye trusted. Greg could then work with an advising physician connected to the American Porphyria Foundation.

I was suspicious. The recently enacted HIPAA laws legally barred him from those records. And only once did he show any real interest in Connye's illness. Earlier in the year, fate seated us next to each other in the audience of a middle-school play in which Christian was performing. It was the courtroom drama *The Three Little Pigs versus The Big Bad Wolf.* Sam asked why Connye hadn't come with me. I told him she didn't feel well enough. He asked some questions about her condition and porphyria in general. I told him that her condition was not terminal—she could theoretically go into remission—but it was chronic and could be fatal. I reminded him that it was hereditary, so Walt and Christian each had a 25 percent chance of inheriting the disease.

To Sam's records request, I replied that there could be only two reasons why he wanted Connye's records. He might want them to help determine Walt and Christian's medical care. If this was the case, I had already mailed him copies of Connye's official diagnosis along with several lab results showing her elevated porphyrin levels. That would be enough to establish her condition and their possibility of having it.

The other reason Sam might want Connye's records was to see what he could find to support a malpractice suit. I told him that he'd first have to provide me with some separate motivation to spur a review of the medical records. He couldn't or didn't provide any such reason. The reasons, he said, would be contained in Connye's medical records.

I refused Sam's request. He had wished Connye dead when they were married. He stole money from her in their divorce. He accused her of fraud when she applied for disability insurance. No way would I let him root around in Connye's private medical records looking to make a convenient buck off her death.

On the morning of Labor Day, I gathered the supplies I needed to divide Connye's ashes. I already regretted splitting her remains. A wife and mother gets pulled in so many directions during life; I didn't want Connye pulled apart in death. But part of her always belonged to Texas and family, while another part belonged to the Northwest and to her sons.

Walt and Chris, who had spent the holiday weekend with me despite Sam's vow, were asleep in the basement. Brad slept on the couch in the living room. From the kitchen, I took a roll of duct tape, a bottle of Super-Glue and a metal funnel smaller than a tennis ball. From the china hutch with the door pane of curved and broken glass, I drew two pieces from Connye's collection of Fiestaware: a small, green sugar bowl and lid and an orange, stoppered decanter. The decanter would go to her parents. It reminded me of a genie bottle; as a young girl, Connye loved the

TV show "I Dream of Jeannie." Brad would get the sugar bowl.
I took the brown plastic box with Connye's ashes from my closet,
where they remained hidden in the months since the memorial
service. Next to the ashes waited a paper maché bowl I'd made
along with the boys once as a winter art project, a blue bowl
decorated with white crescent moons and Matisse yellow stars. In
the bowl, petals from the flowers at the memorial service dried in
the dark.

I set the bowls and boxes and tools on the floor at the foot
of my bed. I opened the east-facing window blind, turned off the
overhead light and lit votive candles on my personal altar shelf.
That's the spot where I knelt in meditation and tried to watch the
fever of grief slowly leave me.

Before starting, I tried to clear my mind. My pulse pounded.
My logical mind said that I would have to actually see Connye's
ashes the day I spread them, so why not see them now? My comic
mind wondered if I might spill the ashes or do something equally
stupid. I didn't want to freak out the boys. I was scared of what I
would find in the brown plastic box. Death is an awful taboo.

With my Swiss army knife I cut the clear packing tape on
the lid of the plastic ash container. Inside the box was pure white.
Bone, I knew, could be white, but not like this. Another moment,
and I recognized the cotton batting stuffed into the top of the box.
It made sense. A linebacker's remains would take up more box
space than a cheerleader. Under the batting, Connye's ashes lay in
a plastic bag closed with a twist tie. I expected the ash to be black,
or at least dark. Instead, it was light sand, beautiful and natural, a
creation I wouldn't expect from the destruction of fire. I planned
to pour the ash straight from the plastic container into the funnel
in the opening of the jug, but that wasn't going to work easily.
From the altar I took a small ceramic bowl with a sea turtle painted

241

on the inside and used it as a scoop. Five scoops equaled about half of the ash. With each scoop I had to tap the funnel to get a small piece of bone unstuck from the spout. The remaining space in the jug I filled with some of the dried flower petals. I brushed Superglue around the opening of the jug, and held the stopper in place for a minute. Brad would get a scoop of ash sealed in the sugar bowl. The remaining ash went back in the brown plastic box, to be spread later. I returned the brown plastic box and bowl of flower petals to the closet.

After Labor Day, the light began to slant into autumn once again. The time had come for Connye's parents to drive their RV back to Texas. I gave Dayne and Janie the orange Fiestaware decanter to bury in the Caldwell family cemetery outside Bryson, along with Connye's framed undergraduate diploma. I wanted her parents to have the proof that she fulfilled her promise. They packed the diploma and ashes in the RV bed space that overhung the driver and passenger's seats. Between Spokane, Washington and Graham, Texas, schools were back in session. Dayne and Janie drove free and open roads all the way home, cruising south with Connye riding above them.

THE MAN WHO SOLD
THE PLANET

At the kick-off dinner for Tom Grant's mayoral campaign, a
retired founder of ESPN asked me if I would consider selling
The Local Planet. He knew an interested party. "Sure," I told him,
"I'm always willing to talk." I promised to deliver the newspaper's
financial information to him. Only a month had passed since
Connye's death, and I was too exhausted to actively market the
paper to buyers. Simply running the business was work enough.
I had already failed several times to sell the paper, usually right
after a particularly stressful period, so I didn't get too excited about
an unsolicited inquiry. I tried to sound upbeat, but by then I'd
made enough pitches to investors and buyers to know not to raise
my hopes.

Not that I didn't want to sell. Aside from losing Connye and
a bunch of money, running the newspaper had become just plain
weird. For instance, a city council member was suing us for the con
side of a pro-and-con set of articles discussing his record and the
upcoming election. Of course, he found the pro side just dandy.
An unemployed nutcase was "renting" some of our empty office
space for his fledgling counseling business. In reality, he was living
in his office. A former fringe mayoral candidate, who lived on

disability payments after head trauma, was using an inheritance from his mother to mail harassing fliers to all our advertisers because I wouldn't refund his prepaid advertising payment. No self-respecting publisher gives cash refunds. I suggested he could donate his unused balance to the non-profit or political organization of his choice. Instead, he wrote the state attorney general's office, who sided with the newspaper.

In the spring of 2001, after just a year of owning the newspaper, I offered the business to a team of local executives. At the time, I was beginning to understand how quickly a start-up newspaper could burn through cash. Connye already resented the stress of the work and the guilt of not being home raising her boys. We were in the midst of restructuring the staff. I would have been happy to let someone else run the business. The execs didn't bite, but from that meeting we hired our first sales manager and landed one of our largest advertisers. Around the same time, I also pitched a model of tight financial integration with one of the television stations in town. I decided to swing for the fences with my proposal. They could buy six pages of advertising space each week at a steep discount, and then resell it to or bundle it with their other advertisers. We'd get a steady income stream and they'd expand their reach and that of their customers'. I thought it was a great idea, and certainly affordable in the television station's budget. However, the station general manager assumed from my aggressive offer that we would soon be out of business, and so backed away. Years later, he apologized for his miscalculation.

After the 9/11 attacks, I listed the paper in the "For sale by owner" section on the website of a Montana newspaper broker. Through that ad I met two guys, Steve and Stu, who had been top executives for a radio station chain that had recently been bought out. They and another partner were investigating a business model that married print and radio in mid-sized markets across the West, something like what I had pitched to the television station. Certainly the idea had merit, and already succeeded in markets like Pittsburgh. But they found no radio station licenses for sale west of the Rockies and eventually lost interest. I offered Steve part ownership of *The Local Planet* and the position of Vice President of Business Development, in exchange for his sales expertise. After the corporate buyout, though, he didn't need a job.

In crafting these and other deals, I learned that profitable newspapers are normally sold for an amount equivalent to their annual gross revenues. The price goes higher if the paper owns real estate or significant equipment like a press. For fledgling papers like mine without profits, property, or physical plants, the math gets sketchy. Each time I offered the business to publishers or newspaper chains in Seattle, Portland, Boise, Phoenix, or Baltimore, the price declined. So did the potential buyers.

Tom Grant joined a mayoral primary that consisted of the current mayor, a former mayor, two current city council members, and the state senator majority leader. Although the mayor's position in Spokane is non-partisan, everyone knew the established politicians' party leanings. The current and former mayors and council members definitely leaned Democratic. Everyone assumed that Tom was another solid Democrat, but often he fit better with the Green Party than with the Democrats. Before the primary, one of the Democratic-leaning candidates approached Tom. He congratulated him on his conviction to run but cautioned that he was the political novice in the race. Tom would likely siphon votes from other Democratic-leaning candidates and hand the election to the Republican state senator. Maybe Tom should withdraw. Tom said thanks for the advice, but he was staying in the race.

Jim West, the state senate majority leader, was the only clear Republican in the race. In the 1980s he served on the Spokane city council. As a state legislator, he'd developed a reputation as a fiscal and social conservative. West introduced legislation to ban homosexuals from working as teachers or day-care providers. He pushed a bill to outlaw all teen sex. He voted against legislation outlawing discrimination against homosexuality. West also had a reputation as a hard negotiator. He got in a smattering of trouble once for leaving a threat of bodily harm on a lobbyist's answering machine.

At *The Local Planet*, we didn't handle election season like the daily papers that let boards of old white men issue endorsements. Instead, we summarized the actual debate of our editorial board, and showed how they voted. We felt that was a better way to highlight the issues. *The Stranger* newspaper in Seattle called their election board "The Death Squad." We loved that but couldn't steal it, so we named ours "The Ministry of Truth."

Our discussion of each proposition and election was always campy. For this issue, we gave all the mayoral candidates nicknames by combining the names of their family pets and the street names from their childhood homes. Normally that's the Porn Star Name Game, but we didn't tell them that. Although we tried to be fun and different, we didn't shy away from tough questions. For instance, we asked Tom "Caesar State" Grant whether the personality of a bulldog investigative reporter, crusading alone for the truth, could be an effective consensus builder and compromiser in the world of politics. He conceded that might pose a problem. But he countered that much of his journalism experience came as a small-town reporter. In Oregon, Alaska, Vermont, and

Iowa he learned to do tough stories in tight-knit towns and still maintain good personal and working relationships throughout the community.

When Tom was editor of *The Local Planet,* he started a Ministry of Truth tradition: the SAT question. We pulled a sample question from the Scholastic Aptitude Test off the Internet and posed it to each of the candidates. They could take all the time they wanted and work out their answer on scratch paper or a dry-erase board. We didn't expect all candidates to answer correctly, but it was useful to observe and compare how they solved problems. The Ministry of Truth SAT question for 2003: "How many three-digit numbers between 100 and 1,000 have five as the tens digit?" (Answer. The tens digit is the second one to the left of the decimal place, such as the 5 in 150. Between 100 and 1,000, three digit numbers with five as the tens digit would be all the numbers containing 50: 150-159, 250-259, and so on. Since 150-159 contains ten numbers, and nine sets of 50s exist between 100 and 1,000, then 10 times 9 equals 90.)

Tom worked the problem using the dry-erase board, but sailed through to the right answer. "It's just a counting question?" he asked.

City Council member Corky Pleasant estimated the answer was 109. His reasoning, though faulty, had some structure to it. Deuteronomy Gulfview, the former mayor, aced the SAT question. In fact, she was the fastest to answer. Senator Jim "Boomer XIII" West also aced our SAT question. I dearly wanted to ask him about the rumors of child sexual abuse that stemmed from his connections to accused child molesters while he was a sheriff's deputy and a Boy Scout troop leader. That gossip had circulated through Spokane for years. An election board wasn't a fair venue for that sort of grilling. Still, I got clammy just sitting next to him.

The most spectacular failure at the SAT question came from the sitting mayor, John "Moosey Pleasant" Powers. When asked the question, he giggled, rubbed his palms on the table, and blurted loudly, "4,500."

I was flummoxed. "Is that your answer?" I asked.

"Sure, why not?"

This man was running our city budget? This man ran an insurance agency? This man practiced corporate and bankruptcy law? There aren't even 4,500 three digits numbers between 100 and 1,000.

At the end of each interview, I asked the candidate, "Is there anything else you feel we should know about you or your candidacy?" In his answer, Mayor Powers worked himself into a frenzy of yelling and table pounding about our negative coverage of his One Spokane anti-poverty campaign. The problem was, he yelled at us for stories that had recently appeared in the daily paper, not *The Local Planet.*

The primary election occurred the third Tuesday in September, right after our Ministry of Truth article. Tuesday night election results always posed a problem for us. We had to send our pages to the printer Tuesday night before all the races were decided. After eating Chinese takeout in our conference room, I visited Tom's campaign party at a homegrown pizza joint next to Gonzaga University. I looked around the restaurant. No sight of the ESPN exec. No response from his interested party on my proposed sales terms, either.

According to early results just after the polls closed, Jim West led the mayor's race. Not surprising—the state senator raised more money than the other mayoral candidates combined. Much of his funding came from outside the county, let alone the city. Tom stood in second place, far ahead of all the Democrats who had worried that he would split their votes. The novice and the senator would meet in the general election. Tom grinned his bulldog grin. He knew that the real work was now starting.

Tom's campaign manager approached me and said, "Isn't this great? Connye would have been glad to see this." The mention of Connye startled me. I recalled her ache of betrayal when Tom left the paper. Would she have been happy? Maybe. She would have wanted Tom to win, would have wanted what his victory would mean for Spokane and for the paper. But it was Tuesday night; I had to return to the office and send another set of money-losing pages to our printer.

I woke up on the second Saturday in October and finally, fully, instinctively knew that I needed out of the newspaper business. No dream spurred me, just an absolute clarity the moment I opened my eyes. Now was the time. I set a goal of selling or closing the paper by the first of November. Sales had declined throughout the summer, almost since the week Connye died. In June, I had set aside some of the life insurance money that the paper received from her policy. Our lease expired in six months, and I wanted the funds for moving to smaller, less expensive offices. But as sales declined, we spent our cash cushion to meet current bills. Now, that cushion was gone.

In selling the business, I wanted just enough to pay my debts and replenish my retirement funds. That came to $85,000, or 10 percent of what I felt the paper was really worth. On Monday morning I conveyed this figure to Mr. ESPN, who sent it to his buyer. He brought back an offer for $85,000 over three years, signed by Paulette. I set the letter in my lap, looked up, and sighed.

This wasn't my plan. For the low price I was offering, I wanted cash immediately, not over three years. Plus, I didn't want to sell to Paulette. She couldn't write a decent lead, let alone run a newspaper. She recently married *The Planet*'s old web designer and was five month's pregnant. Did she honestly think that she could have her third child, care for her other two sons, and run a newspaper? In my heart, had I listened, I knew the right answer to that question. After everything I had gone through, I should have known the answer. But at this point my choices were either sell to her or close the doors. I jacked up my price another $25,000, signed the letter and sent it back. My instincts told me I shouldn't have signed, but I needed out and I wanted the money. I also felt obligated to keep the jobs going for the staff, even if I wouldn't be around.

Paulette agreed to my terms. She would pay 10 percent down and monthly payments for three years, starting with two half-payments in January and February 2004. Mr. ESPN collected $5,000 for his broker's role, which made him giddy like a child and Tom mad enough to bite.

The sale of the paper closed on Election Day, 2003. That Tuesday would be my last time working to assemble a newspaper. But first and foremost, it was Tom's big night. With my staff handling the production work, I headed to the pizza joint once again for Tom's election night party. The polls had just closed, but the numbers already trended in the wrong direction. Jim West led Tom by four percent. Tom's staff repeated the mantra, "It's still early." They expressed hope for a big turnout from the northeast district where Tom had campaigned heavily. Historically, the voters in the northeast district were the poorest and most marginalized, but their district also contributed the most business tax revenue to the city. In this election, they had a chance to elect one of their own as city council president, as well as a sympathetic mayor. If they did, they'd have the largest voting block on the council. But despite this opportunity to seize Spokane politics, the marginalized northeast district decided to stay home and stay marginalized. Another 1,500 voters from that district could have elected Tom mayor. By Thursday, Tom ceded the race.

With the paper sold and Tom defeated, I went home and laid down for weeks. I slept nine or 10 hours every night, took naps every day, and could still barely get up from watching movies while lying in Brad's old bedroom. My arms and thighs hurt like I'd been pumping iron continually for years. Occasionally I'd drive to the store or take Henry for a walk. For some reason, I decided it would be a convenient time to renew my passport. Government ID photos are usually horrible. Mine was frightening. I looked worse than Brad: pale, drained, slumped. Bloodless skin sagged off my cheekbones. Dark circles surrounded my eyes. I wondered if people would recognize me from my picture. I didn't recognize myself. I looked like a stroke victim.

I spent Thanksgiving with my family in Seattle. Brad decided to stay behind in Spokane and celebrate with his aunt and cousins. He didn't feel healthy enough for the five-hour drive across the state. I passed the hours in the car listening to audio books: Garrison Keillor, Bob Newhart, self-help books on grief, old-time radio mysteries.

Brad called me in Seattle on Thanksgiving Day. Paulette had left a printed note in his aunt's mailbox, accusing me of slowly murdering my family members for insurance money. After all, Connye and Brad lived with me full-time, and they were horribly sick. Walt and Christian didn't live with me anymore and they were fine. What a whack job Paulette was. When I returned to Spokane,

I asked her about her note. She dismissed it. "Pregnancy makes me paranoid." She grinned. "It's true—ask anyone."

Paulette took over the paper with the belief that sanitizing the content was all she needed to do before she raked in ad sales. She insulted the existing staff before firing them all. Then, she remade the editorial content according to her tree-hugging, guilty Catholic beliefs. Out went any ads for sex-related businesses like escorts or toyshops. Out went "Cabana Boy," our sex advice column. Out went any swear words or double entendres. She collected all the accounts receivable that came along with the paper. She made her half-payments to me on January 1 and February 1, but by mid-February her bowdlerizing clearly wasn't working. She cut circulation by 10 percent because she didn't want to pay the fees to distribute the paper inside area grocery stores. She stopped keeping distribution records. She didn't pay the rent for months. She kept exclaiming to me that her team had sold $80,000 worth of ads in four months. I explained that those sales stretched into the coming year; she needed to collect at least $80,000 each quarter just to come close to paying the bills.

Around Valentine's Day she told me that she wouldn't be able to make her March payment to me. By the end of March, she owed the distribution drivers three week's pay and didn't have the money to pay me for March or April. Our agreement stated that two consecutive missed payments automatically voided the contract. I gave Paulette a letter on March 31 informing her that I was taking back the newspaper. She withdrew $5,000 out of the newspaper's bank account before filing for Chapter 7 bankruptcy. Her taking the money bewildered me. That wasn't how I treated her when I sold her the paper. Brad was livid when he discovered that Paulette could file for bankruptcy and not repay her debts. But

I told Brad it was all right. She was the one who had to face life stupid and bankrupt.

One of our delivery drivers told me that his father sold their family cement factory in Pendleton, Oregon three times before a deal finally stuck. I called Rob, the paper's former landlord. We struck a gentleman's agreement in e-mail to sell the paper for $65,000 once the business was released from Paulette's bankruptcy. We hurriedly moved offices into an abandoned flower shop that Rob owned near the Holley-Mason building, to beat being evicted from the Wells Fargo building.

Rob asked me whom I thought he should hire to run the newspaper. I suggested Jeremy. He was the only person besides me who had sold ads, written stories, laid out pages, and delivered papers. Rob offered Jeremy the job as business manager. He also hired Chris, our original culture editor, as an interim editor for the spring and summer. Chris planned to attend graduate school at UC-Berkeley in the fall but wanted out of his ad agency job sooner than that. Chris and Jeremy begged me to not sell the paper to Rob. They complained about his unavailability, his abusive communication style and his failure to pay them. I told them that selling the paper was my best option and that Rob was first in line. If they could find another, better buyer I'd gladly entertain offers. In the meantime, I would pay them and collect from Rob later.

The paper cleared Paulette's bankruptcy in less than 60 days. I thought that was quick for anything to happen in the land of lawyers. After the trustee declared that I could sell the business again, Rob said that he wanted the weekend for final consideration. I thought that we already had a deal. I told him that I needed an answer on Monday morning. When Monday rolled around, I placed several calls to him. I left messages, none of which he returned. Rob eventually backed out of the deal, complaining about how poorly he thought the staff that he put in place communicated with him.

Another buyer came forward the day after Rob's Monday deadline. I told this new suitor that I wanted to sell the paper immediately and asked that he give me a preliminary yes/no answer within a couple days. On Thursday, he declined. He dreamed of running for political office and feared that something he might write for a newspaper would return to haunt him. What a spineless prick: "Vote for me, but I won't stand behind what I write." He'd be perfect for politics.

Finally, I closed the paper. I took out a home equity line of credit to consolidate my loan on the minivan and all my business debts. I wondered if I could file for business bankruptcy but decided not to. Filing would require more time and legal fees. Besides, I had the money. I just didn't enjoy parting with it. I paid the bills as best I could. The leasing company repossessed the phone system. Paulette's bookkeeper, who stayed on after Paulette left, sold most of the office furniture and equipment out of the abandoned flower shop. The remaining equipment I sold on the Internet or donated to the Girl Scouts for a computer lab in their new building.

I asked Rob for reimbursement for paying his obligation to Jeremy and Chris. I provided pay slips and tax records to prove that I had paid them legitimately. After ignoring several more calls and messages, Rob finally offered to pay me half of the amount within three months. I agreed mainly to get closure on the deal. Rob waited another year to pay me less than half.

WORDS THAT START WITH THE LETTER P

Inspirational books preach that the only true obstacles to happiness are will and faith. One such book I read recounted the story of Abraham Lincoln. Lincoln suffered depression and nervous breakdowns, lost his fiancée to typhoid, watched three of his four children die young, failed at several businesses including selling whiskey, and lost many political elections. He was even haunted by a nightmare of standing in a somber crowd surrounding a train and, after asking a grieving woman what had happened, learning that the president had been assassinated. If Lincoln had not won the 1860 presidential election, he would have been a mere footnote to history, a moderately wealthy lawyer and state politician from Illinois. Yet because he won that one election, he became a great historical figure. We suppose that he had will and faith. Was Lincoln successful? Eventually. Was he happy? Rarely.

I found inspirational books were wrong, or at least incomplete. Will and faith are vital, but life can also deal you challenges you can't conquer. You can accept them, work with or around them, but not defeat them. Accepting defeat without being defeated, then, becomes as valuable as will and faith. That's what I needed to do after the collapse of love, family and business under the pressure of publishing, parenting, and porphyria.

First, I took stock.

Aside from exhaustion and back problems, I had my health. I was fundamentally capable. After nursing Connye and Brad, I knew that health counted. I could work my way back.

I had a graduate degree and Microsoft experience on my resume.

I had a house that was nearly paid for. It was far bigger than I needed, but even with maintenance, property taxes and interest on my equity loan, staying in the house was cheaper and easier than moving.

I had some money in the bank. All my investments and retirement funds were gone, but I had enough cash to fund some sort of recovery and subsequent job search. Amazingly, people asked me how it felt to be "retired" again, now that the paper was closed. I guessed I fooled them into thinking *The Local Planet* was a financial success. Still, I had more assets than many of my peers. At times I told myself that I'd taken on the right amount of risk in my life. After all, the worst of the worst happened and still I had a solid roof, a stocked pantry, and a positive net worth. But I was only fooling myself. I would have been much better off physically, financially and emotionally by quitting the paper years ago.

I had Brad. Not all my family was gone. Plus, I had three cats and Henry the poodle.

I had friends. Many of my friends from *The Local Planet* left town in search of work, but I still had supportive people who knew my situation and cared about me.

I also had resentment and loathing towards many people and aspects of Spokane. I found the leaders stupid, the politics petty and the buildings dilapidated. If Spokane didn't need my business, then I didn't need it. To hell with supporting local businesses or causes. At the same time, I loathed myself for turning into another oblivious local who wouldn't lift a finger for their community or their neighbors. I had despised that attitude for so long, and now I had embraced it.

So much for my inventory—given my list of resources and responsibilities, what direction did I need to take to reclaim my life?

First, I needed money coming in the door after seven years of watching it go out. I also needed the social and psychological benefits that come along with earning a wage.

Two, I needed a better diet. Years of kid food and stress eating had packed on the weight.

Three, I needed exercise. My abs and back needed to be strengthened. I didn't want any more back spasms.

Four, I needed art and personal expression back in my life. Through all the work and stress and grief and loss, I'd given so much of myself that I felt I had nothing left. For years I hadn't written a paragraph just because I wanted to. I also hadn't listened to music or gone to a play. I'd lost any sense of myself, of who I was and wanted to be. I did this during my second marriage, as well, so I needed to figure out why I let this happen.

Finally, I needed love and affection. After spending much of my 30s alone despite two marriages, I needed a sex life again.

After the trials of publishing, parenting, and porphyria, my life needed some new, positive words that started with P. Thus, I made my 5 P Plan, five food groups for my body and soul:

Paychecks

Late in 2003, I received a call from a local company that sold fire control and alarm systems to the federal government. One of their technical writers needed back surgery and would be on medical leave. Was I interested in a few months of freelance technical writing work?

Definitely.

This company was one of the most dysfunctional businesses I've experienced. They earned most of their revenues selling fire and intrusion protection systems to U.S. Air Force bases. However, the company mission statement did not contain the phrase "save lives." They had an e-mail system that no one used, in part because managers were automatically copied on any message entering or leaving the company. Managers also closely monitored Internet usage, but the computer security was comically lax. I'm hardly a computer whiz, but only a single, easily located option stood between me and downloading files onto their computers from anywhere on the Internet. Plus, their computers had floppy disk drives. I could have easily copied all the U.S. Air Force plane schematics out of the company database and taken them home to sell to terrorists. Not that I did, but I was tempted to send the drawings of the Space Shuttle to my brother, who has always dreamed of going into space.

Maree, my manager, was the company's only female supervisor. Professionally she was very knowledgeable about both the company's technology and the tools and processes needed to document that technology. Personally, she was a black hole of emotional need. A bad week at work warranted cruising the pawnshops for engagement rings others had sold for groceries. Maree shared horrifically inappropriate information with her co-workers. Her stories often concerned her dogs, including a miniature Boston terrier named Cooper. Maree told me once about having a dream that involved enjoying oral sex, and then waking up to find Cooper licking her.

At one point, I heard through the office grapevine that Maree wondered if I might be interested in staying on full-time. There was more than enough work between the hardware, software, and sales documentation. I already knew my answer: I didn't fit in at the company. And by being a misfit, I'd only cause trouble.

The temp agency that I worked through also handled recruiting for a Spokane technology company that made hardware and software to measure, collect, manage, and analyze utility meter data. It was a large and growing company. Utilities never struck me as a sexy line of work, but running the newspaper taught me that distribution can be an interesting and significant business problem. Utilities are primarily concerned with distribution, how to deliver power and water to customers throughout a service area. The pay was good, the people pleasantly normal, and the work challenging yet familiar. Exactly one year after Connye's death I started a new, full-time job writing marketing material for utility data equipment.

I was happy to leave journalism behind and return to working in technology. The company hired me at a salary and vacation level equal with my previous position at Microsoft. At first, that felt like a step backward. In the eight years since leaving Microsoft, I'd earned a graduate degree and lead a start-up company. That should have been worth something. At other times, employment felt like an impossible luxury. I received paychecks and weekends off on a regular basis. Once again I had time, energy and money to dedicate to writing that wasn't work-related.

Protein

In 2004, low carbohydrate, high-protein diets were in vogue. Maybe more protein would help me. Something needed to change. I was overweight and flabby. Out went pasta and rice, two of my favorite foods. In the summer, I could live on pasta and rice salads. I didn't miss garbage pasta like ramen noodles or macaroni and cheese from the days raising Walt and Christian. Pesto capellini, spaghetti puttanesca, linguine with clam sauce—those were the dishes I missed. And rice. White rice with butter, salt and pepper—sometimes that was enough of a meal for me. Or Japanese pot stickers alongside rice sprinkled with soy sauce, sesame oil, seaweed and toasted sesame seeds.

Normally I don't like red meat. In my 20s, I went years without eating it. If I have a burger, it's either ground turkey or a vegetarian patty. Steak leaves me cold. But I figured that a high protein diet gave me license to eat the most disgusting, loveable red meat on the planet: sausage. Summer, thuringer, salami, Genoa, pepperoni: I'll eat it all and only rarely worry about where it comes from or what it contains. Sausage is what I missed during my no-red-meat years. My grill started seeing a lot more action. Dairy products, I realized, also contain high amounts of protein. I added yogurt, soymilk, and cheese to my grocery list.

Did it work? I lost 10 pounds almost immediately. Only God knows what happened to my cholesterol levels, because I certainly didn't have them checked. Then I thought back on my days with Connye in Italy. Breads and pastas, wines and cream puffs were everywhere, but not the kind of obesity you see in America. It's not only what Americans eat, it's how we live: huge portions, junk food, stress eating, no exercise. I started eating pasta again, and rice, along with more fruit and vegetables to balance out my rediscovered proteins. My weight stabilized. I still weighed 20 pounds more than I did out of college, but at least my clothes from two years ago fit comfortably again.

Pilates

Years earlier, my brother and his wife gave Connye a book on modified Pilates calisthenics. Pilates exercises focus on your abdomen and lower back, the core of your body, and support a healthy spine, something that I needed. I started doing floor exercises every morning. I'd throw some water and a tea bag in the coffee maker that I used for making tea, and then twist and stretch and breathe and lift for 20 minutes while the coffee maker chugged and sputtered. Henry and the cats circled around me as I flailed my limbs. Sometimes I bonked them on the head as they passed by.

Connye had performed her daily exercise routine in the living room. She used exercise to work her way back from what we later surmised was her first bout of porphyria. She would flex and clench her neck and jaw like a lizard hunting a fly and grimace like a football player while lifting hand weights. Now I appreciated her dedication to at least a minimum of daily activity. She never nagged or bragged about it but did it to keep herself healthy.

Calisthenics were not enough, I knew. I also started taking Henry for long walks most afternoons. My house sat in the center of a triangle formed by three parks. We would walk to and around a park and then return. Our jaunts covered one to two miles. Henry learned to follow without a leash, to come and heel and sit before crossing the street on command. On weekend or holiday mornings, Henry would stare at me with black poodle eyes and refuse to go relieve himself in our back yard. Only a walk would suffice. Unless, of course, it was raining outside, or heavy dew made the grass wet, or there was too much snow on the ground. He was a poodle, after all.

Once I started full-time work, I joined the YMCA at a discount and returned to swimming. I had spent my youth as a competitive swimmer—a swimming scholarship helped me pay for college. Returning to the pool after 20 years felt comfortable and yet awkward. The locker room routines felt familiar. In the water, I didn't feel the easy rhythm of swimming that I remembered from my youth. I could swim faster than most of the other people in the pool. At first, I couldn't swim as long as they did, and I imagined myself being as un-coached as they looked. I was happy to cover 800 yards twice a week to start, and tried to forget that I once swam races longer than my current total workout. Exercising didn't change my weight, but my back felt better. My muscle tone and stamina improved. My pants started feeling a little loose.

Paragraphs

Paragraphs, and pictures and poetry and plays and punk music: I needed art back in my life. Ironically, years of running a newspaper that covered the arts left me no time or energy for actually enjoying them. The editorial staff and freelancers saw the concerts, read the books, heard the CDs, attended the readings and the openings. I either worked late at the office or went home to care for the sick and the young.

I started writing again. I wanted to resurrect at least parts of my graduate school thesis to create some short stories to submit for publication. Once upon a time I put a lot of effort into that project. Maybe I could assemble an anthology of stories from *The Local Planet*. I started writing the memoir that you're reading now. At first it was just words, phrases, images, people's names, brand names, moments that I knew I wanted to include. Later came timeline, structure, paragraphs and pages and chapters. Connye had always loved memoirs and had been well on her way to writing a great one of her own. She'd be proud if I published one.

I needed music back in my life, as well. The newspaper staff wrote extensively about the entire spectrum of music, but I'd missed a lot of great tunes during those years. The media consolidation sweeping the nation left Spokane with astonishingly mediocre radio stations. Sure, we had more than 20 to choose from, but three companies owned the vast majority of them. None of the owners were local. All the play-lists came prepackaged from media consultants and were built according to the demographics and psychographics of the mid-sized Western market as they understood them. One station replaced all their disc jockeys with a recorded voice to announce the artist and title for each song played. Their ratings soared. Corporate wondered how they could go jockless in more cities. Without radio, I looked for other resources for catching up with music. Digital music services finally started offering affordable selection and quality. I signed up.

Writing jokes, learning the harmonica and snapping digital photos all fell under the P for paragraphs. Not all those came to pass. But it was good to enjoy again, to do things for me just for the sake of doing.

Philandering

Like all of Spokane, I needed to get laid. But I didn't feel ready for the emotional commitment that comes with monogamous relationships. Besides, for various reasons my serious relationships had not been consistently sexually fulfilling for me. Maybe it was time to try a bottom-up approach.

Escort services had advertised in *The Local Planet*. I met some of the escorts when they came to our office to pay their bills. They also advertised in the local phone directory and online. Few people dispute that the line between escorting and prostituting gets blurred. Personally, I think prostitution should be legal and regulated. But here I found myself seriously considering engaging an escort, visiting a certain type of massage parlor, and seeking out other shady ways to scratch my all-too-human itch. It would have been easy, just a phone call or a short car trip. But my story-telling mind and cheapskate nature got the better of me. What if I got busted? I knew that Tom Grant had reported on public officials as they left Joe-Jean's Oriental Spa (Parking in Rear). The city's cable TV channel ran mug shots of people arrested for solicitation. The last thing I needed was *The Spokesman-Review* running the headline, "Ex-*Planet* Publisher Pays Prostitutes." Maybe I could drive to another town, Seattle or Portland, and look up an escort in the local alternative newspapers. Then I started to do the math: cost of service, lodging, meals out, entertainment, gas, travel time, car mileage—certainly there had to be more cost-effective ways to get laid.

If I wasn't willing to pay for a prostitute, maybe I could at least find some no-strings-attached sex. I'm no drinker and can't stand cigarette smoke, so cruising bars was out. Where do closet geeks like me look for meaningless sex these days? The Internet. AdultFriendFinder.com is a large sex-and-swingers website. You post your profile, pictures, and interests, and cruise other people's profiles. You can sort for one-night stands, discreet relations, threesomes, groups, bi-curious, whatever—algorithms don't care what you search for. What the hell. I posted an awful self-portrait from a digital camera, filled in my profile, and started to flirt online with various women 28-45 years old who lived within 25 miles of my ZIP code. Some even flirted back. One 28-year-old single mother expressed interest. She thought that she could get her mom to watch her kid for an upcoming Saturday. But when she mentioned needing money to help her get by, my mind went back to newspaper headlines and cost-benefit analyses.

One woman flirted first with me. Lara said she was 35, blonde, and a former Playboy model. Her ad had no picture. I was skeptical but decided to see where this adventure led. We tried meeting at a coffee shop near one of my neighborhood parks. My heart pounded as I parked my car and walked up to the café. A pounding heart is good, yes? We missed each other. Then she went on vacation to Hawaii. Next, I left for holidays with my family. Eventually we met up at an Applebee's restaurant near my house. Lara was blond, all right. She had a frizzy mop of dyed yellow hair. Mascara spikes set off her big eyes. Her short-waisted white fur coat didn't hide her surgically enlarged breasts. Tight black stretch pants hugged her matchstick legs. If she had ever been a Playboy model, it was during the Johnson administration. Adventure changed to letdown. We took a booth, ordered coffee and tea to warm up, and talked for a while. Lara was obviously bright. She was self-employed managing a number of rental properties. "Monthly income, depreciation, and someone else pays the mortgage—what's not to like?" She was married to a man who drank and traveled too much. She had also volunteered for and donated money to Tom Grant's mayoral campaign and knew my name and story from *The Local Planet*.

I sensed that I could never call Lara again and we'd both understand. After Christmas, though, I did call. We met at her home a few blocks away from the house I bought with my ex-wife when we first moved to Spokane. Although Lara said she was married, she shared the brick bungalow with another altered blond who could have been her sister. There was some other sort of relationship between the two women that I didn't want to know about, even when Lara offered to explain. The three of us sat in her oddly Victorian living room and drank the bottle of red wine I brought. It seemed vaguely Faulknarian. They asked if I wanted to smoke some pot. "Not my thing," I said, "but go ahead if you want." Her roommate retired to watch a movie and Lara led me to her bedroom. Our encounter was perfunctory, almost mechanical, and much briefer than I'd like to admit. We never met again.

I decided to move up a rung on the food chain of Internet romance. Match.com is the largest of Internet dating sites. It's the same sort of profile-and-search arrangement as AdultFriendFinder, except that the women at Match.com like their children, cats, careers, and (oddly enough) fishing. One woman on Match.com stopped me in my mouse tracks: bright green eyes, wavy brunette hair, and big dimples in her smile. She described herself as college-educated, well employed, creative, the mother to two teenaged children. Definitely my type. It was hard to comprehend a visceral connection to a 100-pixel-square photo. I emailed her to introduce myself and ask if she wanted to meet.

"Not my type—sorry," came her reply a few days later. Such is life, I suppose, in Internet dating. I tried not to feel let down, but this was my first upwelling of emotion in a long time. I closed my account on Match.com.

Months later when I started working, I met an attractive brunette with green eyes and big dimples while on the job. At first, I thought she seemed familiar only because she was my type. Then I realized that she was the one from Match.com. One peek online confirmed it. I didn't blab right away. I thought that as she got to know me at work, she'd like me. At times, she seemed like she did. Or was she just friendly with everyone? For months I harbored my crush, until I had to confess. One way or the other, I needed to move on. I invited her to a conference room under the pretext of asking for her help with a work-related matter. She was surprised by my confessed feelings and knowledge of her Match.com ad. I'd like to believe that she was at least a little flattered, but I have no foundation for that belief. I still wasn't her type.

After that, we managed to work well together and develop a mutual connection around parenting struggles—her daughter was starting to get into teenage trouble just as Brad had. She and I would go to lunch and commiserate about the guilt, doubt, and exhaustion of having a screwed-up family life.

During my Internet dating period, I ran into Kimi. She'd been one of the disc jockeys laid off from the radio station that went jockless. In fact, she got axed the day that we put her on the cover of *The Local Planet* as part of our radio coverage. When we met, she was divorcing her husband, who also happened to be the station manager who fired her. She was soon to move out from the guy she was sharing a house with, a latent homosexual CPA with a collection of nipple clamps and bongs. We became "friends with benefits," as the slang goes. We both liked baseball and music and sex and Italian food. We were both politically independent and outspoken. She had been the media coordinator for Tom Grant's campaign. If Tom had won, Kimi would have had a great job in City Hall. For a while she was back on the air in the mornings, playing second fiddle to a raging conservative asshole on AM talk radio. I encouraged her to find another job outside of the broadcast booth. As an ex-publisher, I honestly thought that she could succeed in radio advertising sales. She wouldn't consider it.

Somehow the connection that I craved just wasn't there with Kimi. I told her that straight up. Plus, she was a rabid fan of the Dave Matthews Band, and I never allow Dave Matthews in my house or car. She wanted more and felt more. She would have been happy to marry me, and tried to show how she would take care of me: cooking, cleaning, raking leaves. Once she spent an hour ironing a single shirt of mine. Then her ex-husband got a big promotion to the Baltimore radio market. Their kids could move back east with him. There was nothing keeping Kimi in Spokane. I helped her pack her stuff for the move back to her hometown in Virginia. The last I heard, hers was the top-rated radio show from 7 to midnight in her market.

I'd struck out at all levels of philandering. Maybe it was time to move. Eight years in one place was a long time for an old military brat. Brad wanted to move. I could go back to Seattle and get a job with Microsoft again, which might get me better paychecks. They'd recognize my prior years of service, qualifying me for four weeks of vacation a year and maybe a window office. I'd be closer to my family and there were more women in Seattle. But four Ps out of five in Spokane wasn't bad.

Once I sold the newspaper, started working, and embarked on my 5 P plan, my sense of déjà vu returned. From a young age, I've often experienced déjà vu and now regard it as confirmation that I'm on the designated track, whatever that might mean. During those newspaper years, my déjà vu left me. Whether from fatigue, distraction, or being off track, I don't know, but I noticed its absence. Now, moments on the job seemed too familiar to be simple repetitions. I was glad to have those guideposts back.

BEAUTY BAY

My back muscles started to spasm on the August morning we planned to spread Connye's remaining ashes. I lay on my back on my living room floor, doing my Pilates exercises. Saturday sunshine barged in the windows. I extended my legs and pointed my toes towards the ceiling. As I lowered my legs about six inches off of vertical, I heard a pop and felt my back tense. Then I couldn't flex my back. Damn it, why did this happen on days like this? The night before, I was cleaning out and packing up the former newspaper offices. I hauled three garbage cans of old files to the office dumpster half a block away. Hoisting large cans of paper over my head must have stressed my back. Slowly I got to my knees and then stood, holding onto a coffee table for support. The tensed muscles in my right hip rotated my foot clockwise and pulled it slightly off the floor. But I could walk, so on with the day. We couldn't reschedule. A rented pontoon boat waited for us for a full day on Lake Coeur d'Alene in northern Idaho.

I leaned over the kitchen sink and funneled Connye's remaining ashes out of the brown plastic box from the funeral home and into a black lacquered wooden jar painted with oriental goldfish. Handling her ashes now was easier than originally dividing them had been nearly a year earlier. I rested the wooden jar in the blue paper maché bowl along with the dried flower petals, and then slid the bowl into a paper grocery bag.

From the Coeur d'Alene city boat ramp, we motored the rented pontoon boat due south, away from the resort towering over the shore. August is hot in the Inland Northwest, and on this hot cloudless Saturday the lake swarmed with boats. The water in front of the resort held swells two to three feet high from all the wakes. On board were Connye's parents (back for another summer), her sister Dayna and her family, and Brad and I. At first everyone was quiet, a little tense. Walt and Christian had been invited but were out of town for the weekend. Just after we left the marina, one big swell crested the bow of the boat and soaked Dayna. We all laughed, which lifted the tension. Lake Coeur d'Alene is large, at least 25 miles long. My plan was to find Cottonwood Bay from the water, to see again the house where Connye and I got married. It seemed a fitting place to spread her ashes. Genius me left the map of the lake in the minivan, though, so we weren't sure where we were headed. Dayna's husband Bruce steered us down one long bay that wasn't the right one. Along the way we passed a string of flowers floating near a stretch of rocky shore. Someone else must have spread ashes that morning. It seemed strange to be on the way to solemn business while teenagers in nearby boats sipped forbidden beers and eyed wet young skin. We explored another bay that turned out to be the wrong one as well. Dayna's daughters grew fidgety. All of us dreaded our chore.

Finally, we turned the boat into Windy Bay. I pointed to a forested stretch of shoreline without houses or docks. "Let's go over there," I told Bruce. He drew us close to the shoreline and set the engine in neutral.

I removed my floppy brown hat and took out the paper maché bowl holding the dried flower petals and the lacquered jar.

Our rag-tag family stood quietly, dressed in swimming suits, t-shirts, baseball caps, and water shoes. It felt like we were holding church in the middle of a playground. "I'm glad we all dressed up for this," I joked. "I didn't write anything specifically for this event. But in thinking back, Connye gave me a lot of things: love, acceptance, family, laughter, courage. I think about her and those gifts every day. She would have loved being out here on the lake with us. It's not the same without her. I miss her."

"But we're glad she's not suffering anymore," Connye's mom Janie added. At times I was selfish enough to want her back even sick, without thinking how miserable she must have been. Janie distributed flowers to everyone. I opened one of the short gates in the boat railing. Feeling a little paranoid, I looked around and noticed a large cabin cruiser motoring slowly toward us. I put the bowl and jar back in the paper sack.

The cruiser pulled within shouting distance. The driver called out, "Which way is Coeur d'Alene?" He had gotten turned around. We all pointed north and watched him pull away.

"Bruce, could you troll the boat?" I asked.

As the boat bobbed forward gently, I sat in the gate's gap, loosened the lid of the jar, and poured the ashes into the water. Small pieces of bone clicked against the neck of the jar. A line of white drew out in the steely green water, paralleling the shore. I heard Dayna' youngest girl, Kelsi, ask her mom, "What's ashes?" and wished Dayna would just tell her. One stem at a time, everyone tossed flowers overboard. Kelsi and Sarah took handfuls of the dried petals and flung them towards the water. After a quiet moment, Bruce pushed the boat throttle forward a couple of clicks and we slowly motored back towards the center of the lake.

I went to the back of the boat, sat next to Brad, and put my arm around his shoulders. I looked over my shoulder at the petals floating on the water. "Bye Connye," I whispered. "I love you."

We rounded the southern point of Windy Bay into a small cove where several other boats anchored for lunch. Bruce parked us near the shore. While the Dayna and Janie retrieved fried chicken, potato salad, chips, and other lunch items, I pulled on my water-skiing vest and jumped in the water. At first the cool water shortened my breath. Soon enough I relaxed and enjoyed floating weightless. Our rental boat had no ladder for climbing out of the water. I had to climb up the stern of the boat, which I knew wouldn't help my back.

After lunch we powered the boat back north. Both Brad and Janie were drooping and wanted to head home. Dayna's girls whined, "When can we go swimming?" "Soon," Dayna told them. She diverted their attention by helping them fly small kites off the back of the boat.

After Brad and his grandma disembarked, our mood lightened. We headed east from the resort towards Wolf Lodge Bay. Bruce said he knew of several docks along that shore where we might tie up and let the girls swim at a beach. A beach would be better for my back than climbing up the side of the boat. All the public docks we passed were full. Bruce drove us into Beauty Bay and cut the engine when we found a corner with just a few boats. Brad's grandpa became skipper, keeping an eye on our location while the rest of us played in the water. At first Dayna's girls hesitated about getting wet. After a while we had them in the water floating and laughing, even bobbing under the boat between the pontoons and pretending the space was a pirate cave.

With a water-skiing vest on, I bobbed weightless in the lake. Buoyancy released the tension in my hips. Water lapped in my ears.

Looking up through my sunglasses I saw the cornflower blue skies of northern Idaho. *The Local Planet* was closed. All its bills were paid. Connye's ashes were spread and she didn't suffer any more. I had new friends and a new job. Most of my 5 Ps were going well. Yes, Brad was still sick. I felt unsure about my ability to love again. But, the desperation was gone. *It's done*, I felt in my chest. *It's over*. I had lost my self, but maybe I was finding my self again. Maybe the pain in my heart and the pain in my back came from me splitting open and crawling out like the dragonfly. In my darker moments, I wondered if the stress created by my plans and choices didn't kill Connye, or at least spoiled what little time we had together. But I couldn't erase all that—I did what I did. And I wasn't going to miss out on my life because I missed Connye.

The next morning in bed, I needed more than a minute just to roll over. Sitting up was unthinkable. But no matter how much my back hurt, my bladder still filled up. Somehow, I managed to pour myself from the mattress to the floor and then gingerly crawl into the bathroom. I pulled myself up onto the toilet. Eventually I made it back into bed, huffing and wincing.

"Brad!" I yelled. "Brad!" His sleep schedule was very erratic, but once he was asleep, nothing would wake him.

I missed work Monday. By Monday night, I could stand and walk for about a minute if I was wearing my back brace. Desperate, I telephone my neighbor Barry across the street. Barry is a chiropractor. As the son of a nurse, I'd never done chiropractic, either. I had no idea what to expect. Other people had told me about their "spinal adjustments," which sounded wrenching. I couldn't imagine that snapping my spine around would feel good, but maybe that was what I needed. Barry backed his van into my driveway, loaded me in, and drove me downtown to his darkened office. A large mural of an alpine meadow papered one wall of his exam room. He leaned me face-first into a vertical cushion, and then slowly tilted the cushion down until I was lying horizontal.

Barry practiced low-force chiropractic, I learned. I couldn't see the first devices he used on me. They felt like calipers. I could sense that he was turning knobs on the device to adjust pressure. Then he put a low-frequency energy pulsing device on my lower back and left it there for several minutes. Once that was done, he tilted me back up to standing. Barry loaned me the pulser and drove me home.

Miraculously, the next day I could move. Slowly, cautiously, I could walk. I drove myself to work and made an appointment to see my doctor. An exam and X-ray revealed that I had spondylolysis, a small bone break or defect in my spine that leaves one vertebra partially disconnected from the next. Apparently, one of my lumbar vertebrae can slip forward, pinching my spinal column. When that happens, my muscles spasm trying to protect my spine. There's not much treatment available for spondylolysis, just appropriate exercise and stretching plus maintaining a low body weight. Extreme cases require surgery to fuse the disconnected vertebrae.

Brad yelled to me from the basement, "Did you get those shoelaces?"

I'd just walked in the kitchen door after commuting home early from work and stopping at the store on the way. I opened the door to the basement. Brad stood at the bottom of the stairs, still dressed in sweatpants and t-shirt. "I know—I'm running behind. I'll be ready in 10 minutes." I tossed him the laces.

I knew he'd need more than 10 minutes. I decided to return some phone calls and check the mail: cable TV bill, a straggling ad payment for *The Local Planet*, and several medical insurance statements regarding my back spasms. In 20 minutes, we were due in court to finalize my adoption of Brad. We'd already rescheduled this appointment three times, and were at least two weeks past the two weeks the attorney said the process would require. Because I didn't have a legal relationship with him after Connye died, I couldn't add him to my health insurance through my new employer. We decided that adopting him would be the best way to handle his continuing need for medical insurance and general assistance. His biological father certainly wasn't providing anything.

Brad stomped up the stairs. The black suit and white shirt he first wore to his mom's memorial was poorly assembled on his body. "It's not going to work—my port used to be on the other side." We had his white dress shirt tailored with an opening in the side seam through which he could pass his IV tubing. But after his first chest port became infected, the doctors put a new port on the other side of his chest, opposite from the seam opening.

"Just run the tubing across your body," I said.

Brad growled and went back downstairs. After another five minutes he returned, this time with his shirt, pants, and coat all properly assembled. His tie needed tying.

"What would the guys on *Queer Eye for the Straight Guy* say if they knew you couldn't tie a tie?" I tied his tie, but it hung past the bottom of his belt buckle. It was now officially our docket time, and we were still standing in our kitchen. "We can retie it at the courthouse. We need to go."

While trying to safely speed down the hill and across the river to our appointment, I talked Brad through how to tie a necktie. "Cross the fat part over the skinny part, then wrap it around the skinny part one time." The first time it still came out too long. "Wrap it around again, kind of horizontally this time." The second time, the slipknot of the tie wouldn't slip. I don't know how he accomplished that. "Then pull the fat part up through the opening and push it down through the second wrap." The third time worked just as I was parking the car at the courthouse.

"Sorry I made us late," Brad said while we waited for the elevator.

"That's okay. We'll be just fine."

In the third floor courtroom, Brad, our lawyer Jane and I sat in the front bench of the gallery area and waited. The presiding family law judge was running late. He dispatched various motions and filings ahead of us at the pace of about one a minute. Many of the motions involved restraining orders. We were the best-dressed people in the gallery. I'm always surprised at how ratty some people dress when they appear before a judge.

Once the judge polished off most of the files before him, he ordered the courtroom closed. A trio of people dressed in Hawaiian shirts and missing a sizeable percentage of their teeth entered and was quickly shooed out. Brad and I took seats at the counsel's table facing the bench. Jane stood on the other side of Brad and was sworn in. She was brief, factual: Mr. Spaur was petitioning to adopt his stepson of six years. Consideration of adoption began after his wife's death, when Brad's biological father would not supply support or medical insurance, even when required. From there, adoption came to seem a natural course.

The judge then asked me to raise my hand and swear to tell the truth. I agreed. When he asked me why I wanted to adopt Brad, I said, "We've been through a lot together and have formed a father-son bond. It has been frustrating to be his father in all but a legal sense. Adopting him will make it easier for me to care for him."

The judge looked down at me from the bench. Even through his black robes I could tell he was a thick-chested man. Waves of lightly graying hair framed his large, round face. He could have played Father Christmas for Dickens. "You understand that once I sign this there is no way to revoke it. There are no returns or exchanges. Do you want to proceed with this adoption?" I looked at Brad. I expected to see tears welling up in his eyes. Instead, he was smiling. It was the first time in years that he looked truly, contentedly happy.

Connye had always wanted me relax and enjoy the boys, to parent more out of caring than sternness. I wanted her to know that I was taking good care of her Brad.

"I do," I told the judge.

AFTERWORD

If you made it to the end of my memoir, you probably have two questions:

- Why wait 20 years to publish this story?
- What happened in those 20 years?

I'm glad you asked. I'll take those questions in order.

Now is the Time to Publish

Not publishing this story before now wasn't for lack of trying. This manuscript saw a lot of submissions. But the submission process is often inefficient, manual, time- and labor-intensive. It can be demoralizing for writers. Once, this manuscript sat for two years on an editor's desk at a university press. That was the last straw for me, at least at the time. I decided that literary publishing was a broken market. Too much supply of manuscripts for the limited demand from a highly inefficient distribution system.

I decided to move on. I've never suffered from a lack of things to do. Things like photography and surfing and getting an MBA were always calling to me.

Ok, fair enough. So then, what changed my mind?

One thing was technology. In the intervening years, the mechanics and logistics of producing and distributing a book has become cheaper and easier. Creating a properly formatted manuscript, designing a cover, binding it all together and shipping it to a bookstore or directly to readers is now fairly easy. That physical chore was a big part of what a traditional publisher would handle for an author. Today, an author has options to more easily handle that on their own or hire a third party to handle the work without taking acquiring rights or royalties in the work.

Another thing that changed was my attitude towards the meaning of publishing. Writers are groomed on the idea that being validated by a traditional publisher is the ultimate sign of success. I certainly bought into that for a long time. But over the years I met colleagues who had published various business and leadership books. They typically worked with small or specialty publishers, the types of companies most likely to publish a memoir like mine. Looking at those colleagues' experiences, I saw that no matter their publisher, authors still had to do the bulk of work in promoting their books. Aside from production, promotion was the other main benefit of working with the publisher.

So, I finally accepted that if promotion would always be on my shoulders as an author, then I might as well self-publish my book.

But I'll confess that friction within the publishing process is only some of the reasons I set aside the project for several years.

I've always carried some shame about my checkered history with relationships. No one else in my family has been divorced or widowed. I even joke that my sister was an elementary school librarian and my brother was an Eagle Scout, so I must be the black sheep of our family. Logically this all seems silly, I know, especially in the land of memoirs. Other authors confess actually shocking things in their memoirs that make my failed relationships seem boring. But I needed the time to come to terms with this sense of shame, as well. Even now, while writing this, part of me is panicked at sharing so much about my past.

Beyond that particular emotion, I needed to feel like the time was right to take on this work. Self-publishing, at least for me, is still illogical in some ways. I don't need whatever expenses and work this project might generate. Any money that I make on this will probably be incidental in my overall economics. But publishing this memoir finally feels right. Maybe it will help someone realize something useful, something meaningful to them, about family and friends and perseverance and work and love. I hope it does.

And finally, I needed all that time to decide on the right title for this book, a title that felt right. You'd be surprised at how long that process can take.

What's Happened Since Then?

Twenty years is a long time, especially these recent 20 years. I can't cover all two decades of history in an afterword, but I can catch you up on the major characters in the story.

Matthew

After the utility tech company, I worked for an education nonprofit, another utility tech company, and an HR consulting company. Along the way I earned an MBA degree. Three times in nine years, my marketing job vanished during a company reorganization. Each time, it got harder to find a new job; I blame ageism. Finally, I made the transition to being a self-employed marketing consultant.

I also started narrating audiobooks, another pursuit where I saw the limits of small press publishers and the inevitable need of authors to promote their own work.

I continued to date for several years before finally, and very happily, remarrying in 2016. My wife and I reside in the San Francisco Bay area.

Connye

After Connye passed, I worked with the Association of Alternative Newspapers to establish a cash prize honoring her. I would pay the winners of their annual award for media criticism at papers under 50,000 circulation a $300 stipend. We'd call it the Connye Miller Award for Media Criticism. Connye and her team twice won that award. I thought media criticism was a valuable function for alternative newspapers and wanted to encourage it, along with honoring Connye. I also hoped that my prize would inspire others in the AAN to offer more such prizes. Winning something like that can mean a lot to a young writer. Unfortunately, no one else took up the mantle. After several years and in the face of the 2008-9 Great Recession, I decided to stop funding the prize.

Brad

Brad, part two, could be a whole other book.

He continued to bounce between Spokane and Seattle as he grew into his 20s. He continued to struggle with substance abuse, mental health, porphyria, and eventually AIDS.

I once told a friend that I would be surprised if Brad lived to 30, the way he was going.

"You can't say that," she said. "Don't even think it."

"It's true," I replied.

Brad also developed great friendships, founded and sold an AIDS-positive digital publication, and worked in politics, including campaigning for Hillary Clinton.

Brad passed away in November 2014, at the age of 29, from complications. There were so many for him.

Henry the poodle

While working at the first utility tech company, I was living alone, putting in a lot of hours, and often traveling for my job. That left Henry essentially abandoned for long periods of time. It wasn't fair to him, I thought. And while I enjoyed him when we were together, I had never wanted the responsibility of a dog in the first place.

One of my colleagues at the time had recently lost one of her poodles. Cindy didn't travel for work or keep the same sort of hours that I did. She gladly took in Henry and gave him more of a life than I did.

About a year after taking in Henry, Cindy stopped by my cubicle to say that she'd be in my part of town for the better part of a Saturday. She wanted to know if I'd like to have Henry come hang out with me.

Sure, I said.

After Cindy dropped him off in my front yard and pulled away, Henry stood about 20 feet from me and just barked. He clearly recognized me. His bark had varying rhythms but a medium tone. He went on for more than minute, maybe more than two.

Henry was reading me the riot act.

I got it. I had dumped him. The years had been tough on him too.

Eventually he said his peace. We went inside and had some lap time. I don't recall now whether I took him on one final walk. I didn't see him again.

Brad said that he did see Henry again. Brad had returned to Spokane, but I had moved on to California. One day, he was walking in downtown Spokane and saw a woman walking a black miniature poodle who looked like Henry. Brad being Brad, she stopped the lady and started talking to her. Yes, the dog's name was Henry. It was him. Yes, Henry had had a few previous owners. No, another woman had given her the dog. Cindy must have needed to find him a new home, as well.

Tom Grant

After *The Local Planet,* Tom continued his vagabond journalism career. He anchored television news in Wyoming, thinking that might make a good step towards being a US representative or senator. After all, he would have statewide name recognition and needed to turn out comparatively few votes to win. But media in that market was just as mismanaged as Spokane. For example, Tom told me about how the station manager had hired his mistress as an intern, then fired the weather anchor and put his mistress on the air.

Next Tom landed in Augusta, Georgia as editor of another alternative newspaper. I visited Tom and Mary Ann on my business trips to Atlanta or neighboring South Carolina. Augusta seemed a lot like Spokane, except smaller, poorer, and more overtly racist.

When the Augusta paper was sold to a different publishing, Tom decided to earn his PhD and teach college. He's now back in Georgia as a tenured professor. In some ways, he's reprising his role from *The Local Planet,* guiding a small army of young journalists onto great things.

Spokane

Spokane news media continued to reflect the messed-up state of the national media landscape. It remains one of very few markets where the same company owns both a dominant daily newspaper and a network television station. Dallas is the only other similar major market that I know of. Congress in 1975 passed laws about this type of media cross-ownership. The Cowles Publishing cross-ownership was grandfathered in when the law was written, in part with help from Representative Tom Foley, who would go on to become Speaker of the House.

Spokane mayoral politics continued their turmoil. The town had gone more than 40 years without a two-term mayor. Mayor David Condon finally won reelection in 2015. Once he finished his finished his second term and no longer serve as mayor, he was replaced by long-time local news anchor Nadine Woodward. Tom hadn't been far off the mark after all.

After I moved from Spokane, I held on to my house there for several years and rented it out. I've never liked being a landlord, but it was the right thing to do for a while. In 2015, once I was engaged to my now wife, I decided it was time to finally cut that remaining tie with Spokane. I sold the house for $100,000 more than I'd originally paid. Selling closed out all my remaining debts from *The Local Planet* and left a little money for rebuilding some retirement savings.

Spokane has since enjoyed a bit of a renaissance. In 2020, my old house sold again, this time for nearly twice again as much. Folks priced out of the bigger cities closer to the Pacific coastline discovered Spokane along with Bend, Oregon and Boise, Idaho. Those inland West Coast cities saw spikes in population and housing prices even before the COVID-19 pandemic. Then with more white-collar workers able to work from home full-time, young families moved eastward. Soon Spokane became one of the least affordable housing markets in the country, an ironic twist from my days of covering the local economy.